Making Market Systems Work for the Poor

Praise for this book

'Alan's work was transformational. [He encouraged thinking about] dynamic relationships between many actors and many processes in an ever-changing system of people, policies and institutions. He made an enormous contribution.'

Kim Wilson, Faculty, Tufts University

'In the face of major cuts to development budgets, Alan's advice is especially timely and relevant; we must focus on systemic constraints and underlying causes, invest in relationships and an understanding of the incentives of key actors, and design catalytic interventions that aren't dependent on recurrent subsidy if we are to deliver the lasting change needed to achieve impact at scale.

'I thoroughly enjoyed this book, part trip down memory lane, part look to the future ... This collection of essays captures Alan's passion and drive and also illustrates his lasting and dynamic legacy across multiple fields within international development. Essential reading for anyone interested in market systems approaches to take in over a doughnut and coffee!'

Adrian Stone, Investment Climate Team, Foreign, Commonwealth &
Development Office

'For those of us in the market systems development trenches, reading this book is *almost* as good as having a drink with Alan to debate the best ways to facilitate the evolution of markets that actually work for those living in poverty. From FSD Kenya's perspective, we have learned so much from Alan's prescient insights, many of which are highlighted throughout the chapters in this riveting book.'

Tamara Cook, CEO, FSD Kenya

'This book is much more than a testament to the influence which Alan Gibson had on many people's thinking and lives. It is also a testament to the enduring relevance of market system development thinking. By providing a compendium of updates from those at the far flung frontiers of this field, this book should encourage current practitioners and inspire future ones.'

David Porteous, Chair, BFA Global and Digital Frontiers

'For anyone troubled by the difficulty of translating M4P theory to practice, this book is a must-read. It validates that challenge while making the approach more tangible by orienting the reader to its key elements such as identifying market actors with the incentives and/or capacity to assume functions and roles that will improve markets for the poor. It presents a collection of experience lived by professionals who confirm that successful M4P is, by definition, ever (art) work in progress.'

Candace Nelson, Author and Editor, Savings Groups
at the Frontier and The New Microfinance Handbook

'Market systems development remains as relevant to today's challenges as it was more than twenty years ago when Alan Gibson and others pioneered the approach. As Jim Tomecko observes in one piece in this collection, it is fundamentally 'just good development'. But it is no easier for that. This volume offers an eclectic set of insights and reflections on the practical application of market systems development from some of the many around the world who were inspired by Alan. It provides an invaluable addition to the literature on the praxis of making markets work for the poor and offers much for newcomers to the field and seasoned practitioners alike.'

David Ferrand, Consultant

'Good market systems work is significantly more challenging than more traditional approaches to development. It requires a deeper analysis of root causes, a more humble and limited role for external development agents, and a greater understanding of and comfort with markets. In his pioneering and leadership role, Alan Gibson continually challenged all of us in our thinking and practice of market systems development. This books makes an important contribution to this ongoing learning and practice.'

Chris Eaton, Executive Director, World University Service of Canada

'What mattered to Alan was not branding but to keep the ambition in development, striving to do the best possible job with the available resources, and to not accept the status quo. Alan concerned himself always with the quality of our efforts to contribute to a more equitable world. He pushed us not to shy away from the deep, iterative analysis of the reality of complex systems and the more difficult questions about our role as development actors. Despite the multiple interpretations of what 'market systems development' may mean, it is clear that our collective efforts have improved thanks to Alan's ability to share his great mind.'

Diane Johnson, Independent Consultant and former Springfield Associate

Making Market Systems Work for the Poor

Experience inspired by Alan Gibson

Edited by
Joanna Ledgerwood

Practical
ACTION
PUBLISHING

Practical Action Publishing Ltd
27a Albert Street, Rugby, Warwickshire, CV21 2SG, UK
www.practicalactionpublishing.com

A catalogue record for this book is available from the British Library.

A catalogue record for this book has been requested from the Library of Congress.

ISBN 978-1-78853-141-2 Paperback
ISBN 978-1-78853-142-9 Hardback
ISBN 978-1-78853-144-3 eBook

Citation: Ledgerwood, J. (ed.) (2021) *Making Market Systems Work for the Poor: Experience inspired by Alan Gibson,* Rugby, UK: Practical Action Publishing <http://dx.doi.org/10.3362/9781788531443>.

Since 1974, Practical Action Publishing has published and disseminated books and information in support of international development work throughout the world. Practical Action Publishing is a trading name of Practical Action Publishing Ltd (Company Reg. No. 1159018), the wholly owned publishing company of Practical Action. Practical Action Publishing trades only in support of its parent charity objectives and any profits are covenanted back to Practical Action (Charity Reg. No. 247257, Group VAT Registration No. 880 9924 76).

Photo on back cover: Chris Eaton
Typeset by JMR Digital Solutions, India

Contents

http://dx.doi.org/10.3362/9781788531443.000

This existence of ours is as transient as autumn clouds.

To watch the birth and death of beings is like looking at the movements of a dance.

A lifetime is like a flash of lightning in the sky, rushing by, like a torrent down a steep mountain.

Sogyal Rinpoche
The Tibetan Book of Living and Dying

Foreword

Alan Gibson: Of mice and men

Alan Gibson was found dead on 8 February 2018 having gone walking in the mountains of north-west Scotland and failed to return. This is a loss which is felt deeply by family, friends, colleagues, and development more broadly. To many, Alan was a mentor and friend and every new person one meets in development makes it all the more clear how uniquely talented Alan was.

Climbing mountains in difficult conditions could be a metaphor for Alan's professional life. Alan was a pioneer in market systems development. Never one to take the easy route, he challenged the status quo, questioned convention, confronted naysayers and exposed posterior-coverers, to forge a new path. Many of us are in his debt for doing so.

Alan was not one for sentimentality and so, rather than wallowing in what we've lost, we thought it might be an appropriate moment to celebrate his legacy, with a Gibson-esque holding up of the mirror to development and its ills.

Ten years on from the release of the first Making Markets Work for the Poor (M4P) Operational Guide, where are we? More than £2 bn spent under the banner of M4P and much, much more under 'market systems development' more broadly. We're all systems people now, aren't we? But is there a risk that 'systems' has become a slogan – as Alan would say, 'wholesome ... and meaningless'? Or, to borrow from Shakespeare:

> Told by an idiot, full of sound and fury,
> Signifying nothing.

One fears an emperor's new clothes phenomenon: a lot of hype, but is anything really different? A certain amount of hype might not be a bad thing, you might argue. It's good marketing, helping to spread the message. So long as that doesn't dilute the content, fine. The objective of sustainable, large-scale development impact and finding effective means of getting there shouldn't be compromised. But is that really the case?

With Alan's passing, it is time to revisit the substance of market systems development.

There are four operative terms in the market systems development approach: 1) 'Market': a means to deliver sustainable benefits by leveraging incentives; 2) 'Systems': a means of ensuring scale by transforming the way markets work rather than just the performance of individual actors; 3) 'Development': the use of external aid to achieve an impact on those that need it – poor and disadvantaged people; and 4) 'Approach': a way of working to achieve objectives – the why, what, and how. The market systems development approach can be broken down into three components:

- *A rationale and objective.* To deliver large-scale, sustainable development impact to poor and disadvantaged people (why we do what we do).
- *A framework for analysis.* Understanding the institutional underlying causes of negative outcomes (what we want to change).
- *Guidance for action.* A method of intervening in systems so as to achieve these objectives sustainably (how we bring about change).

As the popularity of market systems development has grown, so has the size of the emperor's wardrobe. In an effort to fill it, developmental tailors have tended to neglect these operative terms. So we see a tendency to focus on:

- *Markets (firms) and not systems.* Firm-centric initiatives ignore scale by providing support to businesses that never have any realistic prospect of going to scale. They ignore the mechanisms through which behaviour change is catalysed; or
- *Market systems with no development.* Harking back to the earlier years of the 'growth is good' doctrine, by seeing growth as an objective in its own right without considering whether poor and disadvantaged people have benefitted from it; or
- *Development with no market systems.* Initiatives look at what is important to disadvantaged people's livelihoods and then deliver the solution, such as subsidizing seeds for people to sell crops, ignoring sustainability; or
- *Technical methods, with little connection to the why, what, and how.* Useful analytical tools have emerged to help understand complex systems. But using them doesn't mean you're going to create large-scale, sustainable change. You have to be very clear about what you're going to do as a result of the analysis and how you are going to do it. Similarly, guidelines have emerged for making deals, providing grants, and measuring results. But unless these are grounded in accurate analysis and guided by clear objectives, you tend to lose sight of what it is that you're trying to achieve.

How can we rectify this trend? When reviewing anything, Alan's first question was always 'so what?' So, let's use the sadness of his passing as an opportunity. Hold up a mirror as you're on your way to the office tomorrow and ask yourself a question: is what I'm doing, saying, or writing really advancing the cause of better development? Will it really make a difference? If not, then maybe you should do something else.

Be brave. Don't be a 'tim'rous beastie'. Ask yourself, what would Alan Gibson do?

Rob Hitchins and Ben Taylor
Springfield Centre

Preface

Alan Gibson was an exceptional athlete with equally exceptional intellectual capacity. He was also pathologically modest and private to a fault; Alan shunned the spotlight in life. The reality is he was a towering mind in his chosen field but likely his good friends on the football pitch knew little of him off the field.

Alan died on 6 February 2018 while hillwalking in northern Scotland having gone out for the day with his brother Neil to 'bag a Munro' (a Scottish mountain over 3,000 feet). Alan spent a lot of time in the hills of Scotland during his childhood growing up in the nearby town of Nairn and continued to do so right up until his death. He was in a good place in the last year of his life; he had cut back to part-time work and was excited about the future, looking forward to continuing work that was 'valid', work that made a difference – and to having more time to hike, travel around British Columbia where his mother was born, walk his dog, and to just enjoy life.

Before his death, Alan and I were in the early stages of writing a book on making financial markets work for the poor. That book is no longer possible for which I am truly sorry, as I believe it would have been transformational; he had much more to say. In its stead, we have, in Alan's memory, created this book, similar to a *Gedenkschrift*:

> a book posthumously honouring a respected person in a particular field. The term, borrowed from German, and literally meaning 'commemorative-writing', can be translated as 'celebration'. A Gedenkschrift generally takes the form of an edited volume, containing contributions from the honoree's colleagues, students, and friends. The essays usually relate in some way to, or reflect upon, the honoree's contributions to their field. (Wikipedia, 2020)

While this book is not a true *Gedenkschrift*, I find the concept fitting. Indeed, Alan was highly respected, and his work deserves much celebration. As Rob Hitchins, his partner of 20 years at Springfield, said: 'Alan was a legend. He was insightful, articulate, passionate and witty. He was courageous and principled. He had conviction and integrity. He made a genuine difference.'

As an intensely private person, I am sure Alan would be somewhat unhappy that this book has been written. Certainly, he would have shunned the personal attention as he did in life. But his untimely death compels me to make sure his work is both remembered and accessible for those who seek to do development better. His significant influence on a market systems approach (M4P) to poverty alleviation is his legacy; it merits our acknowledgement and celebration.

As evidenced by this book, Alan had tremendous impact on the people he met, those he taught, and those lucky enough to work with him. I am very grateful to all of the authors who cared about Alan and about good development enough to take the time to contribute to this book. It is my hope it will support and influence development professionals to carry on Alan's vision and intellectual honesty, and to make a real difference. The seeds he planted have grown and will clearly continue to grow, as demonstrated by these authors and their passion.

Although often frustrated by the inability of people, and particularly aid agencies, to change, Alan consistently insisted on honest, thoughtful work. He didn't shy away from things that were difficult; he set the bar high – for himself, as well as for others. People often said, 'Alan doesn't suffer fools', but the reality was, while he simply would not work with people and organizations that were not willing to change, he had the most incredible patience and willingness to teach and mentor those genuinely eager to learn. As evidenced by the numerous tributes to Alan in this book from his students and colleagues, his influence was truly transformational.

I want this book to memorialize and shine a light on this influence. Had Alan lived beyond his 56 years, I know he would have spent the next 20 continuing to encourage and support others to do better development – in ways that truly made it count for the poor and vulnerable, but also in ways that were kind, incisive, patient, inspiring, and challenging. As demonstrated by this book and the personal comments within, Alan challenged everyone he met to do things well, and to make a difference. We have lost someone who dedicated his life to development because he himself cared so profoundly about reducing poverty and empowering the poor. I thought the story someone shared during his memorial was telling. He said: 'Alan once said to me that he wished he could be invisible so he could live among the poor and really understand how they lived.'

David Ferrand, a good friend of Alan's and himself a leader in market systems development said it best:

> It simply seems impossible that he should have gone – there was always such a vitality about him. I can only emphatically agree that the world was a far, far better place with Alan in it. It seems grotesque that we have lost someone so brilliant. He managed to combine an extraordinary intellectual and moral integrity with a wonderful sense of the absurd, a joyous wit and – so rare – a genuine, deep modesty.

> We need Alan's vision and intellectual honesty more than ever. I worry that without Alan, M4P will become a debased currency. ... writing in honour of Alan sets a very high bar. He himself always wrote with such fluidity, clarity and significance.

Alan influenced and provoked me like no other person in my 30 years in development, and I have never encountered a more brilliant mind. I had deep respect and admiration for Alan, for his intellect, his kindness, and his endless wit. To his family and friends who may not all have fully known the depth and calibre of his contributions to international development, I can attest there is so much to be proud of in him, as a person and as a change-maker. With his untimely and tragic death, Alan leaves his beloved family, his business partners and co-workers, students, mentees, and others who relied on his advice, prodigious work ethic, moral compass, and always his incisive humour, love of hill walks, football, museums, good food, live music, dancing, a new-found love of kayaking, and a good argument that comprised his whole self. All books take thousands of hours and many good hands to create. These hours are my dedication to the person who changed my life, irrevocably, all for the better but for the loss of him.

There will always be the could-haves, should-haves, and would-haves, but look at all that was.

May you rest in peace, Alan.

Joanna

Reference

Wikipedia (2020) 'Festschrift' [online] <https://en.wikipedia.org/wiki/Festschrift#:~:text=An%20alternative%20Latin%20term%20is,is%20much%20rarer%20in%20English> [accessed 8 February 2020].

About this book

It has been more than 20 years since Alan first reviewed and analysed donor-funded business development service efforts for the Committee of Donor Agencies for Small Enterprise Development and, from that, developed a set of good practice principles (Committee of Donor Agencies for Small Enterprise Development, 2001) – the beginnings of the M4P approach. The approach has clearly developed, grown, and been refined over the years. Alan and his colleagues at Springfield have trained multitudes of people and organizations in its application, and in doing so influenced the development sector immensely over the last two decades. While not always successful, the M4P approach has made a significant difference to the lives of many.

The purpose of this book is to document experiences in applying the approach to provide a learning resource for those managing or funding M4P programmes. It is hoped it will also provide the reader with a reminder of the 'good development' that can result from using the approach.

Consistent with Alan's teachings, this book is not a 'how-to' guide; rather it is a collection of experiences and learnings aimed at demonstrating how M4P works, how the application of M4P has expanded over the years, and to share reflections on some of the challenges. The experiences described within are drawn from many different sectors and geographies, shared by Alan's students and colleagues – those who were influenced by Alan's thinking and who challenged themselves, or supported others, to adopt the approach – and who were willing to reflect on their experience. In addition, Alan's own writings about development, in particular, his views on UK aid, are included.

Ultimately, my hope is this book will encourage and motivate development professionals to use, promote, and to value the M4P approach, and that as a community we will continue to learn and to refine its application and benefits.

This book is intended for facilitators, funders, consultants, academics, and others; and in some cases, system actors, whether from the public sector, the private sector, or civil society organizations. It will be useful for anyone seeking to drive sustainable systems change at scale.

Lastly, this book is also about providing space for Alan's friends, students, and colleagues to pay tribute to him.

A note about Springfield: Alan co-founded the Springfield Centre in 1995 with Mark Havers. After Mark left, Alan continued to build Springfield with his new partner Rob Hitchins, and subsequently David Elliott. In 2014, Alan divested his ownership in Springfield although he continued as Associate Director until his death. And while this book is a memorial to Alan's work, I am certain he would want readers to understand that his legacy is Springfield. Because of his death we are honouring his leadership and therefore in this book we refer to Alan's thinking and influence; however, Alan always saw Springfield as a collective endeavour.

Content and structure

Making Market Systems Work for the Poor: Experience Inspired by Alan Gibson is structured into five parts:

- Part I – What is M4P? And how does it work?
- Part II – Expanding the application of M4P
- Part III – Reflections on making markets work for the poor
- Part IV – Alan Gibson on aid, why development fails, and other matters
- Part V – Tributes to Alan

'Part I – What is M4P? And how does it work?' comprises six chapters focusing on the how and the what of M4P and what makes M4P different from more traditional approaches to development. Chapter 1 provides a summary of the M4P approach in Alan's own words. Chapter 2, 'Applying M4P to the informal sector: Scale and sustainability in savings groups', written by Joanna Ledgerwood, provides a good example of how to apply the M4P approach to a specific sector and considers how facilitators can best support system actors to ensure a sustainable system. Chapter 3, 'Market system diagrams: Or, how I learned to stop worrying and love the doughnut', written by Jake Lomax, discusses the importance of developing and using the infamous doughnut (aka market system diagram) to investigate and address the root causes of market system underperformance in order to effect sustainable change. Chapter 4, 'Measuring what matters: Monitoring and results measurement', written by Ben Fowler and Jake Lomax, examines the shift in M4P programmes from monitoring and evaluation to monitoring and results measurement to inform decision-making and understand system-level change. Chapter 5, 'Getting to scale in M4P programmes', written by Gareth Davies, explores scale, one of the core principles of the M4P approach, and how programmes can maximize the chances of reaching scale. Chapter 6, 'The art of market facilitation: Lessons from FSD Kenya', written by Joanna Ledgerwood, synthesizes Alan's seminal paper on FSD Kenya's work facilitating the financial market system in Kenya. The chapter consolidates lessons from his paper to build understanding of the M4P approach and to provide guidance on key, practical questions facilitators face when applying the approach.

'Part II – Expanding the application of M4P' documents experience in expanding M4P beyond purely private sector development to support more inclusive systems in non-traditional sectors and fragile markets. Chapter 7, 'Making markets work for the poo-er: Water For People's pathway to market systems development', written by Kate Fogelberg, examines the why, the how, and the so what of changing the culture and practices of an international NGO working in the sanitation sector to adopt the M4P approach. Chapter 8, 'Can M4P work everywhere? M4P in thin markets', written by Aly Miehlbradt, looks at what we have learned from the experience of applying M4P in thin markets and suggests it requires using the principles of M4P creatively rather than sticking to a rigid 'rule book'. Chapter 9, 'M4P and gender inclusion', written by Linda Jones and Joanna Ledgerwood, examines the need for pro-active inclusion of gender and women's empowerment in market systems programmes and provides guidance to do so.

'Part III – Reflections on making markets work for the poor' shares reflections on using the M4P approach and how it has developed over time, including the importance of understanding and acknowledging the incentives and capacities of both development actors and system actors to change. Chapter 10, 'Market systems thinking in inclusive finance: Influencing the influencers', written by Mayada El-Zoghbi, describes CGAP's decision to promote the M4P approach (and Alan's support to CGAP in doing so), highlighting limited progress and suggesting the current political economy of aid does not support good practice. Chapter 11, 'Just good development: Why did it take us so long to get there?' written by Jim Tomecko, describes how business development services/enterprise development thinking shifted since its genesis in the late 1990s to become 'good' development. Chapter 12, 'Shame on you! A soteriology of making markets work for the poor', written by Julian Hamilton-Peach, shares the author's experience using the M4P approach in the DFID-funded programme PrOpCom to effect long-lasting and large-scale economic change in Nigeria.

As many people know, Alan was a passionate critic of the UK government's aid efforts, most particularly the commitment to spend 0.7 per cent of gross national income on international development. 'Part IV – Alan Gibson on aid, why development fails, and other matters' includes various blogs and 'soapboxes' written by Alan, all of which reflect his customary wit and substantial intellect. The final paper in this section is a report Alan wrote in 2016 assessing (and criticizing) Scotland's international development efforts. The paper was submitted to ministers in the Scottish parliament to read and, a week after his death, the Scottish *Herald* wrote two pieces about the report encouraging readers to question Scotland's overseas aid. While it is unlikely Alan knew his paper would play a role in his country's politics, it is fitting he had the 'last word'.

'Part V – Tributes to Alan' shares the tributes made by Alan's friends, colleagues, and students on the Springfield website upon learning of his death.

Alan's thinking and vision for a market systems approach to poverty alleviation and economic development was transformative and far-reaching. His brilliance and remarkable ability and generosity to share his insights were a gift, to which this book is testament.

Reference

Committee of Donor Agencies for Small Enterprise Development (2001) *Business Development Services for Small Enterprises: Guiding Principles for Donor Intervention* [pdf] <https://www.enterprise-development.org/wp-content/uploads/BDS-Guiding-Principles-2001-English.pdf> [accessed 9 October 2020].

PART I

What is M4P? And how does it work?

CHAPTER 1

Introducing Making Markets Work for the Poor (M4P)

Joanna Ledgerwood

Abstract

The Making Markets Work for the Poor (M4P) approach is a practical approach to development that increases the likelihood of achieving sustainable positive impact at scale. The approach acknowledges that people live in complex systems and thus provides frameworks to help break down complexity through a process of iterative analysis and strategic planning. The purpose is to go beyond initial symptoms of problems to identify underlying causes. This introduction provides an overview of the approach in Alan's own words.

Keywords: market systems, sustainability, facilitation, incentives, capacity, core, supporting functions, rules, intervention

This book is about Making Markets Work for the Poor (M4P). It is thus fitting to begin with a description of the M4P approach.

In 2017, I was writing a paper on increasing financial inclusion using the M4P approach and mentioned to Alan that I wanted to briefly describe M4P for readers unfamiliar with the approach. He kindly offered to write a 'few pages' for me to include in the paper. The following summary was the result and I think provides a good overview of the approach – useful both as a primer for readers to whom M4P is new and, as well, for those needing a concise reminder of the key elements of approach. These few pages, in Alan's own words, summarize the essence of M4P.

A summary of the market systems approach

> *There is an alluring but misleading simplicity to M4P, to its rationale and to its objectives, all helped by the sense of all-encompassing worthiness of its title 'Making markets work for the poor'. This can encourage facilitators to believe that anything they do related to markets and the poor – which is pretty much every-thing – is M4P in practice. However, M4P is more than a title or a slogan. It is an approach which has disciplines and frameworks to guide it and which challenges facilitators to make sense of it in their own environments.* (Gibson, 2016: 26)

http://dx.doi.org/10.3362/9781788531443.001

This summary proposes the market systems approach[1] as the most effective way to develop a well-functioning market system for the future that is sustainable and at scale. In it, the essence of the market systems approach is set out; this covers both the reasons for adopting the approach (the rationale) and the key elements of the approach in practice (what it is). In doing so, a reference framework is established – a lens through which development experience can be better understood.

This is a summary only[2] and runs the risk of simplification, but nonetheless the substance of the approach can be reduced to a number of key points.

Why a market systems approach?

The late 1990s and early 2000s was a period in international development circles characterized by much reflection and discussion about the approach that development agencies should follow, especially in the private sector development field.[3] Prompting this was a sense of widespread frustration at the efficacy of conventional approaches, then dominated by a narrow supply-side perspective emphasizing subsidy/support for delivery.[4] Reviews of experience with this approach showed it to result in very low levels of long-term outreach and limited sustainability, with partners struggling to move beyond donor support. This was development as small puffs of virtuous, fleeting impact which, in aggregate, amounted to very little.

It was the self-evident 'smallness' of projects, in terms of potential and ambition, that prompted frustration in DFID and other agencies and a search for a different approach – a new paradigm – that would stimulate more substantial, meaningful change rather than simply 'buy impact'. Although not a panacea, nor without challenge in implementation, the market systems approach is increasingly recognized as a logical path to follow.

The market systems approach: What is it?

The market systems approach is based on creating the foundation for lasting change where the market system – its functions and players – is equipped to meet future challenges and continue to meet the changing needs of the poor. The result is *sustained* impact, rather than impact that is short-lived or dependent on further injections of aid. If sustainability is not considered in the context of the market system – and the functions and players within it – change will not be sustained and, ultimately, will not improve the lives of poor people. This means for the private sector, sufficient returns must be provided such that it is in their interest to continue providing (and expanding) the service without continued subsidy. For public sector and not-for-profit actors, change must achieve other objectives such as meeting constituent needs, reducing systemic risk, or providing increased social benefits. Key to sustainability is the *incentive* of market actors to continue to perform the function without ongoing support.

When taking a market systems approach, development organizations are *facilitators* of market development – external change agents whose role is to support market actors to change their behaviour. The primary role of facilitators is to address constraints to catalyse the market system to function more effectively and inclusively. Facilitation is therefore a temporary role. In the longer term, the strategic purpose of facilitation is not to have any continuing role in the market system.

The approach is a way of both understanding the world that poor people face and of taking action to bring positive change to that world. Three overarching features define this as an 'approach', rather than simply a development tool: objectives, analytical framework (or lens), and guidance for intervention.

Objectives. The market systems approach has similar goals to all development initiatives – that is, contributing to a positive development outcome that is sustainable in the long term and reaches large numbers of the target group. This sets the ambition of the approach but also recognizes the reality of poor people (always) being part of a bigger system. Real change is about changing the system, not just individuals themselves. M4P is therefore a systemic approach and the role of development actors is to facilitate the development of the system.

Analytical framework. The approach is underpinned by common frameworks to both describe and analyse market systems. The starting point here is to frame the overall market system as 'multi-function, multi-player'. As Figure 1.1 shows, the system has three main parts:

- *Core function:* the main transaction or exchange between supply and demand.
- *Rules:* both the formal rules (laws, regulations) and the 'informal rules' (attitudes, norms, power relations) that together shape the incentives of key players.
- *Supporting functions:* the collection of other functions required to foster exchange – such as services, information, infrastructure, and advocacy.

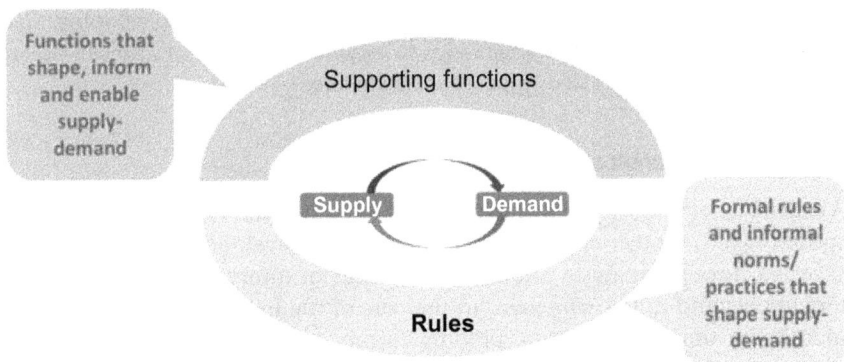

Figure 1.1 The market system

Each of the rules and supporting functions can be seen as systems in their own right. Ultimately, how a market performs – what happens in the core – is dependent on the supporting functions and rules. Changes in the core are a consequence of changes in the wider market functions that surround the core. No matter the point of intervention, consistent with M4P's theory of change, for change to be systemic is has to be manifested in change in supporting functions and rules.

For systems to be inclusive, the variety of market functions must be efficiently and effectively performed by different market actors, not by development actors. While Figure 1.1 provides a means of organizing information related to the structure and functioning of a market system, it does not provide insight into where the constraints are. For that, analysis is needed to throw light on what's *not working*.

Guidance for intervention. The market systems approach provides guidance to facilitators. These 'good practice' guidelines have been developed as experience has grown. Building on market analysis, they deal with the detailed 'how to' issues of intervention, such as how to engage with different actors and encourage behaviour change. The role of development actors is to facilitate change in the system – not to be a player in it, even if that may be necessary in the short term. Facilitation aims to 'crowd in' or stimulate wider and lasting activity beyond the immediate partners/functions that a facilitator works with directly.

A common theory of change

The underpinning logic of the market systems approach is manifested in a common theory of change. This articulates the strategy (based on the analysis) and vision for achieving a sustainable system. The theory of change outlines the anticipated process that will occur from the facilitators' intervention(s) to market system changes, to increased access and usage, and finally, benefits for poor people at a household level (e.g. reduced vulnerability and/or poverty alleviation and/or increased economic opportunities). Developing and monitoring the theory of change helps to establish whether linkages between interventions and intended impacts are plausible.

Understanding market systems

A central tenet of the market systems approach is that it is led by analysis. More specifically, the constraints that are inhibiting the development of the system, revealed through analysis, should be the focus of interventions. This means looking beyond initial *symptoms* (in the core of the market in Figure 1.1) and identifying underlying *causes*, probing further in supporting functions and rules (and asking further why these 'aren't working'). Often this process leads to constraints related to two essential market system truths: markets do not develop because:

- people/actors do not know *how to* change (capacities) and/or
- people/actors do not *want to* change (incentives).

Both of these are also of course shaped by their awareness of the need for change. Commonly, however, successful interventions to develop market systems are shaped by a close understanding of the capacities and incentives factors at the heart of system behaviour.

Developing a future vision

Accompanying a detailed market system analysis, successful intervention should be shaped by a clear vision of how it is envisaged a market system will function in the future without development agencies. This requires matching market functions with market actors and identifying who currently does these and who currently pays for (or resources) these. And if it is development actors currently doing and/or paying, then one needs to consider who *could* do and who *could* pay for these in the future. In doing so, a future direction is set out that informs decision-making by facilitators and provides a starting point for operationalizing sustainability. This 'who does?/who pays?' consideration can be adapted into a simple but useful framework and tool for planning and assessment and for highlighting the role of (and dependence on) donor-funded support.

Interventions to catalyse change

The purpose of understanding the market system and of developing a future picture is to help shape effective interventions. *Interventions* are activities undertaken by a facilitator, usually with partners, to effect market system change. Interventions may be with one partner or involve multiple partners. Facilitators intervene with market actors to support them to, for example: develop and offer new or improved services to new or underserved clients; upgrade their capacity and performance; take on new roles in the system; change the way they relate to other system actors; or change the way they formulate or enforce rules. From a market systems perspective, for intervention in the core to be valid it has to cause change in the wider market system – for example in attitudes to risk, in information available on products, or in willingness to invest in specialist services – which in turn catalyses further development in the core of the market.

The process of intervention is not formulaic, but it is one where facilitators can be guided by substantial learning from experience, manifested in a number of 'good practice' principles. These relate to a number of key aspects of intervention, for example:

- *Who to work with*. Selecting the right partners and adapting interventions to their situation.
- *'Right-sizing' activities*. Developing interventions such that they are the appropriate scale, intensity, and type to induce a positive response.
- *Transactional relationships*. Ensuring that interventions are based on a quid pro quo relationship with partners that tests commitment and ownership.
- *Designing for wider change*. Shaping activities with individual specific partner activities to stimulate a wider response from others, a 'crowding-in' in the market system.

Measurement to guide actions

A key aspect of the approach is continual assessment of the validity of assumptions and of the effectiveness of interventions, adjusting interventions accordingly. Indeed, the non-prescriptive-/analysis-led character of the approach – facilitation rather than simple delivery – means measurement is even more important. Measuring and validating intervention results and tracking and verifying the link between interventions and financial inclusion objectives is a fundamental, integrated part of facilitating systemic change. This means asking the right questions and using the right tools to generate useful information, and then acting on this. Result chains are an important tool for measurement, as well as for overall planning and intervention management.

The above factors frame the key characteristics of the market systems approach. Together they can also be seen as the main features of a lens through which experience can be assessed. Of particular importance here are considerations (understanding market systems and developing a vision) related to the characteristic role of donor-funded support and the degree to which development interventions genuinely address underlying systemic constraints, for example in relation to capacities and incentives.

Notes

1. The approach is referred to by various names – most commonly Making Markets Work for the Poor (M4P), market development, market systems development, and the systemic approach.
2. There are a number of more comprehensive guides to the approach, most notably *The Operational Guide for the M4P Approach* (Springfield Centre, 2015) and other M4P resources; see for example, the BEAM Exchange, the SEEP Network, the Swiss Agency for Development and Cooperation (SDC), and the Donor Committee on Economic Development.
3. Some of this was manifested in new guidelines from the Donor Committee for Enterprise Development.
4. Other aspects of support included research and service delivery development.

References

Gibson, A. (2016) *FSD Kenya: Ten Years of a Market Systems Approach in the Kenyan Finance Market* [online], Nairobi: FSD Kenya and Durham, UK: Springfield Centre <http://fsdkenya.org/publication/fsd-kenya-ten-years-of-a-market-systems-approach-in-the-kenyan-finance-market/> [accessed 9 October 2020].

Springfield Centre (2015) *The Operational Guide for the M4P Approach*, 2nd edn, Durham, UK: Springfield Centre.

CHAPTER 2

Applying M4P to the informal sector: Scale and sustainability in savings groups

Joanna Ledgerwood

Abstract

Despite the seemingly large number of savings groups in existence and clear evidence of benefits to members, the reality is that the system is underperforming in terms of its potential. Market estimates of the demand for savings groups by women in sub-Saharan Africa alone are as high as 125 million, and the potential market for savings groups worldwide may be as large as 400 million. This chapter outlines how the market systems approach can be used to support the development of a well-functioning system where savings groups effectively reach all those who seek participation. It provides a good example of how to practically apply the approach, benefiting from various discussions with Alan on how best to create a sustainable savings group system at scale.

Keywords: savings groups, implementors, facilitation, sustainability, scale

In early 2017, I was invited by the SEEP Network to write a paper on applying the Making Markets Work for the Poor (M4P) approach to the formation and operation of savings groups (SGs). Savings groups are informal financial service providers (FSPs) that serve, primarily, people who are excluded from or underserved by formal FSPs, including the rural poor, women, youth, and other vulnerable populations.[1] At the time, donor funding to international NGOs for SG formation was drying up yet there remained significant demand for SGs throughout sub-Saharan Africa and, to a lesser extent, Asia. I asked Alan if he could help me structure the paper and specifically how a sustainable system could be developed whereby SGs would continue to exist and to be formed without aid funding. He was, of course, extremely helpful as I worked through the paper, providing input both formally – as a peer reviewer for SEEP – and informally as my discussion partner. One of his first comments was to suggest I consider if there was a potential role for government in group formation. I wasn't sure there was. Three years on it is indeed where much of the thinking in the SG sector is going.

Alan was instrumental in shaping my early thinking for the original paper. However, after reading the final draft, he thought it could be better.

http://dx.doi.org/10.3362/9781788531443.002

He suggested there was a need to sharpen the explanation of the market systems approach, especially as a lens for analysing the SG system and for intervening in it, and then to more rigorously apply this lens in the analysis of current experience and into the recommendations. He said:

> Readers need to see sustainability not just as things continuing pretty much as they are without external support – this is a limiting and static view – but rather that the system continues to develop and grow in response to opportunities and needs – a more dynamic and accurate view. That is, that the capability of the SG system in different countries to not simply 'stay' at its existing level but to develop and grow by itself to offer more benefits to more poor people.

Unfortunately, Alan died before the paper was published (Ledgerwood and Johnson, 2018). The paper was then revised in 2020 and published as a SEEP Learning Brief (Ledgerwood, 2020) which is the basis for this chapter. I have tried to address Alan's feedback as much as is possible to do without the benefit of his continued wisdom.

Introduction

In 2011, Stuart Rutherford, author of *The Poor and Their Money*, told the audience at the Arusha Savings Group Summit that success for the SG sector will come when SGs are indigenous, akin to ROSCAs (rotating savings and credit associations), a model widely known and easily adopted by anyone seeking its benefits. But SGs are not only more complicated than ROSCAs, they have become much more than a method of financial intermediation, often adopted by a wide range of development programmes, targeted by formal FSPs for additional financial services, used as channels to gain political favour, and to disseminate government messages. As 'informal' providers, facilitating change in the SG market system needs to consider the incentives of the numerous and varied stakeholders and how this may differ from working with the formal sector.

Historically, the SG sector has been heavily dependent on *development actors* including *donors* (bilateral and multilateral development agencies, private foundations, and development finance organizations) who provide funding to *implementers* (generally local and international NGOs, faith-based organizations and community-based organizations) to form, train, and, in some cases, provide additional support to SGs. The ongoing and relatively high costs (especially given the size of demand/market) of this model amplify concerns for the sustainability of the SG system to achieve scale, highlighting the need for an alternative to continued donor subsidies. There is simply no prospect of enough donor funding to meet the large unmet demand based on the current model of funding implementers to form, train, and support groups (see Box 2.1).

Box 2.1 FSD Kenya: placing SGs into a market system framework

In 2005, savings groups were increasingly seen, globally, as serving an important purpose in enabling poor people to manage their finances and their lives. However, in Kenya they were relatively undeveloped. According to the FinAccess survey (2006), almost three-quarters of the population were excluded or reliant on informal finance. FSD Kenya knew that a more inclusive finance market could not simply rely on formal FSPs; other sources, such as SGs, potentially had a key role to play.

FSD Kenya regarded existing standard approaches to developing SGs as expensive and overly dependent on external, donor support. From FSD Kenya's perspective, the problem with this standard approach was that it was sourced in a view of small-scale, expensive, donor-NGO delivery rather than facilitation of change aimed at unleashing potential for larger-scale, more sustainable impact. For that to happen, not only did the cost of forming groups have to be substantially reduced, but the function of group formation had to be more embedded in the norms and practices of rural society – rather than being one which only (external) NGOs could do. After a protracted period of negotiation, working with NGO partners, primarily CARE and Catholic Relief Services, FSD Kenya, here as an informed funder of facilitation rather than a facilitator itself, initiated a process of project design, experiment, and innovation that spanned eight years. Intervention was aimed primarily at developing training/group formation – a supporting function with a public character – and on this basis enhancing digital information resources and links with banks. In doing so, a better environment would be established for the successful operation of SGs.

Seeing traditional roles in a market systems context: This initial step of putting SGs into the framework of market systems has been most valuable. Group formation can be seen as a legitimate one-off, public good – an investment in social capital – but considering it in this frame rather than seeing it as an aid-funded deliverable instigates a series of questions which interventions should seek to address. How can the process of developing SGs be placed more into the community? How can the system of group formation replicate itself with little (or no) external support? Are the inevitable quality compromises that will arise from reduced NGO control – and the emergence of market norms – acceptable? Much of this revolves around 'right-sizing' group training so that there is more scope for groups to develop as an embedded (if informal) institution rather than a slightly artificial external creation.

Developing a vision of the future: After eight years of intervention and US$6.2 m invested, having made the step to place SGs into a market system framework, and undertaken research on the efficacy of different channels, an important question with SGs (as in any M4P context) is to consider the future vision towards which intervention is proceeding. For example, how can groups be linked with Kenya's formal finance providers? Bringing together disparate parts of the existing market system, narrowing the formal–informal divide, would potentially be a major step to meaningful inclusion but depends critically on whether this represents a feasible business model for banks. This is especially important to avoid the familiar trap of development support for endless group formation.

FSD Kenya has achieved partial success in developing the group formation/training function with momentum created in embedding this into the market context. It is clear, however, that substantial further outreach depends on public/donor resources – but a research base to guide this has been established.

Source: Gibson, 2016: 24–26

That SGs require external subsidies is not a new concern; initially it was argued that the potential for independent groups after one year (thereby limiting the required subsidy) and spontaneous or promoted replication (expanding the value of that subsidy) justified the 'investment'. Nevertheless, concern about the capacity for donor funding to meet what is estimated to be an enormous need, drove efforts in the beginning of this century to both reduce the cost of group formation and to expand outreach. That experience taught us several important lessons: 1) not all groups become fully independent after one year with some requiring ongoing support; and 2) efforts to drive the cost down resulting in an emphasis on quantity over quality led at times to compromised group quality, posing a threat to the credibility and viability of SGs and the system itself.

> Experience indicated that an initial subsidy by development agencies was required to train and establish trainers who would then go on to form and support savings groups. The premise held that once a notional 'critical mass' of trainers and groups was established, the 'system' would take care of itself. Aid funding was regarded as a one-off 'priming of the pump' with no need for recurrent subsidy. However, it became increasingly evident that many groups remained dependent on the services of their trainer after the initial period of training and support, particularly at the time of share-out and to help resolve problems that inevitably arose from time to time. (Elliott, 2016: 5)

If the SG system is to truly reach *scale,* it is necessary to find a way to achieve *sustainability*; that is, the capability of the system to adapt and provide benefits to more people without continued donor funding. Yet catalysing or motivating system actors to assume functions currently performed and funded by development actors can be daunting. Numerous experiments to date have encouraged this transfer. And while some show promise, most have not yet fully demonstrated clear incentives for market actors.

This chapter begins with an analysis of the current SG system, providing an informed judgement of where and why the system is not performing to its full potential. It then considers the incentives and capacities for *system actors* to take on roles currently being performed or paid for by *development actors*, followed by suggestions for how market facilitators can support system actors to develop a sustainable system at scale.[2] The purpose is to propose a practical, although somewhat still theoretical, application of the M4P approach to a sector where there is great demand but very little sustainable experience.

Understanding the savings group system

Facilitation begins with analysis of the functions within a market system. The first step is to define the functions; the second is to determine who is performing the functions and who is paying for them to be performed. Figure 2.1 provides an illustrative view of the SG system and its functions.

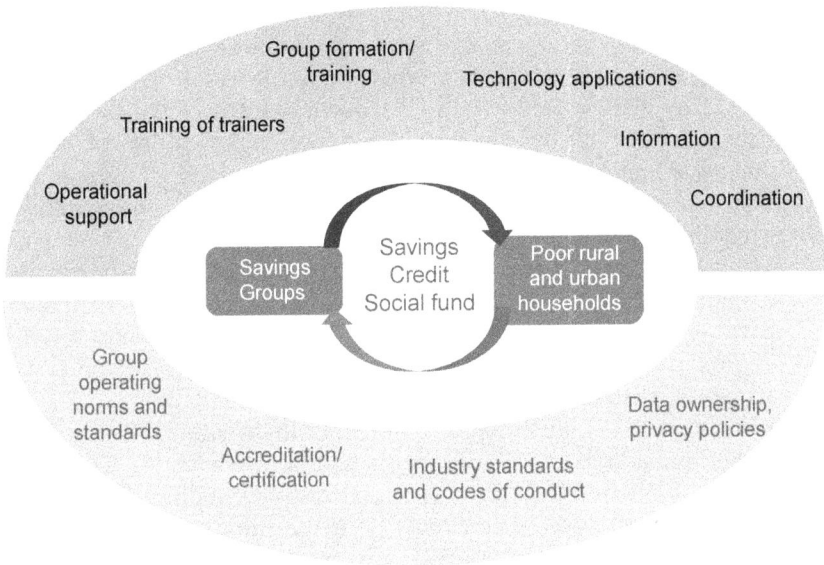

Figure 2.1 Illustrative savings group system

Performance and stability in the core is demonstrated by size and out-reach – the number of members and the number of SGs operating; and by depth and quality – the level of poverty of the members and the degree to which services meet member needs. Supporting functions and rules are necessary for the core to operate effectively. The following describes each of the supporting functions and rules depicted in the SG system. It is through addressing constraints in the supporting functions and rules that increased transactions in the core result. In Alan's paper analysing FSD Kenya's first 10 years, he wrote:

> From a market systems perspective, for intervention in the core to be valid it has to ensure that the underlying causes are addressed in supporting functions and rules. Interventions seek change in the wider market system – for example in attitudes to risk, in information available on products, or in willingness to invest in specialist services – which in turn catalyses further development in the core of the market. No matter the point of intervention therefore, consistent with M4P's theory of change, for change to be systemic it has to be manifested in change in supporting functions and rules. (Gibson, 2016: 6)

The SG system provides a great example of this. While many assume the solution is just to train more groups, this does not happen without changes in the supporting functions and rules.

Supporting functions

- *Group formation and training.* SGs require formation and capacity-building through a structured process of training which takes place over 9 to 12 months. In addition, an unknown number of SGs are formed through 'viral replication' or peer-to-peer training.
- *Training of trainers.* In order to have an expanding cadre of trainers able to form and train SGs and provide support, ongoing training of trainers is required.
- *Operational support.* After groups complete the training, they become safe places for members to save, and increasingly function on their own. However, many SGs require periodic ongoing support, to ensure rules are understood and followed, help with complicated calculations (i.e. share-out), or to help resolve disputes.
- *Information.* There are two primary areas of information within the SG system: providing *data* regarding SGs and their operations (i.e. name, location, number of members, savings, loans outstanding); and providing information regarding *external services* (i.e. information on products or services such as formal financial services, health services, agricultural inputs and practices).
- *Sector coordination.* Coordination among sector stakeholders is necessary to support development of the system. This may include sharing training resources and technology advances, standardizing methodologies, and hosting databases and coverage maps.
- *Technology applications.* Various tools reduce complexity and reinforce and supplement skills, thereby increasing efficiency of group operations. Technology applications to support record-keeping serve to improve both accuracy and transparency as well as collect data as either the primary purpose or as an ancillary benefit (e.g. client information to support access to formal FSPs).

Rules

Because SGs do not intermediate non-member funds, formal regulation has not been necessary. However, SGs face risks related to poor group quality and, more recently, from exposure to external actors, including formal financial service providers (Wheaton, 2018).[3] As SGs are likely to remain informal and, thus, outside of direct oversight, consumer protection needs to be embedded in the SG system.

- *Group operating norms and standards.* Groups require rules that govern operations, and members require the capacity to follow these rules to ensure no harm. Operating norms and standards are typically documented in individual group constitutions which govern how the group functions including rules related to savings and credit, and the rights and responsibilities of members. In addition to formalized rules, group operations are also influenced by informal norms related to gender, age, and particularly trust among group members, between members and trainers, and members and external service providers. Groups are often connected through other affiliations (livelihoods, familial bond, faith, geography, etc.) which may influence informal rules.

- *Accreditation/certification.* Some group formation and training models include a certification process to certify trainers to ensure quality standards. Accredited institutions observe and examine trainers, who are then certified if they meet the criteria. Certification formalizes group operational standards somewhat and may support a more sustainable system although quality depends on how the accreditation is done and by whom.
- *Industry standards and codes of conduct.* At present, standards and codes of conduct relate predominantly to development actors; in a sustainable system, codes of conduct or standards for market actors, particularly external service providers, are required.
- *Data ownership and privacy policies.* Policies regarding how individual and group data is gathered, used, shared, and stored, as well as ownership of data and member understanding of how it is being used and by whom, are necessary to protect group members. Policies are generally enacted by government; however, data ownership and privacy standards may also be included in industry codes of conduct.[4]

'Who does?' and 'who pays?'

Figure 2.1 provides a means of organizing information related to the structure and *functions* of the SG system. Table 2.1 outlines who currently *performs* (does) these functions, and who currently *pays* for these functions, and assesses the effectiveness of current performance.[5] This assessment allows us to identify constraints which are keeping the SG system from performing on its own at scale; that is, which functions are being performed and/or paid for by development actors and, therefore, where change needs to happen.

Developing a sustainable SG system

To facilitate the development of a functioning sustainable SG system that operates at scale, development actors must work towards a future that does not include them. This requires a realistic assessment of which system actors (private sector, government or civil society organizations (CSOs)) have the incentives and the capacity to do and/or pay for functions currently being performed or paid for by development actors (identified in bold in Table 2.1). Determining this provides a possible future vision for a sustainable SG system and helps market facilitators intervene appropriately to develop the system.

Table 2.1 The current SG system: Who does? Who pays?

Function	Who does?	Who pays?	Performance
Core (supply–demand)			
Savings, credit, social fund	*Supply:* SGs *Demand:* Members	Members	SGs are reasonably sustainable themselves, but the overall system is not sustainable; and it is not reaching its potential for scale. Quality varies depending on training and support.
Supporting functions			
Group formation and training	**Implementers (and partners)** Fee-for-service trainers	**Donors** Members	Sustainable once fee-for-service trainers are trained. Not reaching full potential of scale. Not sustainable in the long term if paid by donors.
Training of trainers	**Implementers (and partners)**	**Donors** Trainers	Donors pay for initial training of trainers to train groups and other trainers. Not sustainable in the long term if paid by donors. Not reaching scale.
Operational support	**Implementers (and partners)** Fee-for-service trainers	**Donors** Members	Operational support is provided by the same actors who do group formation/ training. Potential for sustainability if members perceive value and pay; not sustainable if paid by donors or if trainers leave the area.
Technology applications	Private sector developers **Implementers (and partners)**	**Donors** Private sector Members	Mostly donors pay, through implementers, for development, management and trouble-shooting of technology applications. Not sustainable if implementers 'do' and donors 'pay'. Not reaching scale.
Coordination	**Implementers (and partners)** Trainer networks/associations	**Donors** Trainers	Potential for sustainability if trainers and/or government perceive value and pay. Not sustainable if done by implementers and paid by donors.
Information: data collection and provision; linkage to external services	**Implementers (and partners)** Trainer networks/associations	**Donors**	Information collected by development actors less relevant for market actors. Potential for sustainability if government or private sector perceives value and does and/or pays. Not sustainable if done by implementers and paid by donors.

(Continues)

Function	Who does?	Who pays?	Performance
Rules			
Group operating norms and standards	Trainers SGs	**Donors** Members	Largely informal but often documented. Quality varies related to quality of group formation, training, and operational support. Essential for consumer protection.
Accreditation-certification	**Implementers (and partners)** Government	**Donors** Trainers	Certification of trainers is not necessary but may contribute to quality assurance and trust. Not sustainable if paid by donors. Quality varies depending on provider.
Industry standards and codes of conduct	**Implementers (and partners)** Industry bodies/networks	**Donors**	Related to consumer protection. Will shift to local industry networks when development actors are not performing key support functions and rules.
Data ownership and privacy policies	**Implementers (and partners)** Government	**Donors** Government	Not exclusive to SGs but necessary to protect members as groups become digitized, connect with formal FSPs. Sustainable if government 'does' and 'pays'.

This chapter advocates for implementers to shift their focus from *implementing* to *facilitating*. The role of facilitators is to work in partnership with system actors to align incentives and to develop their capacity to do and to pay for support functions and rules currently performed by development actors. In all cases viability needs to be tested based on various assumptions regarding costs and revenues/benefits to determine the numbers and capacity required to make it viable in the long term. Learning through experimentation is key.

> A common theme throughout FSD Kenya's work with SGs was working in partnership. It sought partnerships with organisations that had the track record, momentum, incentives, and capacity to achieve significant change. Within these partnerships, FSD Kenya's role was consistent: it helped partners to test and learn, giving them the confidence to invest further resources to scale up. FSD Kenya did not simply sub-contract its partners to deliver results, as might have conventionally been the case. Instead it used a variety of instruments – research, technical assistance, funding – to influence the thinking and behaviour of its partners. It ensured learning emerged, and was presented, discussed, and debated with key stakeholders throughout the process. This influencing approach has been successful in bringing about lasting change. (Elliott, 2016: 12)

Who could do and who could pay?

When considering 'who *could* do' and 'who *could* pay' in the future, the incentives for each type of system actor must be realistically and practically assessed. For the private sector (whether firms or individuals), incentives most often relate to financial viability and employment (and possibly social standing). For the public sector, incentives relate to developing the economy and managing risk. For CSOs, their objectives are to ensure social good and benefit. Once incentives are aligned, capacity can be developed. This is an appropriate role for development actors in a facilitation role.

Group formation, training, training of trainers, and certification. In recent years, efforts by implementers to create a more sustainable SG system have focused on developing approaches to reduce the cost of group formation and training through a cascaded 'fee-for-service' model whereby independent trainers are paid by the groups rather than the implementer.

As this model evolved, two types of independent 'fee-for service' trainers have emerged: 'lead trainers' and 'community-based trainers' (CBTs).[6] Lead trainers are trained (and often certified) and then train groups. They also identify potential CBTs from existing SGs (or another search process) whom they train and support to form and train additional SGs. CBTs may initially receive training and a stipend from the implementer, but in a sustainable system, they: 1) pay a lead trainer for training; and 2) are compensated exclusively by the groups.

This 'cascade training' approach has worked well to expand the number of SGs beyond those trained by implementer staff and has reduced the cost of group formation and training substantially and contributed to the sustainability of the system; however, it does not address the ongoing need for donor funding to train the first groups of SGs and for training of lead trainers (and certification) to train and supervise CBTs. Thus, neither sustainability nor scale has been achieved, particularly as defined by Alan above.

These early efforts to privatize group formation and training demonstrate the challenges of limited markets, limited capacity, and misaligned incentives. Private certified trainers work in markets limited by how far they can travel to reach new communities and organize new groups. Eventually operating in a saturated market, these trainers have an incentive to keep existing groups dependent on their services.

Privatizing the training and certification of lead trainers has yet to be tried. For a private training institute to offer training for lead trainers on an ongoing, sustainable basis, there must be a viable business case; that is, enough people must be willing to pay sufficient tuition to become lead trainers. For an FSP or fintech to train lead trainers, it must make commercial sense either through developing the market for additional services or to reach new market segments. Individual social entrepreneurs willing to become lead trainers (and pay to be trained) need to be confident there will be enough revenue in training groups and managing CBTs to make a viable business opportunity.

Based on experience to date, it is therefore not clear that 1) training new groups and 2) training of trainers can be fully commercially viable – which means it is unlikely to be just about private actors. Government entities with a social protection or community development mandate,[7] ideally with deep local outreach, may have a role to play in paying for their staff (or quasi staff) to become lead trainers, either by sending them to a private training institute or by developing capacity in-house. These civil servants could then be deployed to local government offices to train CBTs (non-staff), who then train and support SGs. Governments may also be willing to assume the responsibility of group formation and support in the context of social protection programmes which often include cash transfers and reach significant numbers. Such programmes will be more effective when their participants are motivated and facilitated to save. Governments may also recognize the value of SGs in increasing employment and financial inclusion and be willing to accredit (and possibly fund) a training institute to certify lead trainers to reduce risk in the SG system.[8]

Similarly, local CSOs, such as faith-based organizations, are excellent candidates for group formation and training but the 'who pays' question remains. In this case, public–private partnerships may not have received enough attention to date.

Once potential partners have been identified, facilitators can support the development/refinement of training curricula, programme design, materials and processes, and capacity building. Facilitators can also support partners to develop a certification process and seek accreditation from the government to ensure the certificates are meaningful and support quality control. It is of paramount importance, however, that internal capacity be built to maintain and update training materials and to develop new lead trainers in the long term without ongoing support (and funding) of the facilitator – whether in government, private sector, or civil society.

Through supporting an organization(s) to offer training on an ongoing basis to produce lead trainers, create and support CBTs, and maintain and update training materials, facilitators have a clear exit plan; once the training programme is established and its viability demonstrated, development funding is no longer required.

Information, coordination, and technology. Currently, data on group activities is collected primarily by trainers during routine monitoring visits. This data is used by implementers to report to their funders. When training is complete, SG data often ceases to be collected. However, within a sustainable SG system, information is still required. Knowing the number of groups and members and their location, as well as aggregated financial data, and in some cases, individual or transactional data, is useful for governments and others to assess how many people are 'financially included' through SGs (and in some cases, to determine the volume of savings and loans outside of the regulated financial system). This information is also useful for those forming and training new groups and for those interested in providing external services to SGs and their members, such as formal FSPs, local health centres or sales representatives for other products. Who collects and manages this data and who pays for this depends on who has the incentives and capacity to do so.

If a private training institute provides training for lead trainers, they may be willing to collect, aggregate, and manage data if they can sell the information or if it advances their business case. And while a formal FSP is unlikely to take on this role, a fintech or software firm may be willing to do so, particularly if they developed the technology, so long as someone is willing to pay. Governments may be willing to pay for data given their interest in increasing financial inclusion, and national networks may be willing and able to collect it as a fee-based service. The reality is, however, that data collection is expensive and group members themselves do not have an incentive to provide information, particularly if they believe sharing information could result in government oversight or interference.

With respect to SG access to formal financial services, the market actors are clear; a wide range of FSPs could supply financial services in response to the demand from SGs and their members. However, with SGs, FSPs face client acquisition costs that are both higher than and of a different nature from normal bank processes. They involve extensive client education, specialized product design specific to this market, outreach to isolated rural communities, and the need to gain their trust. To date these client acquisition functions have been carried out by implementors and, hence, subsidized. Donor investments are attempting to foster this market by bringing actors together, educating both sides, and building the digital and accounting systems that can facilitate service delivery. However, it is not yet clear that the overall market or nature of its demand (i.e. based more on the need for safe saving facilities than credit) is robust enough for FSPs to fully assume these costs once donors and implementers exit.

The need for information is closely connected to the need for coordination. Various stakeholders currently play a coordination role, generally funded by donors and implementers. In a sustainable system, the focus moves to sharing learning, coordinating geographic coverage, and ensuring best practice by, and among, system actors. The private sector may be willing to take on the coordination role for a fee or to strengthen their offer to various stakeholders, while the government may see it as a public good given their interest in financial inclusion and resiliency. Networks/associations could see value to their members in coordinating the sector in order to share updated materials, information, advanced training, new technologies, bulk purchasing, and so on.

For the most part, the development and maintenance of technology for SGs has been led by implementers funded by donors and developed by the private sector. More recently, investment in 'digital SGs' has been led by implementers, paid for by private investment, donor funding, and user fees (from members/groups and institutional users), and developed by fintechs. Going forward, there will be a continued need for technology applications to be developed, managed, and paid for by system actors. Private sector actors may see the business case to develop, manage or pay for technology applications, including FSPs for example who may be willing to pay for applications that provide information on SG members' financial history to allow them to sell other products. Governments may have the incentive to invest in technology to improve the efficiency of SGs and enable improved sector coordination and data collection. And while civil society actors may support development (i.e. convene their members to test or provide input), it is unlikely they would have the capacity to manage, develop or pay for such technology.

Once organizations are identified, facilitators can support capacity development. Determining the breadth and depth of information to be collected and the frequency of collection may also be an appropriate role for a facilitator to take on given their neutrality and ability to ensure all stakeholders' needs and demands are considered.

Industry standards, codes of conduct, data ownership, and privacy policies. Consumer protection is a vital part of the SG system to ensure quality groups continue to operate and provide value to members. In particular, as groups become digitized, measures are required to protect against online theft of funds and to protect member data, privacy, and digital identity. Currently, the ownership of group and individual member data is not clear. Without development actors present, it is ever more critical that stakeholders agree and adhere to standards and codes of conduct that ensure the safety of SGs and their members. Who develops, monitors, and enforces these standards and codes of conduct, and implements policies in a sustainable system needs to be determined.

The government obviously plays a significant role here given the potential risk that poor-quality groups pose to those excluded from the formal financial sector. Private sector actors including trainers and external service providers may adhere to industry standards if they recognize the need for sustainable quality groups in order to have a long-term client base. Part of the mandate of associations or networks of trainers is to advocate for standards and codes of conduct that ensure group members are protected, as well as policies regarding, for example, data ownership and privacy to protect SGs and their members.

Facilitators can support CSOs such as trainer networks or industry associations to develop effective standards and codes of conducts and work with the government to ensure policies are in place to protect SG data and privacy and that capacity exists within government to enforce these policies.

Vision for the future

Based on this analysis, Table 2.2 summarizes a potentially sustainable SG system where donor-funded implementers are no longer required and the system continues to operate and expand on its own. And while this chapter clearly limits its consideration of SGs as financial entities, it is important to note that the aforementioned multiple uses of SGs may complicate the transfer of supporting functions from what can be multiple development actors engaged with the same groups, to system actors.

Conclusion

The SG model holds much promise; indeed, it has already been transformational for millions of members around the world. Because they do not require external capital, replicate easily, and prepare members to access formal financial services, savings groups have been a more cost-effective investment to increase financial inclusion than many other approaches. Yet none of these qualities can guarantee their future nor meet the significant demand. Recognizing the imperative to build a sustainable system, a range of development actors and SG stakeholders have pioneered ground-breaking experiments with results that are interesting but flawed. While it may not have been obvious when I first asked Alan, that a sustainable SG system would require engagement of a range of system actors including the government, it is now. And while some system actors are slowly recognizing their incentives to support the growth of SGs, they also face huge hurdles to responding with the vision and resources needed. Alan never said it would be easy, but he provided us with the tools and the guidance to try. And the M4P approach is the right one to take. If we can get to a point where SGs effectively reach all those who seek participation, I believe we will have truly 'made a difference'.

Table 2.2 A future sustainable SG system: who could do? Who could pay?

Supporting function	Who does?	Who pays?	Who could do?	Who could pay?
Group formation and training	**Implementers** Fee-for-service trainers	**Donors** Members	Lead trainers and CBTs from: public; FSPs; government; CSOs	Group members; FSPs; fintechs; government; CSOs
Training of trainers	**Implementers**	**Donors** CBTs	Private training institutes; FSPs; fintechs; government; trainer networks; associations; other CSOs	Social entrepreneurs; FSPs; fintechs; government; CSOs
Operational support	**Implementers** Fee-for-service trainers	**Donors** Members	Lead trainers and CBTs	Group members
Technology	Technology companies **Implementers**	**Donors** Members	Technology companies	FSPs; fintechs; government; CSOs
Sector coordination	**Implementers** Trainer networks associations	**Donors** Trainers	Trainer networks; associations; government	Lead trainers; government
Information: data collection; information on external services	**Implementers** Trainer networks associations	**Donors**	Lead trainers; CBTs; private training institutes; trainer networks; associations; other CSOs	FSPs; fintechs; other service providers; government; CSOs
Rules	**Who does?**	**Who pays?**	**Who could do?**	**Who could pay?**
Group operating norms and standards	Trainers	Members	Lead trainers and CBTs	SG members
Accreditation-certification	**Implementers** Government	**Donors** Trainers	Private training institute; government; trainer networks; industry associations	Lead trainers; private training institute; government; CSOs
Industry standards and codes of conduct	**Implementers** Industry bodies	**Donors**	Trainer networks; associations; government	Government; trainer networks; associations
Data ownership and privacy policies	**Implementers** Government	**Donors** Government	Government	Government

Acknowledgement

This chapter is based on a paper published by The SEEP Network (Ledgerwood, 2020).

About the author

Joanna Ledgerwood is an independent consultant specializing in women's financial inclusion and market systems development. She is the author of numerous books and publications and is active on a number of boards and committees. Joanna first met Alan in September 2007 in Chiang Mai at a BDS seminar and they remained close until his death.

Notes

1. For an introduction to SGs, see Allen and Panetta (2010).
2. While SGs are sometimes used as conduits for development programming – in health, education, or agricultural extension, for example – this chapter is focused solely on the provision of financial services through SGs. Furthermore, it does not discuss the sustainability of individual SGs as ongoing financial service providers. Rather, the intention is to help develop a common understanding of the SG *system* and its potential, and to encourage stakeholders to adopt an M4P approach in order to achieve scale, sustainability, and impact.
3. As groups and group members begin to access formal financial services, these services carry their own set of rules, i.e. 'Know Your Customer' (identification requirements, proof of address), credit history, collateral requirements, contract enforcement, etc. This set of formal rules around external financial services is not covered in this chapter.
4. While rules and policies for data ownership and digital identity may not be specific to SGs, relevant standards and policies are needed to mitigate risks when member data is collected and shared externally.
5. Table 2.1 provides a generalized analysis of the SG system. National and sub-national systems may differ with respect to the functions performed and paid for by system actors.
6. Independent, fee-for-service trainers are referred to in different terms depending on institutional affiliation: private service providers, village agents, and community-based trainers are the most common.
7. To identify potential government agencies, looking beyond federal agencies may be useful. For example, traditional structures based on tribal affiliation could provide training of lead trainers or, at a minimum, be leveraged to form, train, and support groups, and potentially provide local consumer protection measures.
8. A robust process of trainer certification helps ensure continued group formation, quality group training to ensure norms and discipline that foster safety and transparency, operational support, and, ultimately, high group quality and consumer protection.

References

Allen, H. and Panetta, D. (2010) *Savings Groups: What Are They?* [online], The SEEP Network <https://mangotree.org/Resource/Savings-Groups-What-Are-They> [accessed 9 October 2020].

Elliott, D. (2016) *Formalising Informality: Savings Groups, Community Finance and the Role of FSD Kenya* [online], FSD Africa and Springfield Centre <http://www.springfieldcentre.com/wp-content/uploads/2017/02/2017-04-FSD-Kenya-Savings-Group-Case.pdf> [accessed 9 October 2020].

Gibson, A. (2016) *FSD Kenya: Ten Years of a Market Systems Approach in the Kenyan Finance Market* [online], FSD Kenya and Springfield Centre <http://fsdkenya.org/publication/fsd-kenya-ten-years-of-a-market-systems-approach-in-the-kenyan-finance-market/> [accessed 9 October 2020].

Ledgerwood, J. (2020) *A Market Systems Approach to Savings Groups* [online], The SEEP Network <https://mangotree.org/Resource/A-Market-Systems-Approach-to-Savings-Groups> [accessed 9 October 2020].

Ledgerwood, J. and Johnson, D. (2018) *Applying a Market Systems Approach to Savings Groups* [online], The SEEP Network <https://www.findevgateway.org/paper/2018/09/applying-market-systems-approach-savings-groups> [accessed 9 October 2020].

Wheaton, A. (2018) *An Empirical Risk Assessment of Savings Groups* [online], The SEEP Network <https://mangotree.org/Resource/An-Empirical-Assessment-of-Savings-Groups> [accessed 9 October 2020].

CHAPTER 3

Market system diagrams: Or, how I learned to stop worrying and love the doughnut

Jake Lomax

Abstract

Doughnuts (aka market system diagrams) are central to market systems analysis, and to the way of thinking that seeks to investigate and address root causes of market system underperformance. But we rarely see them being used, and still less see them used well. Why is the defining framework of the Making Markets Work for the Poor (M4P) approach not used more, and why is it not used more consistently? This chapter starts by getting under the hood of the doughnut to see what's really going on in there and describes how it needs to sit alongside other M4P tools. It then details three common examples of doughnut-related malpractice and the real implications this has for our ability to deliver sustainable change at scale in market systems. Finally, the chapter analyses the incentive and capacity constraints that prevent programmes making better use of doughnuts, and suggests how these may be addressed.

Keywords: market systems analysis, M4P, development, diagnostics

Introduction

Like many of us working in the field of Making Markets Work for the Poor (M4P), I had the pleasure of an M4P pupillage at the hands of Alan Gibson. It was the autumn of 2014. I'd started a job at the Springfield Centre the day after submitting my PhD thesis. And a few days after that, still barely aware of what M4P was, I found myself on a flight to Bangkok to find out. Here, in the King Power Hotel, the scepticism about development practice that I'd carefully accumulated over the preceding years in academia were chipped away.

It turned out people had actually been *doing* something about the problems of implementing development programmes. They had understood the critiques, figured out why development wasn't working, and set out principles and steps to follow in order to avoid those pitfalls. Alan was clearly one of the heroes of this movement, and rapidly became one of mine. His railing against the incompetence and inadequacy of conventional development was devastating and often hilarious. But it wasn't just the familiar critique of failure. It was much more powerful; an outline of a solution – largely of

http://dx.doi.org/10.3362/9781788531443.003

his own creation. And what was the antidote to decades of malfunctioning development aid? The doughnut!

Of course, I'm oversimplifying. It was much, much more than the M4P market system diagram (familiarly known as the doughnut). But if we want one visual image of what M4P is, it's the doughnut. It's everywhere in M4P training. It's everywhere in explanations and definitions of M4P. What's different about M4P? Doughnut! How do you do M4P? Lots of doughnuts! This is understandable – we're in the business of transforming systems, and doughnuts are the only diagrammatic representation of the system outlined in the approach. They are the lens for understanding what a system is, and how it is underperforming. They are central to market systems analysis, and to the way of thinking that investigates and addresses the root causes of market system underperformance.

But once I started working more closely with M4P programmes, it seemed that all the doughnuts had dried up. Scrabble round through old programme documents and you might find one, but it was usually pretty stale. It seemed that the doughnut was an occasional tool of external M4P consultants rather than a tool for regular systems analysis by M4P programmes. And on closer analysis, doughnuts were variable beasts: you can find all sorts of things written in the spaces, value chains stuffed into the centre, actors appended in various places.

What is going on? Why is the defining framework of M4P not used more, and why is it not used more consistently? And why is this a problem?

What's in the doughnut?

A quick primer for the uninitiated. The doughnut has been around in various forms since 2004 (see Annex for a potted history). The system is defined in relation to a set of actions that form the core (see Figure 3.1). Generally speaking, these are a set of production and exchange actions that link producers on the supply side to consumers on the demand side for a given good or service. The core will usually include the actions of the target group.

The system represented in the doughnut then comprises factors identified as important in determining how effectively the core operates. These factors are grouped into either 'functions' (the services or resources required for the actions in the core) or 'rules' (those functions that are specifically related to the formal or informal institutions that shape decisions in the core).

In this manner, the systems analyst using a doughnut can proceed rapidly to specify factors which are causing underperformance in the core. Then each causal factor judged to be important may be framed in terms of supply and demand and put in the core of an additional doughnut for analysis. And so on until we've got to the root of things.

The doughnut is a tool for action. Spend too long sweating over whether a factor is a supporting function or a rule and you're missing the point. And I spent quite a lot of time missing the point. Coming from years immersed in

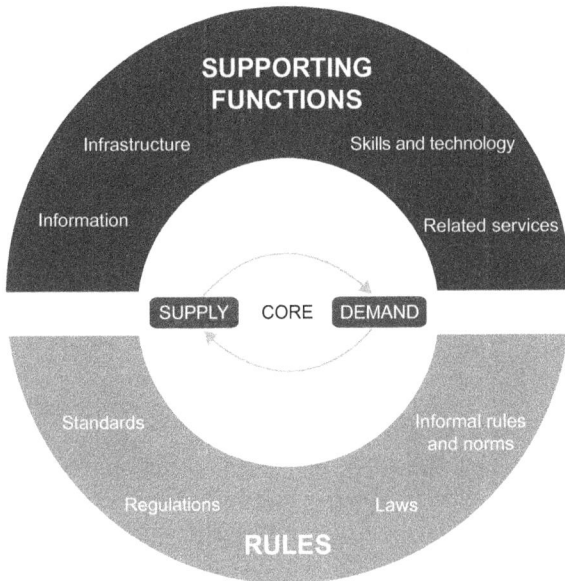

Figure 3.1 The doughnut. Best consumed as part of a balanced diet that includes other system analysis tools

the micro-level analysis of human behaviour, I wanted my concepts nailed down. The doughnut made me uncomfortable, with its loosely aggregated, unspecified sets of actions in the core, and all sorts of different things apparently eligible to be 'supporting functions'. Institutions-based 'rules' are a familiar concept for economists, but what actually *are* supporting functions again? And if they're so important why is this concept nowhere else in social science?

And ... then I got over it. Because of two key realizations. This imprecision is actually quite useful. And the doughnut does not stand alone in the representation of systems in M4P.

Conveniently imprecise

The conceptual ambiguity I found so problematic is exactly what enables rapid, good-enough analysis of complex social phenomena. We're framing an investigation, not a 100,000-word dissertation. Doughnuts are the ultimate quick 'n dirty systems analysis tool – great for getting to the interesting stuff fast. When using doughnuts we don't need to spend time mapping out in detail the actions and actors that comprise the basic value chain. We can skip straight to the causes of underperformance and start analysing what underlies those causes. The analyst armed with a doughnut is able to quickly get into regulatory issues in the licensing of refrigeration trucks while the value chains analyst is still figuring out farmers' profit margins on milk.

Separating out 'rules' from the broader set of supporting functions means the temptation to look for simplistic, input-based answers is countered by the requirement to set out a number of factors that may explain why the system hasn't changed, and may ultimately cause any eventual intervention to fail. It's like having a fisheye lens on your camera. Doughnut-led analysis helps keep an eye on the wider picture throughout. Focusing our initial understanding of systems on the broad spectrum of what is required to make the core operate effectively is its great strength. In fact, it's tempting to butcher some Billy Joel lyrics to emphasize that the doughnut is almost more of a way of thinking than it is a conceptual framework.

> *I'm just looking for reasons*
> *I left the rest behind*
> *I'm in a Doughnut state of mind.*

Not only is it a tool for action, its focus is *on* actions. However, actors are nowhere to be seen. This keeps the analytical focus on what is happening in the system before we have to be precise about who's doing what. This is opposed to an actor-centric view of systems, where analysts may become paralysed mapping out a hugely diverse set of actors – even mapping out individual actors – with the risk that this doesn't actually help to determine interventions. But it is important to remember that the doughnut does not stand alone, and analysis of actors in the system comes once you've decided on the actions that are important.

A dynamic duo

The status of the doughnut as M4P poster child may be deserved, but it is also problematic. There is the risk that some will believe that completing a doughnut-led analysis, and producing a 'market system diagram' (aka the doughnut), is sufficient for understanding and representing a market system, and thus their work is done. It may be the glitzy doughnut that gets all the attention, but it needs a more solid and reliable partner in crime. Like Sherlock Holmes, doughnuts are the massive brained, investigative wunderkind, but they risk becoming a cocaine-addled wreck with limited communication skills unless partnered by something a bit more sensible.

The 'Who Does Who Pays' (WDWP) framework is our Doctor Watson. It's just a table. No curves, no exotically ambiguous concepts. It's boring to look at, but essential for telling the story of the system (Figure 3.2).

For here we get at lots of rich detail about the system that is absent in the doughnut. Just as it says on the tin, we present who is *doing* each of the functions (or creating the rules), finally getting to the detailed actor level but only after we've prioritized important supporting functions and rules to look at. And we present who is *paying* for this work. This lays the groundwork for the focus on sustainability that is at the centre of the M4P approach. But there's more. It may not have made it into the WDWP title, but we're also analysing

		Current picture	
Function/rule	Who does?	Who pays?	Inadequate, mismatch, absent?
Core function			
Supporting functions			
Rules (formal/informal)			

Figure 3.2 Who Does Who Pays. Less appetizing but more nutritious than the doughnut

the nature of the underperformance of the functions. Taken together, this simple table is getting across a great deal of essential information about what's going on in the system. And while doughnuts are more commonly used for framing our understanding of a system, it is the more tangible WDWP that, I think, is rather more useful for this purpose.

Underperformance in doughnut use

We've seen what doughnuts are, what they're useful for, and what they should be used alongside. But as we suggested in the introduction, the use of doughnuts in M4P programmes is often not up to scratch – the full potential of doughnuts is not being realized. Some of the ways in which this is the case are set out below, before we get into possible explanations.

Stale doughnuts

It's not uncommon that a doughnut is produced in the inception phase of a programme then occasionally dusted off and presented to visiting dignitaries as an 'I'm doing M4P' badge. Understanding the system is not a one-off activity. It's a lifestyle choice. The system isn't standing still – even if your interventions aren't effective, it's still changing. And your understanding of the system is never complete – not only because it is changing, but also because the system does not reveal its mysteries on the first date: there are aspects of the system that are difficult to find out and take significant time working within a system to discover. Get your deerstalker on and keep looking for new important reasons the system isn't working effectively. And keep your doughnuts (and your WDWP) fresh.

Unconsumed doughnuts

Even if you have a perfect understanding of the system, represented in doughnuts and a duly completed WDWP, this doesn't mean you have an M4P programme. The diagnostic is happening for a reason – so you can facilitate change in the system. Too often programmes fail to leverage their understanding of the system when it comes to figuring out how to change it. There is a disconnect between diagnostics and intervention.

To bridge this disconnect, first, you need to create a vision. Each of those under-performing functions specified in the doughnut and WDWP needs someone to do them differently and on an ongoing basis. And they need someone to pay for them, also on an ongoing basis. (See the *Operational Guide* (Springfield Centre, 2015) for more detail on the Who *Will* Do, Who *Will* Pay table. Stretching our analogies beyond breaking point, if WDWP is Dr Watson, WWDWWP is the time-travelling Doctor Who.) The system actor who, in our vision of the future, is doing and the system actor who is paying both need to have the incentive and capacity not only to change behaviour so that the function starts performing as required, but also to continue doing so on an ongoing basis. Which is why they should be actors that are part of the system rather than development actors whose funding will run out in a few years.

So there is a need to analyse the incentives and capacities of system actors to determine who may have (or may acquire) the incentive and capacity to *do*, and who has the incentive and capacity to *pay* for changes to each underperforming function on an ongoing basis. This then allows programmes to determine how to intervene, and which actors to partner with, to align incentives and develop the capacity to drive behaviour changes required to attain the desired vision system state. If interventions are not directed by this analysis, there is little scope to attain the sustainable behaviour change at scale that is the underlying ambition of M4P programmes.

Other people's doughnuts

Contact lenses are extremely useful for the person using them. They make the world around you less fuzzy, and help you move around with a clear sense of direction. But take them out and stick them on the side of the sink, and they're not especially interesting for your housemates to look at. With doughnuts too, you need to be *using* them to get the benefits.

So where staff charged with delivery of an M4P programme are not comfortable just getting out there and finding things out for themselves, then there is a risk that producing doughnuts – or indeed any kind of information-gathering – is seen as a formal research exercise to be contracted out. But it is very problematic to outsource diagnostics. The deep understanding of the system that comes through diagnostics then remains only with people outside the programme. Only so much depth of understanding can be effectively presented in a document. The doughnut a consultant produces will mean a lot to that consultant; it will mean much less to the programme. Diagnostic information is much more useful if it is embedded in the minds of intervention staff, rather than sitting in a report on a shelf. Programme staff should be bakers of doughnuts rather than just consumers.

This is not just about the communication of diagnostic information. It is also about the process. System diagnosis is an investigation, and pathways for analysis emerge and are discarded as you know more. If, each time you have a line of enquiry to pursue, you have to write a TOR (terms of reference) and recruit consultants to gather data, analyse it, and write it up, you're not only losing valuable time, you're losing much, much more. You're not out there building relationships that will be useful when it comes to implementation. You aren't getting to know potential partners. Your organization's name is being used, and time and patience of potential partners in the system is being used up by whatever researcher the contracted firm allocates. You can't follow up on interesting information that comes up, and probe deeper. Instead you are reliant on whatever the consultant thinks is interesting. Not only are you not getting any of the rich, non-verbal cues, you're also not getting any information the researcher didn't think was of interest.

Incentive and capacity constraints to improved doughnut usage

What is it that stops programmes improving their use of doughnuts? 'Incentives and capacities' analysis was mentioned earlier. This is usually used by M4P programmes to understand the prospects of system actors changing behaviour to perform a function more effectively (or to pay for it). But this section uses incentives and capacities to determine why M4P programmes are not performing and using doughnut-based diagnostics more effectively.

And as always with incentives and capacities, it is important to be clear about the behaviour change we're seeking – what is it exactly that constitutes improved doughnut usage? I won't go so far as to set out a detailed vision for the system of doughnut use, but I think it's clear that the behaviour change we want involves programmes doing the following:

Use doughnuts to analyse the reasons the system isn't working. Do this *internally* and *regularly*, and *use the findings* from this analysis in creating and adapting programme strategies and intervention design.

Capacity of programmes to use the doughnut

Brain size. How big does your brain have to be to use doughnuts? Alan's brain was bigger than most, and he had the ability to look at a problem holistically; keeping in mind the sheer breadth of factors that doughnuts suggest might be important is certainly a challenge for the little grey cells. No one said understanding why economies don't work better was going to be easy. But doughnuts are for everyone. Don't be intimidated by uncertainty about how to use them, just ensure you maintain a spirit of inquiry and keep your focus on what's most important. If you're doing things right, you'll in any case already be looking for reasons why things aren't working better. Use a doughnut or two to help frame your answers and provoke new questions. The problem is not so much capacity as usage and practice. Eat doughnuts and sleep doughnuts. Get into the doughnut mindset. Instil a doughnut culture in your organization.

Staffing. While doughnuts *are* for everyone, there are some who are going to be more adept at doughnut-led diagnostics than others. If you've got a choice about how you staff your programme, then get people in with an investigative mindset. While I would argue that in-house research capacity is essential (and someone with formal research training will be very useful), this doesn't mean you should necessarily recruit a whole team of dogmatic academic researchers unwilling to spend less than a year analysing their data. Better mix in those with the skills of journalists or journalists' stringers – people used to getting out there, asking questions, building rapport, getting to the root of any kind of story quickly, intuitively understanding what is important and probing further. You need people like this who are able to set up trusting, open dialogues with all the types of actors in the sector you work in, and those who can get CEOs of big corporates to open up about their problems *may* be different from those who can easily relate to marginalized female onion collectors.

Information about doughnuts. Doughnuts don't exist outside M4P. They are nowhere else in development programming or social science. As such, there is relatively little information about how to use them outside the M4P bubble – and I believe there isn't enough information within it. The Springfield M4P training course (that Alan was instrumental in designing and leading) covers use of doughnuts, but there is a lot of other information to cover in two weeks so trainees may not emerge with enough information to be confident doughnut users. Similarly, the *Operational Guide* (Springfield Centre, 2015) contains useful information about using doughnuts, but there is scope to add more detailed and more diverse guidance. I suspect the circle of regular doughnut users is actually fairly small, and many of them spent significant time with Alan, learning directly from him through practical work in diagnosing system constraints.

Alan's death only increases the need to consolidate and clarify the information we have about the tools and approach he created. While this chapter sets out how I overcame some misconceptions of my own, it would be useful to consolidate practical understanding on an ongoing basis that can support a growing community of practice in doughnut-led diagnostics. One way would be to have more of the often-excellent learning documents produced by M4P programmes focus on practical tips and experience of using doughnuts, and for the various forums on M4P practice to draw out more clearly the sum of information already available, and add new guidance as it is produced. Better understanding of what it is to use doughnuts and WDWP may reduce the incidence of misuse, and support more people being willing to give it a try.

Conceptual confusion. Part of the strength of the doughnut lies in its ability to encompass aggregated and simplistic representations of complex processes. A whole lot of stuff can go in there without too much hand-wringing. Lots of difficult-to-articulate actions, often around information exchanges, can be aggregated into 'supporting functions'. This allows things like 'market coordination' to be bunged into a doughnut even if we can't easily nail down *exactly* what it entails. This simplicity has advantages – it's often closer to how we see things in real life, and it enables us to move quickly. It is especially useful for exchanges rather than production – even if there are many important production actions that lead up to transactions in the core of a doughnut, these are wrapped into 'supply'.

But there are costs to this. It makes it difficult for the uninitiated to readily understand what's going on and creates a barrier to entry for those not familiar. Programmes often create a more tangible 'business model' of how parts of the system operate, and this is done using ad hoc diagrams that are disconnected from the doughnut and WDWP. Beyond individual programmes, it creates a language barrier between M4P and the social sciences as well as other development approaches. This contributes to a lack of clarity as to what systems are and what systemic change is.

This is not a criticism of the doughnut per se – as I've argued throughout this chapter, doughnut-led analysis is integral to the M4P approach and good development generally. But I believe it does indicate a possible gap within the M4P approach. I believe there is space for tools to go alongside the 'supporting function' framing of systems that set out visually exactly who is doing what within the system, breaking down 'supporting functions' into their constituent actions. Disclaimer: I've had a go at this myself (see Lomax, 2018).

I believe there are at least two advantages of an additional representation of systems that integrates both actors and actions. First, it can help to translate between the system level doughnut and the tangible set of actors with whom programmes are actually interacting. This may help to reduce the marginalization of doughnuts that can result from programmes not seeing the explicit connection between their day-to-day work and abstract 'supporting functions'.

Second, a more precise understanding of what comprises a supporting function helps in the application of the M4P approach and doughnut-led diagnostics to unfamiliar and new sectors. Similarly, it should help programmes to integrate the wider body of research they commission (e.g. political economy research, gender research, and so on) directly into a unified understanding of the system.

Incentives for programmes to use the doughnut

As always, addressing capacity constraints will only get us so far in shifting behaviour – incentives are key. If all implementers were as inherently interested as Alan was in developing and deepening their understanding of the broader system they were trying to change, we'd all be knee-deep in doughnuts. But something of the spirit of inquiry that M4P depends on sometimes evaporates on contact with the bureaucracy of the aid industry. And so we must look at what underpins the lack of incentives to use the doughnut.

Disconnection of doughnuts. Building on the conceptual confusion set out above, there are two things that in my experience tend to focus the thoughts and actions of M4P programmes. First is partnership agreements. Second is intervention monitoring and measurement. Both are about relationships: relationships with the partners who often become responsible for delivering numbers, and relationships with donors to whom the programme is accountable. These human relationships often take precedence over the more abstract understanding of systems.

Programmes often become very partner-centric, rolling out agreement after agreement with one partner as they capitalize on the relationship that has been built; it is easier to continue cost-sharing new behaviour changes with one partner than look beyond that partner to the supporting function or rule of which it is part. The incentives for programmes are often to get numbers as easily as possible. Working with new partners involves difficulty, hard work, uncertainty, and cost. Working with new partners in new supporting functions or rules still more so. 'Better the devil you know' becomes a way of thinking (not least because the system-wide doughnut analysis was done three years ago by someone else), so if the numbers are doing OK, why bother analysing the system?

Which brings us to monitoring and measurement. 'Diagnose down, measure up' is an oft-repeated mantra, but I think this is problematic. With doughnuts and incentives and capacities analysis, we diagnose down to where the programme forms a partnership. Then set up logic models and measurement plans based on that partnership through to impact on the target group. What's missing? Some kind of measurement of the performance of *supporting functions* and hence of the *system*. Why is this a problem? As another noted Glaswegian intellectual once noted:

> I often say that when you can measure what you are speaking about, and express it in numbers, you know something about it; but when you cannot measure it, when you cannot express it in numbers, your knowledge is of a meagre and unsatisfactory kind … (William Thomson, Lord Kelvin, 1883)

This is often simplified as 'what gets measured gets done'. Which isn't always true, but in the case of programmes accountable to donors, the basis of measured outcomes usually is. This points to a problem whereby programmes are not accountable for changing systems because systems are not measured – not at the diagnostic stage, and not later even if there are sporadic efforts to capture 'expansion' of benefits. I think 'diagnose *and measure* down, measure up' would produce a healthier, system-centric accountability framework for programmes. If system diagnostics are incorporated into ongoing measurement systems, then there will be greater incentives to keep the focus on the system throughout the programme lifecycle. And hopefully to use doughnut-led diagnostics to continually understand both progress within the system and reasons for its underperformance.

A dearth of donor desire for doughnuts. Programmes are responsive to donor priorities. What might it take for donors to start incentivizing doughnut use? Donors' technical skills in diagnostics are – at least in my experience – inadequate to hold programmes to account in their identification and prioritization of important reasons why systems are not working. We've a couple of options for addressing this, though they may be fanciful. First, if donors used doughnuts themselves they might understand them better, and so be better able to interrogate the lack of, or poor quality of, programmes' doughnut-led diagnostic processes. In principle you might imagine that donors who understand and endorse the M4P approach would use doughnuts to understand national-level priorities for the poor in a given country, and commission programmes within that framework. You might also imagine this would best be a coordinated process between multiple donors and national government in a given country, producing a unified overall understanding of why the economy is not functioning for the poor. This in turn could be extended and deepened to include coordination with and between implementers working on specific programmes.

But we must return to reality. The second, slightly more feasible, option is to return to the 'what gets measured gets done' principle and push for consistency and transparency in the methodology of doughnut-led diagnostics. We have said diagnostics represent an investigation, not a lengthy dissertation. But the principles of research, whereby we state our methodology explicitly so that others can interrogate the process we followed to collect information and reach our conclusions, are not incompatible with market system diagnostics. A clearer set of methodological principles around a diagnostic process that establishes best practice for measurement of the underperformance of supporting functions would not only help the sector learn about how best to conduct their diagnosis, it would also render the process more transparent and set the basis for accountability, coordination, and incentives. There are of course risks here; we don't want to prevent inquisitive thinkers from getting to the root of problems and turn diagnostics into an audit process. The inquisitorial spirit of the doughnut must be retained, even if we advocate for the trailblazing truth-seekers to be armed with the best tools for gathering information, and be pursued by someone laying down some more tangible tarmac.

Conclusion

The doughnut facilitates deep investigation of the underlying causes of problems in market systems. It should be used more widely, certainly beyond the confines of what currently comprises M4P programming. Moreover, it should be used much more frequently within M4P programmes. Though a high-quality doughnut-led diagnostic process does not by itself guarantee a good M4P programme design, it certainly is a key step that is more likely to be useful to the programme when done internally and regularly, and when the findings are properly and consistently integrated into the work of the programme.

The 'supporting function' concept that underpins the doughnut is what allows for the diagnostic process that embraces complicated aspects of market systems and allows the M4P analyst to find root causes without getting bogged down in conceptual murk. This chapter has made a case that incentives and capacity for increased doughnut use might be improved through breaking down supporting functions into 'actions' that are more readily understood at the actor level and hence more easily integrated into the intervention and measurement plans. Increased effective use of doughnuts also depends on the necessary skills being present in the programme team and might be supported by more and better doughnut guidance, including more transparent diagnostic methodologies.

Take the necessary steps that will allow you to embed doughnuts in your thinking as a programme. Learn to love them, as I did, and you will be rewarded with a better understanding of what's going on in the market system. This, if embedded alongside other steps of the M4P approach, will give you better interventions and ultimately lead to better, more sustainable outcomes that will benefit the poor.

Through the set of tools Alan left us, he has helped the rest of us see the world as clearly as he did, and helped so many of us to do more good in the world. We must cherish these tools, and make sure we keep trying to improve our understanding and application of them.

Annex: A brief history of doughnuts

Early documents of M4P, for example Department for International Development (DFID) (2000), do not present visualizations of markets or market systems. It was in 2004 and two papers written by Alan with Springfield Centre and DFID colleagues that early forms of doughnut seem to have been produced, although the recipe wasn't quite what we enjoy today. First, in February 2004 came an early iteration where we have a core transaction and supporting functions. Rules are not differentiated from supporting functions here – regulation appears as a supporting function. Producers and consumers are actors in the core function, connected by 'delivery' and 'consumption'. And the whole thing looks rather unsatisfying to eat (Figure 3.3).

Later that year, something slightly more familiar – if no more edible – emerged, where 'institutions' we now know as 'rules' were distinguished from 'services and infrastructure' that are now referred to as 'supporting functions' (Figure 3.4).

.

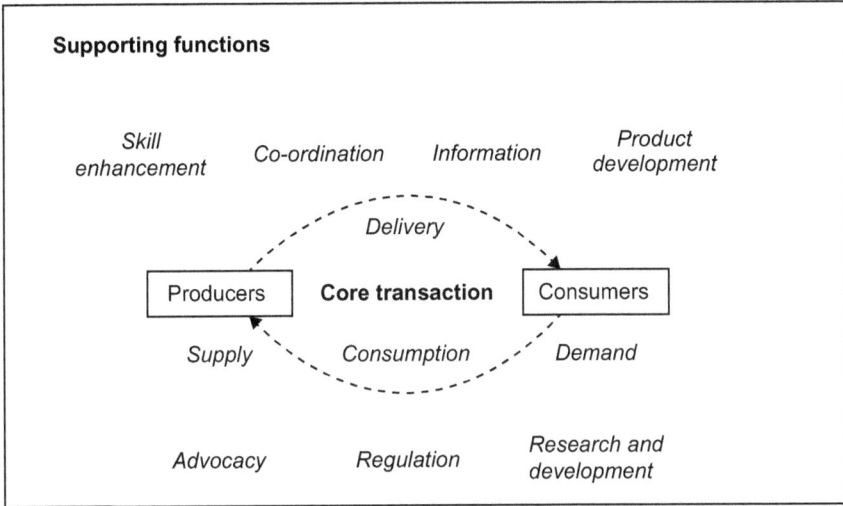

Figure 3.3 Doughnut exhibit A
Source: Elliott and Gibson, 2004

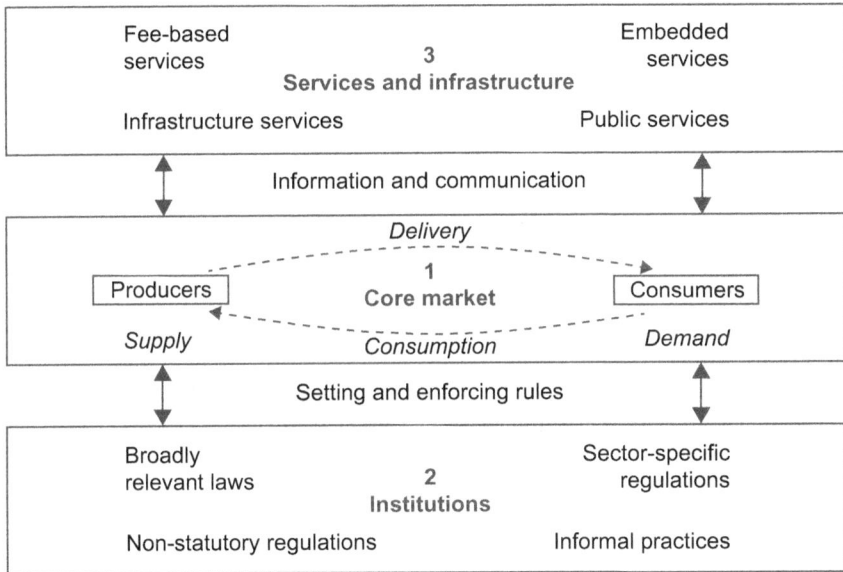

Figure 3.4 Doughnut exhibit B
Source: Gibson et al., 2004

By April 2006, the more familiar representation and terminology had emerged, presented in a Springfield paper by de Ruijter de Wildt et al. (2006) (Figure 3.5).

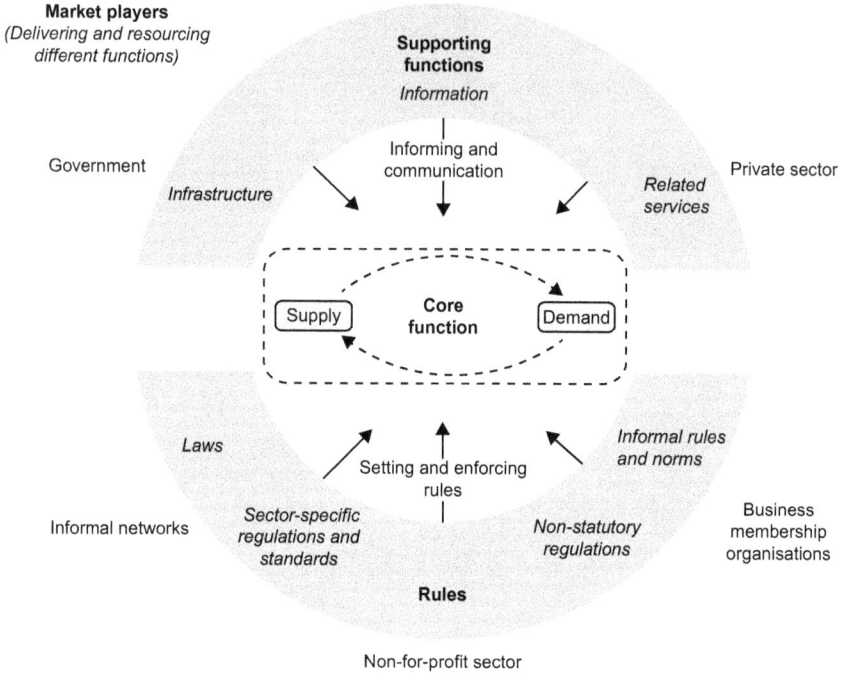

Market players
(Delivering and resourcing different functions)

Government

Private sector

Informal networks

Business membership organisations

Non-for-profit sector

Supporting functions

Information

Informing and communication

Infrastructure

Related services

Supply   **Core function**   Demand

Laws

Setting and enforcing rules

Informal rules and norms

Sector-specific regulations and standards

Non-statutory regulations

Rules

Figure 3.5 Doughnut exhibit C
Source: de Ruijter de Wildt et al., 2006

Here, producers and consumers have disappeared from the core transaction (now called a core function), but actors have appeared in greater diversity, floating rather amorphously round the edges of what is now definitely a more edible doughnut. And here they remained at least in one instance in the 2008 *Operational Guide*, before disappearing in the 2015 edition, which also removes the text informing how rules 'setting and enforcing rules' and supporting functions 'informing and communicating' connect to the core function. The 2008 *Operational Guide* also includes an instance of the doughnut with a value chain in the middle, as well as several versions that point towards the 2015 version (Figure 3.6).

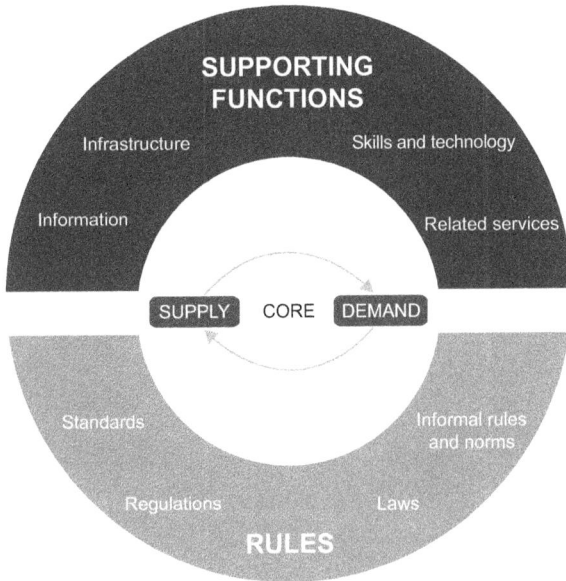

Figure 3.6 Exhibit D: the satisfying form of the 2015 doughnut
Source: Springfield Centre, 2015

About the author

Dr Jake Lomax is a systemic change researcher and consultant, and founder of 3sd Research. He has been an employee and subsequently a close collaborator of the Springfield Centre since 2014, and it is through Springfield that he learned the core principles of M4P from Alan Gibson.

References

de Ruijter de Wildt, M., Elliott, D. and Hitchins, R. (2006) *Making Markets Work for the Poor: Comparative Approaches to Private Sector Development*, Bern: Fauno Consortium/SDC.

Department for International Development (DFID) (2000) *Making Markets Work Better for the Poor: A Framework Paper*, London: DFID.

Elliott, D. and Gibson, A. (2004) *'Making Markets Work for the Poor' as a Core Objective for Governments and Development Agencies*, Woodmead, South Africa: ComMark Trust.

Gibson, A., Scott, H. and Ferrand, D. (2004) *'Making Markets Work for the Poor' An Objective and an Approach for Governments and Development Agencies*, Woodmead, South Africa: ComMark Trust.

Lomax, J. (2018) *Mechanisms of Social Change: Outline of a Conceptual Framework* [online], 3sd Research Briefing Paper 1 <http://dx.doi.org/10.13140/RG.2.2.22279.85920/1>.

Springfield Centre (2015) *The Operational Guide for the Making Markets Work for the Poor (M4P) Approach*, 2nd edn, London: DFID/SDC.

Thomson, W. (1883) Lecture on 'Electrical Units of Measurement', 3 May 1883, *Popular Lectures* I: 73.

CHAPTER 4

Measuring what matters: Monitoring and results measurement

Ben Fowler and Jake Lomax

Abstract

The greater complexity and uncertainty of Making Markets Work for the Poor (M4P) programming has led to monitoring and results measurement (MRM) as a replacement for traditional monitoring and evaluation. MRM shifts the emphasis towards analysis-based learning and more frequent measurement to inform decision-making and understand system-level change. This change has not always been straightforward. We have learned that MRM must be internally owned and well resourced, evaluation methods need to keep up with advances in development practice, and donor requirements such as the value for money agenda can block progress. Building on these lessons, this chapter outlines opportunities for further advancing MRM practice within M4P, including putting the market system at the centre of measurement efforts, building theory on a deep understanding of incentives and capacities, and using that theory to analyse when and how interventions are working and making changes when they are not.

Keywords: monitoring and results measurement (MRM), monitoring and evaluation (M&E), systemic change, impact, adaptive management, theory of change, results chains

We first met Alan Gibson when attending the Springfield Centre's Making Markets Work for the Poor (M4P) training course. From the start, he made quite an impression. Who was this wiry Scotsman questioning so much development orthodoxy? Alan's insistence on the need for sustainable change that truly benefitted the poor has had significant influence on our careers. In pioneering the M4P approach, he advocated for programmes to measure and monitor results to *improve* impact, not just to report to funders. As a consequence, M4P programmes employ practices for monitoring and measuring results that differ significantly from traditional methods.

Introduction

The monitoring and reporting function within development programmes has traditionally been referred to as 'monitoring and evaluation' (M&E). Yet, as many seasoned M&E professionals have discovered working on their first M4P

http://dx.doi.org/10.3362/9781788531443.004

programme, the M4P approach represents a significant shift to monitoring programme performance, commonly referred to as monitoring and results measurement (MRM). This chapter summarizes some of the key attributes of this shift in measurement outlining some of the challenges and lessons along the way and identifying opportunities to advance the field.

What is different about monitoring and evaluating M4P programmes?

There are two important distinctions in M4P programmes, relative to direct delivery approaches, that drive this shift in the monitoring function from M&E to MRM. The first is there are usually more system actors of various stripes involved in the causal logic between intervention and impact, along with the behaviour changes desired of all actors reflected in the 'market system change' step in the M4P theory of change. Relatedly, there is inherent uncertainty about what those actors will do, and whether the intervention will succeed in facilitating desired behaviour changes. This means longer impact chains, more uncertainty, and a consequent need to test and iterate interventions. And second, M4P programmes are concerned with indirect effects, and thus to design interventions with an eye to the indirect effects on behaviour changes in the wider market system. The first of these requires a shift towards a stronger role of theory in measurement. The second requires system-wide measurement. Both are substantively different from traditional M&E.

A shift in emphasis towards theory-based learning that informs decisions

Crudely, a traditional M&E system has a programme level logframe and a set of indicators to measure once a year. This creates too slow a feedback loop, in which key market systems changes for individual interventions are missed. Because of the added complexity of M4P, it is critical to have theory-based learning that is developed at the intervention level. And given the complexity of market systems, MRM must measure more frequently and more granularly to test, make adjustments, and improve. For MRM systems, theory underpins both intervention strategy and measurement and connects the work of intervention and MRM teams. While both M&E and MRM share the same double purpose – to improve the programme and prove its impact to donors – MRM systems prioritize the 'improve' side. This allows the programme to take a more experimental approach to learning what works, abandoning or altering interventions that are not working, and designing new interventions along the way in response to market behaviour.

The theory is based initially on information gathered in diagnostics, and is expressed in intervention-level results chains (see Figure 4.1) that outline – and enable subsequent testing and measurement of – the anticipated causal pathway between the programme's activities and its anticipated results. Intervention-specific indicators are developed for each box in the

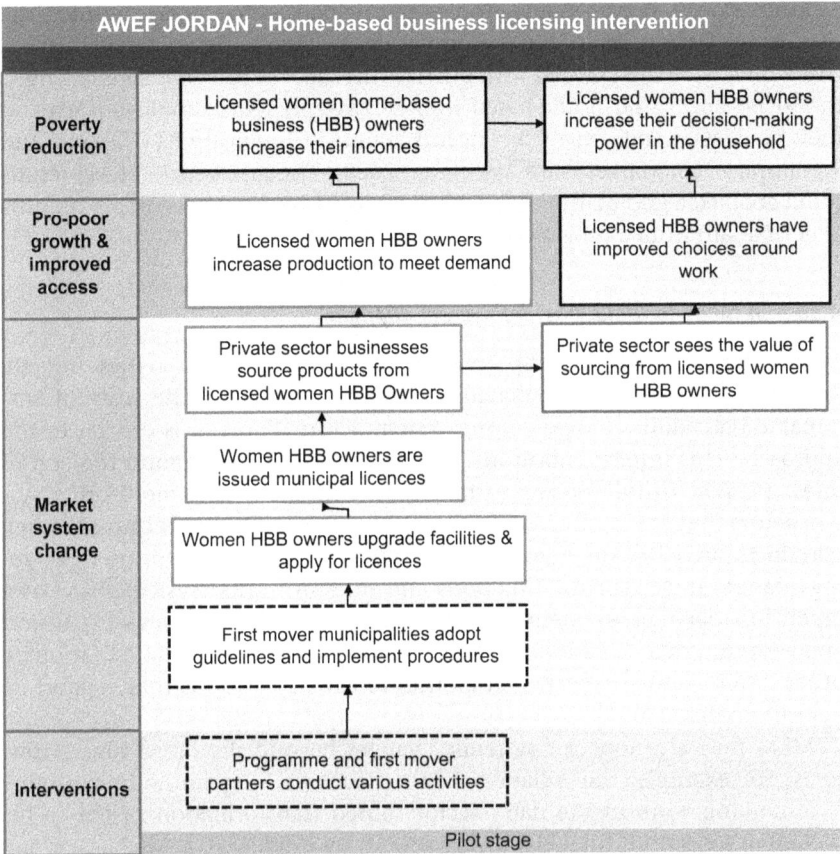

AWEF JORDAN - Home-based business licensing intervention

| Poverty reduction | Licensed women home-based business (HBB) owners increase their incomes | Licensed women HBB owners increase their decision-making power in the household |

Figure 4.1 Simplified results chain

results chain. These indicators are monitored to determine the validity of the intervention theory, and the theory is adapted as stronger evidence is gained through monitoring.

For example, the DFID-funded Arab Women Enterprise Fund (AWEF) sought to support formalization of women entrepreneurs operating in the informal sector whose business growth was limited by their informality. AWEF worked with municipalities to introduce a new licensing process for home-based businesses (HBB). The intervention theory was initially built on an assumption that the new process itself and women's knowledge of it would be adequate for adoption. However, two months after launch AWEF's intervention monitoring found low uptake – the results chain box 'Women HBB owners upgrade facilities and apply for licences' was largely not happening in practice.[1] Through focus group discussions, AWEF discovered women were not registering given fears of tax implications, and strong social norms that discouraged women from expanding their businesses. Based on these findings, AWEF adjusted its intervention. It partnered with five municipalities to jointly subsidize the cost of registration for an initial group of 100 women to demonstrate the benefits which were then shared with others. This cadre of role models challenged the social norm that home-based women entrepreneurs should not expand their businesses and dispelled concerns about tax implications (Hakspiel and Scarampi, 2020; MarketShare Associates, 2020). The intervention-level results chain enabled a granularity of insight that would have emerged many months later (if at all) from a programme-level logframe.

A shift in focus to include wider system change

Intervention theory for M4P does not just go from activities directly through to system actor behaviour changes to impact. The scale of sustainable behaviour change among system actors involved is central to the approach. This implies monitoring programme partners beyond the end of direct support to fully assess sustainability and scale, and monitoring system actors that never received direct support. Given the significant role they play in influencing the core function, MRM requires monitoring of ongoing changes in supporting functions and rules. An MRM system thus has a much broader measurement focus than M&E and incorporates expansion and adoption of innovations throughout the market system via imitation by other system actors, as well as responses to the innovations that support its institutionalization.

MRM may also look for systemic changes beyond the target market systems. For example, the Alliances Lesser Caucasus Programme in Georgia's longstanding work in the dairy sector caused transformation of the sector including significant financial benefits for dairy producers, as well as, among other impacts, significant expansion in the local retail sector. These were captured via an outcome harvest that explicitly defined the boundaries of the system of interest geographically, and hence was able to identify a number of systemic changes that would not have been captured by looking for changes specifically in the dairy market system (MarketShare Associates, 2016d).

Putting MRM into practice: What have we learned?

There are many lessons we have learned in developing MRM systems that are adapted for M4P; a few key lessons are highlighted here.

A strong MRM function must be owned internally with adequate investment in both human and financial resources

MRM has to be within teams; it has to be owned; it has to be part of the way (a programme) works. Moreover, (a programme) needs to have an MRM resource specialist – not as a convenient place to deposit measurement responsibilities but, in the context of an organisation wishing to put measurement at the heart of its culture, as a useful support to managers. (Gibson and Barlow, 2016: 14)

Because monitoring an M4P programme means testing a longer causal chain, assessing wider system impacts and getting quick feedback, programmes must measure more things more often compared to measuring a few logframe indicators annually. This requires a bigger MRM team, more resources, and everyone in the programme needs to play a role (e.g. in keeping an eye on wider system changes).

Effective MRM involves the programme's technical staff as well as MRM specialists. Technical staff play a critical role in collecting information and understanding the market system and its functions as well as its players, designing and adapting interventions; the MRM specialists support technical staff to clearly think through the causal links from activities to impact, designing assessments and facilitating learning.

Establishing an MRM system that can support consistent and effective learning, facilitate adaptive decision-making, and meet funder reporting requirements requires a committed team with a myriad of required skills, as well as a programme budget with sufficient resources.[2] This requires M4P programme staff to be comfortable with both complexity and flexibility, where the future cannot be predicted with any certainty; to avoid descending into 'analysis paralysis' while trying to craft the perfect results chain, teams that succeed at MRM must be able to live with 'good enough'.

The range of skills needed for quality MRM is extensive, including strong qualitative and quantitative research skills, the ability to motivate technical team members to undertake monitoring tasks sometimes viewed as outside their job description, the ability to extract and effectively disseminate insights from data, and an ability to operate in a context of ambiguity. Finding all these skills in one or a couple of individuals is often a difficult task, compounded by the inconsistent commitment to MRM by staff and leadership. Full buy-in from programme leadership, the board or other governance bodies, the funder (at least to the extent of agreeing that MRM merits adequate funding), and by the entire programme team is necessary (MarketShare Associates, 2016b). A lack of support in any of these areas will greatly limit the ability to develop and sustain an effective MRM system. While sometimes at odds with the prevailing work culture, staff need to be willing to accept and even embrace failure as part of the route to discovering what works.

Longer causal chains make it difficult to evaluate and assess the impact of M4P programmes

External evaluations complement MRM systems by providing independent validation of reported results, examining results following programme closure when the MRM team is no longer operating, and identifying broader impacts beyond the boundaries defined by the programme. However, the utility of external evaluations is limited in part by a scarcity of evaluators familiar with the M4P approach. As Alan once put it, 'evaluation methods that emerge outside a sound knowledge of "good practice" in development can produce answers that so completely "miss the point" that they drive development practice backwards' (Gibson and Elliott, 2012). Accordingly, one review of 14 M4P programme evaluations from 2013 (by now somewhat dated) described them as 'generally weak' in terms of data quality, triangulation practices, aggregation of results, and the consideration of unintended negative effects (Ruffer and Wach, 2013).

M4P programmes do not generally work directly with target beneficiaries; thus, there are longer causal chains between programme activities and anticipated results. As Figure 4.2 makes clear, the inclusion of the 'market system change' step in the causal logic increases the number of external factors that may also have influenced the observed change, making attribution to the programme interventions more difficult to establish than programmes working directly with target beneficiaries (Fowler and Dunn, 2014). Addressing this challenge has sparked a lot of rich learning around estimating counterfactuals (i.e. what would have happened without the intervention) in ways that are compatible with using an M4P approach (for example, see Posthumus and Wanitphon, 2015). This starts by validating the intervention theory by testing if the anticipated changes have occurred, then applies a method for estimating the counterfactual that would satisfy a 'reasonable, but sceptical observer'. Deciding what is good enough is ultimately a balance between practicality and rigour, aiming to select the most rigorous approach possible taking into account the nature of the intervention, the scale of the impacts created, and the availability of other data (Sen, 2018). Randomized control trials, the so-called 'gold standard' of attribution measurement, are very rarely appropriate (Ripley, 2015).

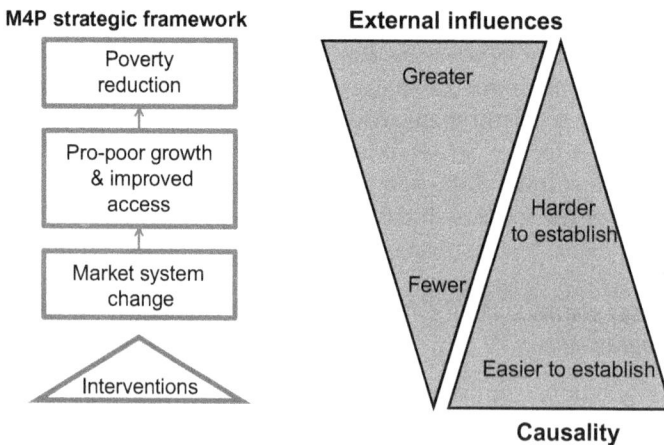

Figure 4.2 Attribution and M4P programmes
Source: author adaptation of DFID and SDC, 2008

The push to justify 'value for money' frequently undermines good MRM

Many funders require programmes to report against tailored metrics to demonstrate value for money (VfM). DFID, for example, has elaborated a '4 Es' framework of economy, efficiency, effectiveness, and equity to assess VfM, as presented in Figure 4.3 (DFID, 2011). The 4 Es examine how much is being spent on inputs (economy), how much it is costing to achieve project outputs (efficiency), how much it is costing to achieve outcomes (effectiveness), and who is benefiting from the outputs and outcomes (equity).

While M4P programmes would be expected to have better VfM relative to non-M4P programmes focused on the same issues when assessed at the end of the programme or a few years after, VfM measurement has tended to focus more heavily on economy and efficiency indicators that can be measured early on in a programme's implementation. This provides an incomplete picture and may well be premature. First of all, M4P programmes tend to spend a larger proportion of their budget on items typically defined as overhead (primarily staff). Secondly, systemic change may take longer to produce beneficiary-level results than direct delivery programmes. Often the most impactful systemic changes take the longest to occur. Given the typical three- to five-year timeframe of an M4P programme, this means the greatest change may happen after closure, meaning external evaluations will not capture critical programme impacts.

The focus on VfM has also resulted in contracts that mandate payment by results (PbR). PbR makes the payment of a portion of the total contract conditional on meeting certain performance milestones, creating a strong pressure for programmes to agree only to output indicators that are within their control and can be easily counted (e.g. number of people trained), rather than market system changes, increased access, and impact. As one study of funders' ability to manage adaptively noted: '[t]he need to fit specific results with commercial appetites for payment risk [can] easily lead implementers to propose lower targets and accept lower quality work from partners' (MarketShare Associates, 2016b). This orientation creates perverse incentives for implementers to implement (and hence measure) activities that can guarantee outputs on a timeline established by donors and reduce or eliminate measuring the wider system and systemic change.

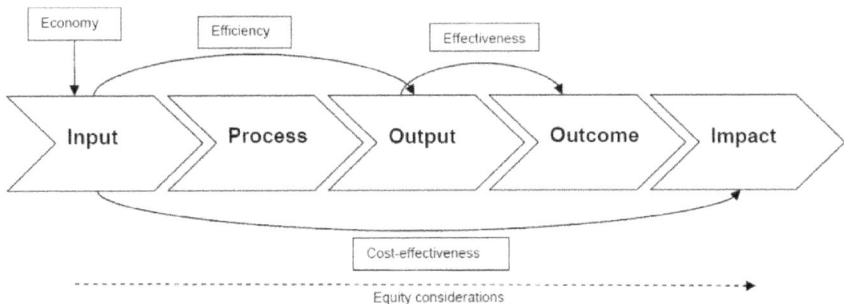

Figure 4.3 DFID's '4 Es' VfM framework

Looking forward

Reflecting on the evolution of learning in MRM, there is a lot of room to be impressed by how far the field has come. Looking forward, there remain a number of underexplored opportunities to further bolster MRM's value add for M4P programmes.

Put the system at the centre of MRM

Measuring system change is difficult, partly because there is a disconnect between information gathered as part of the system diagnostic process and measurement of system-wide change. This is related to weakness in diagnostics (see Lomax, Chapter 3, this volume), as well as how the role of MRM is conceived. M4P practitioners are told from the start to 'diagnose down and measure up' (Springfield Centre, 2015)[3] but this misses a key step. The result is an MRM-based view of the system that is intervention-centric rather than system-centric. We lose sight of what is going on in the wider system, and efforts to find out tend to be partial 'number-grabbing' exercises to find examples of wider adoption of innovation that can be added to impact reports.

Instead, we need to 'diagnose down *and* measure down, as well as measure up'.[4] That is, we need to identify the underperforming supporting functions and rules through diagnostics, but we then need to *measure* the underperformance of functions and rules we select for intervention to produce a system-level baseline. This system measurement (like the diagnosis) should be regularly updated to assess how the wider system changes over time. For example, the USAID-funded Inova programme in Mozambique conducted a market system-level baseline to understand key dynamics of the market systems, including the level of business innovation and trust and cooperation underpinning commercial relationships. Alongside continuous intervention monitoring, Inova has periodically repeated these analyses to understand whether and how its target market systems are evolving (DAI and MarketShare Associates, 2019).

Expand the evidence base for the sustainability and comparative efficacy of M4P

In the context of increasing pressure on development budgets, there has perhaps never been greater need for evidence that M4P 'works'. A key tenet of the M4P approach is that it yields sustainable results at scale. However, as previously mentioned, these results often take time, as per the so-called 'hockey stick' curve of continuing sustainable impacts post-programme (see Figure 4.4).

While efforts to measure results once the programme is no longer actively engaged have been relatively limited, evidence we do have is interesting. For example, one USAID-funded ex-post assessment found that desired changes in the market system had continued to grow five years following programme

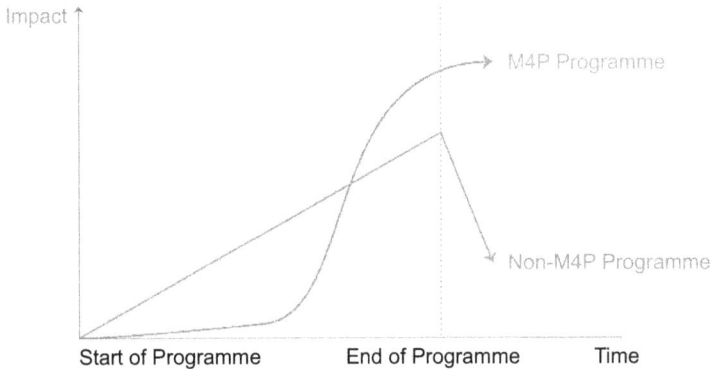

Figure 4.4 The M4P impact 'hockey stick'
Source: MarketShare Associates

closure (MarketShare Associates, 2016c). Bolstering this limited evidence with more ex-post evaluations is warranted, as well as analysis of relative performance of M4P programmes and other approaches aiming to achieve similar goals in similar contexts with similar resources.[5]

But seeking evidence that M4P works is not enough. To honour the spirit of the approach and the theory-led principles discussed earlier in this chapter we need to go further to seriously investigate *when* and *how* M4P works. To do so we need to understand what is actually different about M4P in terms of the detailed mechanisms by which it influences the system sustainably and at scale, rather than in terms of good principles and process steps that development actors should follow.

Rightsize MRM

Alan's focus on practicality and common sense pushes us to ask tough questions about whether every element of our MRM systems is actually needed. In too many cases, programmes underinvest in their MRM systems and do not build adequate capacity for learning (or as sometimes happens, generate a lot of great data that are not used to inform programming). In other cases, MRM systems are too granular and measure too many indicators via overly detailed results chains that overwhelm the MRM system and the MRM team. Further, when MRM systems are focused on programme needs only, they can overburden system actors while providing little value to them.

Rightsizing MRM should start with a continued and ruthless examination of the minimum information that meets learning, reporting, and system actor needs. System actors' preferences can provide a helpful reality check on what information is actually useful. This means reassessing how detailed results chains should be and how many indicators each intervention requires. Technology – particularly the growing availability of mobile phones – can help to streamline how much MRM data is collected while also reducing costs and increasing speed.

Strengthen theory and learning through deeper analysis of incentives and capacities

We set out at the beginning the central importance of theory and intervention results chains in driving M4P programme learning, adaptation, and ultimately impact. Yet we consistently find programmes with weak results chains that have important gaps – especially at the market system level – or steps where there is no clear associated actor, or dubious behaviour change logic, or unstated assumptions. The most straightforward way of embedding better theory into results chains is to make sure that incentives and capacities for each desired behaviour change are analysed and evidenced from the perspective of the actor. This requires evidence on how actors themselves perceive the change.[6] Analysing the success and failure of interventions in overcoming different types of incentive and capacity 'blockers' of behaviour change will support M4P implementers' ability to learn what works for whom in what context.[7]

Structure MRM to improve the market information supporting function

M4P programmes conduct market systems analyses during design and then use their MRM systems for ongoing learning about their target market systems. They use these findings as a value add when brokering partnerships. This is useful to system actors because many have limited understanding of their customers – an indication of a poorly working market information supporting function. M4P programmes have an opportunity to create MRM systems that support learning and improvement not only for themselves but also for system actors. They can do so by identifying the information to better understand and meet the needs of system actors' customers, then build these actors' capacity to collect this data themselves. In this way, MRM itself becomes a way to strengthen market system functioning. As an illustration, in Mozambique the USAID-funded Inova programme diagnoses each partner's priority knowledge gaps about their customers. It then supports its partners to design and apply lean and rapid methods to gather that evidence for their own decision-making. For instance, one agricultural input supplier identified the key performance drivers of the new input delivery business model they are testing and captured quick data on its performance. It then used the findings to reform several aspects of the model and undertake additional tests they are now carefully monitoring (DAI and MarketShare Associates, 2020).

Conclusion

Alan's pioneering work in developing and applying the M4P approach has had an outsized influence on monitoring and measuring results. The shift in emphasis towards learning to improve decision-making, tools, and processes, and measure market system change, ultimately leading to more impact, has been profound and worthy of continued meaningful investment in MRM systems that facilitate consistent and effective intervention.

About the authors

Ben Fowler is a co-founder of and Principal at MarketShare Associates, a global firm bringing actionable insights to economic development. He has 17 years experience designing, implementing, and measuring social impact initiatives for investors, firms, and governments. He is an auditor of the DCED Standard for Results Measurement. Ben first met Alan Gibson at Springfield's M4P training.

Dr Jake Lomax is a systemic change researcher and consultant, and founder of 3sd Research. He has been an employee and subsequently a close collaborator of the Springfield Centre since 2014, and it is through Springfield that he learned the core principles of M4P from Alan Gibson.

Notes

1. This is a simplified version of a results chain used on the AWEF programme.
2. Five to ten per cent of total programme resources is a rule of thumb with variation based on programme size, structure, etc.
3. 'Down' the diagnostic cone from the target group to intervention, and 'up' the results chain from the intervention back to the target group.
4. Similar points have been made by MarketShare Associates (2016a), Lomax (2020), and Posthumus et al. (2020). All of these documents provide processes to measure systemic change.
5. Such a comparative analysis would rely on a defensible definition for distinguishing M4P and non-M4P programmes or interventions. In practice, making this distinction has not always proven so easy as many programmes and interventions exist on a continuum of application based on context (e.g. thin or strong markets), the behaviour of other system actors (e.g. the prevalence and nature of subsidies being offered by other development and governmental programmes), etc.
6. For a tool to support embedding incentives and capacities into programme theory see Lomax and Shah (2020).
7. For more detailed description of blockers of behaviour change, see Lomax and Shah (2018).

References

DAI and MarketShare Associates (2019) *Feed the Future Mozambique Agricultural Innovations Activity (FTF Inova): Monitoring, Evaluation and Learning (MEL) Plan*, Washington, DC: USAID.

DAI and MarketShare Associates (2020) *Inova Quarterly Report*, 2020 Q2, unpublished.

DFID (2011) *DFID's Approach to Value for Money (VfM)* [pdf] <https://assets.publishing.service.gov.uk/government/uploads/system/uploads/

attachment_data/file/67479/DFID-approach-value-money.pdf> [accessed 12 October 2020].

DFID and SDC (2008) *The Operational Guide for the Making Markets Work for the Poor (M4P) Approach*, London: Department for International Development; Bern: Swiss Agency for Development and Cooperation.

Fowler, B. and Dunn, E. (2014) *Evaluating Systems and Systemic Change for Inclusive Market Development* [online], LEO Report No. 3, Washington, DC: USAID <https://marketshareassociates.com/evaluating-systems-and-systemic-change-for-inclusive-market-development/> [accessed 12 October 2020].

Gibson, A. and Barlow, S. (2016) *End-Term-Review, 2011–2015: Main Report*, Durham, UK: Springfield Centre, unpublished.

Gibson, A. and Elliott, D. (2012) *Excellence, Evidence and Elephants* [online], Durham, UK: Springfield Centre <https://www.springfieldcentre.com/excellence-evidence-and-elephants/> [accessed 12 October 2020].

Hakspiel, J. and Scarampi, A. (2020) 'Using data to promote women's empowerment in MSD programmes: the experience of AWEF' [online], BEAM Exchange <https://beamexchange.org/community/blogs/2020/2/11/data-and-womens-empowerment-msd-programmes/> [accessed 12 October 2020].

Lomax, J. (2020) 'The antidote to systemic change frameworks: Six practical steps to assess systemic change (and improve your strategy)' [online], Briefing Paper 3, UK: 3sd Research <https://www.researchgate.net/publication/338775196_The_antidote_to_systemic_change_frameworks_six_practical_steps_to_assess_systemic_change_and_improve_your_strategy> [accessed 12 October 2020].

Lomax, J. and Shah, R. (2018) *Unpacking Incentives and Capacities: Factors Affecting Actor Behaviour Change* [online], Durham: Springfield Centre <https://www.springfieldcentre.com/unpacking-incentives-and-capacities-factors-affecting-actor-behaviour-change/> [accessed 12 October 2020].

Lomax, J. and Shah, R. (2020) 'The Building Blocks of programme theory: how to get better at driving behaviour change' [online], Briefing Paper 5, UK: 3sd Research <https://www.researchgate.net/publication/340849411_The_Building_Blocks_of_programme_theory_how_to_get_better_at_driving_behaviour_change> [accessed 12 October 2020].

MarketShare Associates (2016a) *Disrupting System Dynamics: A Framework for Understanding Systemic Changes* [online], LEO Report No. 47, Washington, DC: USAID <https://marketshareassociates.com/disrupting-system-dynamics-a-framework-for-understanding-systemic-changes/> [accessed 12 October 2020].

MarketShare Associates (2016b) *Getting There from Here: Knowledge, Leadership, Culture, and Rules Toward Adaptive Management in Market Systems Programmes* [online], London: BEAM Exchange <https://marketshareassociates.com/getting-there-from-here-knowledge-leadership-culture-and-rules-toward-adaptive-management-in-market-systems-programmes/> [accessed 12 October 2020].

MarketShare Associates (2016c) *Scaling Impact: Cambodia MSME Ex-Post Assessment* [online], Washington, DC: USAID <https://marketshareassociates.com/scaling-impact-cambodia-msme-ex-post-assessment/> [accessed 12 October 2020].

MarketShare Associates (2016d) *Testing Tools for Assessing Systemic Change: Outcome Harvesting – The ALCP Project in the Georgian Dairy Industry* [online], Washington, DC: USAID <https://marketshareassociates.com/testing-tools-for-assessing-systemic-change-outcome-harvesting-the-alcp-project-in-the-georgian-dairy-industry/> [accessed 12 October 2020].

MarketShare Associates (2020) 'AWEF systems change reporting: Jordan licensing intervention', London: Department for International Development (unpublished).

Posthumus, H. and Wanitphon, P. (2015) *Measuring Attribution: A Practical Framework to Select Appropriate Attribution Methods, with Cases from ALCP in Georgia, MDF in East Timor, Propcom Mai-Karfi in Nigeria and Samarth-NMDP in Nepal* [pdf] <https://www.enterprise-development.org/wp-content/uploads/RMMeasuring_Attribution_Overview_Case_September_2015.pdf> [accessed 12 October 2020].

Posthumus, H., Shah, R., Mielhlbradt, A., and Kessler, A. (2020) *A Pragmatic Approach to Assessing System Change* [online], Springfield Centre <https://www.springfieldcentre.com/pragmatic-approach-to-assessing-system-change/> [accessed 11 November 2020].

Ripley, M. (2015) *Fooled by Randomisation: Why RCTs Might be the Real 'Gold Standard' for Private Sector Development*, Geneva: International Labour Organization.

Ruffer, T. and Wach, E. (2013) *Review of M4P Evaluation Methods and Approaches* [online], London: Department for International Development <http://www.value-chains.org/dyn/bds/docs/849/M4P_Evaluation_Review_ITAD.pdf> [accessed 12 October 2020].

Sen, N. (2018) *Guideline to the DCED Standard for Results Measurement: 3b Estimating Attributable Changes* [online], Cambridge, UK: Donor Committee for Enterprise Development <https://enterprise-development.org/wp-content/uploads/3b_Implementation_Guidelines_Attribution.pdf> [accessed 12 October 2020].

Springfield Centre (2015) *The Operational Guide for the Making Markets Work for the Poor (M4P) Approach*, 2nd edition [online], funded by SDC & DFID <https://www.enterprise-development.org/wp-content/uploads/m4pguide2015.pdf> [accessed 12 October 2020].

CHAPTER 5

Getting to scale in M4P programmes

Gareth Davies

Abstract

Scale is a core principle of the Making Markets Work for the Poor (M4P) approach, but what is the evidence on getting to scale, and how can programmes maximize the chances of reaching scale? One of the last papers written by Alan Gibson, FSD Kenya: Ten Years of a Market Systems Approach in the Kenyan Finance Market, *contains a fascinating account of two contrasting interventions. In both cases FSD Kenya had succeeded in supporting first movers to adopt new practices and improve their performance, but in only one intervention was there any wider crowding-in. From this initial case study, this chapter identifies the general assumptions required for the replication or demonstration effect to hold and explores the different scaling strategies available. The most important lesson for practitioners is that programmes cannot assume that the demonstration effect will work automatically. Project staff need to think through carefully at the start of the intervention not just whether there are sufficient first movers to partner with, but also who the second movers are likely to be and the capacity and incentives of these second movers, the visibility of the demonstration effect, and whether a knowledge transition mechanism exists.*

Keywords: scale; first movers, systemic change, demonstration effect, rules, SACCOs

Alongside his many theoretical and conceptual contributions to international development, one of Alan's most important contributions was to raise the level of ambition of donors and practitioners. For Alan it was simply not good enough for development programmes to build the capacity of a few microfinance institutions or distribute agro-inputs to a few thousand farmers. Instead programmes should aspire to transform entire sectors by catalysing and leveraging the resources and dynamism of local systems and actors. 'Scale' and 'systemic change' are central tenets of the Making Markets Work for the Poor (M4P) approach, and starting in the 2000s M4P programmes demonstrated that it was indeed possible to reach millions of poor smallholders in places like Bangladesh, and revolutionize financial services for the poor in places like Kenya.

Alan was also driven by an irrepressible desire to learn and improve. He was not content with only trumpeting success – he also wanted to understand the failures. This is evident in one of the last papers he wrote, examining

http://dx.doi.org/10.3362/9781788531443.005

Box 5.1 What does it mean to reach 'scale'?

Despite 'scale' being a commonly used term in development, there is no agreed definition of what it means to get to scale. This is not surprising given the greatly different contexts in which development programmes operate: from Vanuatu (population 276,000) to India (population 1.3 billion). Two programmes referred to in this chapter, Katalyst in Bangladesh (population 165 million) and PrOpCom in Nigeria (population 191 million) have reached over a million people with a single intervention. This is obviously much harder to achieve in a country like Liberia with a population of only 4.7 million (2 per cent of the population of Nigeria) and 'thinner' markets, not to mention impossible in Vanuatu. The size of the programme budget also has an influence on the scale and outreach achievable.

For the purpose of this chapter, what constitutes getting to scale has therefore been left deliberately vague: getting to 'scale' means reaching a large number of poor men and women (as producers, consumers, or workers), with 'large' being dependent on the country context. As a rule of thumb, with the exception of very small countries, this means reaching people in the hundreds of thousands, rather than the thousands or tens of thousands.

---

the experience of the Financial Sector Deepening (FSD) Kenya programme (Gibson, 2016). The paper spends as much time exploring disappointments and missed opportunities as it does examining the successes (of which there are many).

Two of the case studies contained in the paper – one a success and one a failure – inspired much of my own thinking around 'scale'. Starting with the success, Equity Bank had been a building society which, from the 1990s, had started on a process of change aimed at reaching the millions of unbanked and underserved in Kenya. It was the first bank in Kenya to recognize the potential value of being more customer-driven (rather than product-led). Equity Bank received concentrated technical support from 2002 to 2008 from several different sources. The shift in strategy at Equity, supported by FSD Kenya and others, led to a significant improvement in performance, and Equity quickly grew in terms of customers, revenues, profitability, and market share. This success led to a response in the rest of the sector (some organic, some facilitated), with a sizable number of local and regional banks jumping on the Equity bandwagon. 'We have taken financial inclusion on board because of Equity. It was they who saw the importance of the bottom of the pyramid', according to the CEO of one competitor quoted in Alan's paper. Rival banks emulated Equity by investing in their own technical capacity; several directly poached Equity staff.

Turning to the failure, savings and credit cooperatives (SACCOs) are member-based, not-for-profit organizations strongly embedded in Kenyan society. In 2005, when FSD Kenya started working with SACCOs, there were an estimated 3,200 SACCOs with approximately 1.6 million members. SACCOs were seen by FSD Kenya to be an important financial service provider for the poor, but their performance was highly variable, and they were often poorly managed. In Phase 1, FSD Kenya provided direct capacity-building to eight of the best-run SACCOs, spending US$2.3 m in SACCO capacity-building overall.

By 2010 FSD Kenya recognized that the strategy had not led to the desired sector-wide transformation. As noted in Alan's paper, working with individual SACCOs 'at best produced isolated pockets of excellence but there was no spread beyond these'.

Contrasting these two cases led me to the intriguing question of what explains the difference. In both cases FSD Kenya had succeeded in supporting first movers to adopt new practices and improve their performance, but only in the case of banks was there wider crowding-in. Drawing on the material in Alan's paper, a number of factors that would seem to support crowding-in in the banking sector, which were absent in the SACCO sector, stood out:

- The industry structure was more conducive to crowding-in – a small number of large, well-resourced banks, concentrated in the capital Nairobi – as opposed to a large number of small, generally poorly resourced SACCOs scattered across Kenya.
- The high visibility of the Equity demonstration effect: through the bank's reported profits, rapid expansion of branches, new-look marketing campaigns, and conversations in tightly knit industry networks, the success of Equity was clearly visible to other banks in the industry – as opposed to SACCOs, which were more dispersed, less visible, and less densely networked.
- Competitive pressure among banks, driven by the profit motive and the desire to maintain or win market share, created a strong incentive for other banks to copy the Equity model – in contrast to SACCOs, which typically lacked any strong incentives to improve performance or compete and generally enjoyed local monopolies; the traditions and values (informal rules) around SACCOs also diluted any external pressure for change.
- There was a clear transition mechanism for second movers: high staff turnover in the banking industry and the poaching of Equity staff, and the dissemination of lessons and insights through industry networks and forums – in contrast to SACCOs, with low staff churn, a weak association, and limited networks.

Organic replication (or lack thereof?)

Contrasting the two examples from the FSD Kenya paper, one of the clear lessons is that programmes cannot assume that crowding-in will happen organically or with minimal support. Alan and others at the Springfield Centre had made this same point in several other case studies. For example, a case study of Katalyst, an agri-business market systems programme in Bangladesh, found regional limits to the organic replication of the maize 'super-contracting' model:

> Systemic change programmes often expect that expansion of benefits will occur 'organically' as a result of the incentives of the partners, since these should be aligned to increasing the number of beneficiaries,

and information regarding those incentives encourages competitors to crowd in. Yet in many cases this does not happen, especially where, as in this case, marked regional markets for maize meant either the capacity or the incentives of the initial implementing partners are lacking in new areas. (Lomax et al., 2016)

In my own experience I had seen many M4P programmes rely on organic or light-touch crowding-in as the pathway to scale, often with disappointing results. The FSD Kenya and Katalyst case studies prompted me to look more closely at the assumptions underpinning this strategy and the conditions in which they might or might not hold. In my own paper, *Getting to Scale*, I identified three assumptions that need to hold for the demonstration effect strategy to work:

1. Success for the first movers is visible to the second movers, and second movers attribute this success to the adoption of the 'innovation' by the first movers.
2. Second movers have the incentives, capacity, and resources to copy the innovation, and barriers to adoption are low (or not insurmountable).
3. Second movers are able to access the know-how in order to replicate and adapt the innovation (for example, via a knowledge 'transition mechanism' such as staff poaching, or reverse engineering).

During my research for the paper I could find relatively few cases of programmes getting to scale through the demonstration effect. Looking at the three assumptions, this is perhaps not surprising: one or more of these assumptions may fail to hold in practice for a variety of reasons.

Taking the first assumption, there are many reasons why the innovation – and the success derived by the first mover – may not be clearly visible to outsiders. This is especially likely for 'process' innovations, or innovations that generate secondary benefits (such as reducing customer churn or increasing agent loyalty). This was cited in another Springfield case study (PrOpCom Mai-Karfi, 2014) as one of the reasons for disappointing levels of replication around the Notore small-packs innovation in Nigeria:

> When company executives see rival firms innovating, but have little information on how the innovation affects the rival firm's performance, they may be reluctant to emulate it ... One challenge in encouraging more firms to invest in marketing fertiliser to poorer farmers is that the cause of Notore's success remains partly hidden. Industry-wide and even within Notore, small packs remain a small percentage of total fertiliser sales. Yet small packs, by allowing new customers to test Notore's product, often lead to sales of 50kg bags in future years ... unless a fertiliser company executive understands both small pack sales and their effect on 50kg bag sales, they might underestimate the attractiveness of investing in small packs. (PrOpCom Mai-Karfi, 2014)

Even proactive communicating of the Notore success to the rest of the market failed to spark the desired spontaneous crowding-in, requiring PrOpCom Mai-Karfi to work intensively with second movers to promote replication.

Even if the success of first movers is visible to the rest of the market, second movers may lack the incentives, capacity, and resources to replicate this success (assumption 2). In the theory of the diffusion of innovation developed by Everett Rogers in the 1960s, Rogers suggested that the distribution of different types ('innovators', 'early adopters', 'early majority', 'late majority', and 'laggards') in any population follows a uniform bell-curve. However, there is no reason why this should be so in practice: in many contexts in which development programmes work, the distribution may be heavily skewed to the right, with a small number of innovators and early adopters, and a large number of 'laggards' (as seemed to be the case with SACCOs in Kenya).

The knowledge transition mechanism between first and second movers may also be weak (assumption 3). This will be the case in industries that are loosely networked and have weak associations or professional bodies, low levels of staff churn, and high geographic dispersion (again the case with SACCOs in Kenya).

To take another programme example, the Market Assistance Programme in Kenya (K-MAP) provided support to a number of mid-sized agro-dealers with the aim of driving wider replication across agro-dealers in Kenya. As with FSD Kenya's SACCO intervention, various industry factors meant all three assumptions required for wider replication failed to hold in practice. Despite notable successes with several agro-dealers, very little wider crowding-in was observed. Although the reasons behind this were never fully explored at the time, it seems that both the push and pull factors were insufficient to drive crowding-in. Although the K-MAP 'star' partners were enjoying good returns and reasonable sales growth, their success was not widely visible to geographically dispersed agro-dealers (assumption 1) and was not enough to entice typically unadventurous and conservative agro-dealers to shift from the status quo (assumption 2). In rural areas, farmers often have limited agro-dealer options, meaning that effective competition between agro-dealers is limited, further dampening the incentive, or imperative, to change (assumption 2). While some of the practice changes could easily be copied or reverse-engineered by interested second movers (such as improvements in shop layouts), various internal 'process' improvements (such as stock management and book-keeping) were less easy to copy, and aside from receiving support from K-MAP or other donor programmes, no clear transition mechanism existed (assumption 3).

Alternative strategies for getting to scale

So, what can programmes do to reach scale if the assumptions required for organic replication do not hold?

Big actor strategy

The simplest strategy for getting to scale is what I call the 'big actor strategy': working with one or two market actors that by themselves have the ability to reach large numbers of poor men and women. At the start of the intervention, this means identifying and partnering with 'big actors' with deep pockets who are able to mobilize significant financial and human resources to develop and roll-out the innovation. These big actors may also already have extensive distribution or sales channels. Beyond helping these firms develop and test the initial innovation at the pilot stage, at the scale-up stage programmes may provide additional support to help these firms overcome internal scaling barriers (such as technical advice on how to recruit and train new stockists or agents, or providing additional finance). Through the big actor strategy programmes can get to scale even without any further competitive response or crowding-in by other market actors.

Many of the well-known cases of getting to scale in market systems development (MSD) programmes broke the one million mark through a single big actor: PrOpCom with Notore (Nigeria), Katalyst with Syngenta (Bangladesh), and FSD Kenya with CBA (Kenya). However, the big actor strategy is obviously not an option in countries with thin markets and fragmented economies, where actors with sizable, country-wide reach and deep pockets may be thin on the ground. Achieving scale through just one or two actors also comes with its own risks. One obvious risk is that of putting all your eggs in one basket: if the partnership stalls, the whole intervention may be jeopardized, as nearly happened with PrOpCom and Notore:

> Notore faced long delays at Lagos port when importing NPK, and a plant failure affected urea production. The government's GESS voucher scheme tied up most available stock and working capital, leaving little for small packs ... A key lesson of Notore's 2013 performance is that even successful business models are vulnerable to external shocks – especially when they depend on one business. For development programmes that are serious about sustainability, this highlights the importance of working with more than one market player, and favouring innovations that are attractive enough to withstand shocks. (PrOpCom Mai-Karfi, 2014)

By supporting just one actor initially, even if the intention is to support a wider number of second movers later on, there is also the risk of creating a dominant market position. This can happen when there are strong network effects, or the first mover is able to erect barriers to entry (for example through exclusivity deals with agro-dealers, or through political machinations). For example, although it may seem churlish to question the huge success of M-Pesa, a legitimate question can be asked as to whether the development support given to Safaricom to develop M-Pesa should also have been offered to other mobile network operators quicker than it was in order to create a more level playing field.

Strengthening the demonstration effect

Another option is to try to strengthen the demonstration effect. For example, the programme might develop a business case study highlighting the success of the pilot and disseminate the study to the rest of the sector through industry events or one-on-one channels. To be effective, these case studies need to be couched in terms that will be compelling to the interests and motivations of market actors. For commercial actors, this might include evidence of increased sales, improved customer loyalty, reduced costs, and ultimately greater profitability.

Although programmes may wish to see as much crowding-in as possible, it is typically not in the interests of a commercial actor to support crowding-in by competitors. This tension often manifests itself in partnership negotiations, with programmes having to balance their quest for scale with the wishes of the partner for exclusivity and non-disclosure. There is also a limit to how much programmes can expect partner firms to contribute to and participate in efforts to trumpet their success to the wider industry. Having said that, there are examples where individual champions have been willing to do just that; the incentive often appears to be peer recognition for the individual champion (rather than the commercial interests of the wider organization). It may also be possible to find non-competing players to lead the promotion of new models, such as industry associations.

If this fails to promote the desired crowding-in, a programme can provide more direct support to second movers. The aim is to either reach scale through a combination of the first and second batch of programme-supported actors, or to create a further demonstration effect or reach a tipping point that will lead to scale through the spontaneous crowding-in of a third wave of actors.

There is a common belief among MSD/M4P programmes that having achieved 'proof of concept' with first movers, any support to second movers need not (or *should not* as a matter of principle) be as intensive as the support provided to the first movers. While it is obviously desirable to do the least possible to catalyse the desired response, there is no a priori reason why second movers should require less intensive support than first movers. In fact, if second movers have lower capacity, are less innovative, have shallower pockets, and are more risk averse than first movers (which is plausible given they are second movers and not first movers), they may require *more* intensive support, not less. This seems to be backed up by programme experience: when reviewing the case study evidence, we found plenty of examples where second movers required the same or more intensive support, not less. For example:

Katalyst. Following the successful pilot with Syngenta, Katalyst entered into partnerships with other inputs suppliers interested in replicating the model. Syngenta was chosen in the first place partly because it already had some experience in delivering training to stockists, and the innovation fit within its overall strategy and ethos. There were no second movers with a comparable level of existing capacity or strategic alignment, requiring Katalyst to offer a similar intensity of support:

> Katalyst have initiated new projects – *on a similar basis* – with two other input suppliers who are (to some degree) competitive with Syngenta; Bayer Crop Science and East-West Seeds ... This is a major strategic change in approach for both firms. Neither has any previous experience of retailer training. (Gibson, 2005; emphasis added)

PrOpCom. When the success of the Notore mini-fertilizer innovation failed to spread organically to the rest of the sector, the successor programme (PrOpCom Mai-Karfi) developed partnerships with two other fertilizer companies, TAK and Springfield Agro. Springfield Agro required similar levels of support to Notore. The pilot phase was bumpy, but as of 2014 Springfield Agro had increased investment and commitment. With intensive programme support TAK launched a pilot, but the pilot failed to take off and was later abandoned (PrOpCom Mai-Karfi, 2014).

Developing service providers

Another option is for programmes to work with service providers in the wider market system in order to catalyse the desired industry-wide change. So rather than the programme directly providing support to second movers to promote the uptake of an innovation, it may be possible to create or strengthen a set of service providers to do the job for you. For example, rather than the programme attempting to provide technical support to dozens or potentially hundreds of agro-dealers to adopt a particular innovation, the programme could instead partner with a small number of service providers to develop training or consultancy services that will then be provided to agro-dealers.

Although this strategy offers an eloquent solution to getting to scale, unfortunately we could find more examples of where this strategy failed than where it succeeded. As with the organic replication strategy, there are a number of conditions that need to hold for the service provider strategy to work:

On the demand-side:

- Sufficient ability and willingness to pay for services exists among target 'intermediary' organizations (e.g. agro-dealers).
- Accessing the support service will catalyse the adoption of the pro-poor innovation.

On the supply-side:

- There is sufficient interest among potential service providers to develop a service offering.
- Service providers have sufficient capacity to provide a 'good enough' service offering.

- The service and target market is lucrative enough (relative to alternative options and segments) for service providers to sustain and expand the service offering.

Programmes often encounter difficulties on both the demand and the supply side. For example, halfway through ENABLE1 – a business environment reform programme in Nigeria that used an MSD/M4P approach – the programme started work with a variety of service providers to pilot a number of different fee-for-service offerings for business member organizations (BMOs), such as media relations and advocacy training. Although it was possible to catalyse initial transactions through a combination of facilitating linkages and providing cost-sharing to incentivize take-up, a sustainable service market targeting BMOs never emerged. On the demand-side, the vast majority of BMOs did not have sufficient interest in the service offering to pay for the service. In the case of advocacy training, the service offering also did not lead to the desired practice change, which cannot be achieved through a standardized one-day training of the type offered by service providers. On the supply-side, the BMO market was simply not lucrative enough for service providers to invest sufficient effort or resources in developing new and improved service offerings or winning new work. For example, it proved much easier to provide media relations services to large corporate and government clients than cash-strapped BMOs.

Similar experiences have been recorded in K-MAP and FSD Kenya. In the case of K-MAP, despite a handful of project-brokered transactions, marketing service providers found rural and peri-urban agro-dealers an insufficiently lucrative market segment to justify the effort of targeting these out-of-the-way consumers. Katalyst did record success in fostering the sustainable provision of training to agro-dealers, but it is interesting to note that while agro-dealers paid a small fee to book their place, this training was delivered at a loss by Syngenta: the company was motivated by wider concerns, such as using the training to increase brand loyalty among retailers; the training also fit within their wider corporate social responsibility (CSR) and public relations strategies.

In the case of FSD Kenya, the programme worked with the Cooperative College of Kenya and individual providers to develop practical SACCO training programmes and other services; on the demand-side, a SACCO Fund was launched to support the uptake of these offerings by SACCOs. However, as with the ENABLE1 example, a 2015 review found that despite a high subsidy, demand from SACCOs was weak, with no signs of a sustainable market for services emerging. The review also found that SACCOs that had received training or capacity-building were just as likely to be non-compliant with regulations as SACCOs that had not.

Influencing the rules

Similarly, a programme might target the barriers to entry that prevent new entrants from offering or expanding a given product innovation or help to put in place regulations that provide greater certainty to firms. For example, the development of mobile money in Kenya provided a challenge to regulators who were uncertain how to regulate the new product, and who should be responsible given that mobile money cuts across the jurisdiction of a number of different regulatory bodies. FSD Kenya worked closely with regulators to develop an appropriate regulatory regime, thereby giving Safaricom and others in the market the confidence to invest in and expand new mobile money products.

New rules and regulations can also be used to put pressure on and therefore change the incentives facing organizations to upgrade their business practices and adopt pro-poor 'innovations', such as improved policing of the sale of counterfeit or substandard agro-inputs, or putting in place minimum quality standards. Programmes might also try to influence informal rules and norms, for example through encouraging the naming-and-shaming of substandard agro-input suppliers. The strategy here involves an attempt to reshape incentives to adopt pro-poor changes in situations where the incentives are currently not strong enough for more than a small number of innovators. By improving the enforcement of rules against poor quality or counterfeit agro-inputs, it can become more risky and more difficult for businesses to engage in those practices, whereas in an unregulated environment it may actually be more profitable to sell bad products. The incentive for change is the 'stick' rather than the 'carrot'.

Reform to rules and regulations offers the promise of influencing a whole sector or industry. However, a key lesson from programmes is that regulatory reform can be very challenging. There are often vested interests that benefit from the status quo, requiring programmes to have a good grasp of the political economy dynamics. The regulatory process in many developing countries can also be very slow. To get to scale, it is also not enough to achieve reform-on-paper: changes need to be implemented and enforced on the ground. In its work with SACCOs, FSD Kenya worked with the regulator to put in place tighter regulations that would compel SACCOs to upgrade their systems and processes and hence adopt some of the innovations being promoted by FSD Kenya. However, it became apparent that the regulator lacked teeth, with limited political will to enforce tougher standards. The impact of regulatory reform was therefore minimal. In sectors with weak regulatory or standard-setting bodies, and high levels of informality in practices, it will generally be difficult to promote widespread uptake of innovations through regulatory reform. There is also a risk that enforcement agencies use new standards to extract rent from firms rather than drive up standards in a fair and even-handed manner.

Before trying to promote scale through reforms to rules and regulations, programmes therefore need to ask a number of questions:

- What are the potential barriers to scale in the wider rules and regulations? Can the innovation reach scale without reform? Would reform improve the resilience of the innovation?

- What are actors' current incentives, and how exactly will the regulatory change impact incentives to make pro-poor changes? Will the incentives be strong enough to make a difference?
- What is the nature of the reform required? Are new laws or regulations required, or would incremental improvements to coordination and enforcement be sufficient?
- What is the feasibility of reform given the political economy dynamics? Who are the key actors that require influencing, and does the programme (or its partners) have the ability to do so effectively?
- Once passed, what is the capacity of the relevant bodies to enact and enforce the new rules or regulations? What is the culture of compliance in the sector – will actors take notice of the reforms?

Country-level factors and industry structure supporting getting to scale

Reflecting on the evidence from Kenya, Nigeria, Bangladesh, and elsewhere, a final lesson is the importance of context – both at the country-level and industry-level.

Country-context has a significant bearing on the ability of innovations to reach scale. Although more evidence of successes and failures in getting to scale are needed, from more countries, the following country-level factors seem to be important:

- *'Thicker markets', with a range of large, well-resourced players.* This increases the choice of first movers and makes crowding-in by second-movers more likely.
- *High population and population density.* This reduces the cost of reaching large numbers of bottom of the pyramid (BoP) consumers, improving the commercial viability of BoP innovations and associated distribution models.
- *A more developed financial sector.* Improved access to financial services makes it easier for first movers to invest in developing and rolling out innovations and makes organic replication more likely by second movers (who cannot rely on soft financing from donors).

Looking at the first two factors in particular, it is perhaps not surprising that many of the examples of getting to scale come from Bangladesh and Nigeria. Where these factors are absent, getting to scale can be challenging. For example, the BOSS (Business Opportunities and Support Services) project in Timor-Leste cites the importance of contextual factors in their ability to reach scale: 'Operating in thin markets, shaped by a history of conflict, colonisation and occupation, it proved difficult for BOSS to move beyond small-scale pilots towards a credible strategy for large-scale change' (Ripley and Major, 2015).

Even within countries, differences in industry structure can have a significant bearing on scale outcomes, as the example of Equity Bank versus SACCOs in Kenya illustrates. Generalizing from the FSD Kenya examples, three industry-level factors seem particularly important:

- *Market concentration.* It seems easier to reach scale in sectors with a small number of large players: programmes can already reach large numbers through working with one or two players directly, and the wider demonstration effect is more likely to hold.
- *Intensity of competition.* In highly competitive markets, competitive pressures are more likely to compel firms to innovate and copy successful innovations. Note that what matters is less the number of firms, but the degree of overlap in customer segments and geographic reach. For example, competition between three national mobile operators may be more intense than between hundreds of agro-dealers if those agro-dealers effectively enjoy local monopolies.
- *Density of networks.* Where actors and individuals are tightly networked, ideas and innovations flow more readily. Geographic concentration helps (for example, the tendency of banks to all locate their headquarters in the same district of the commercial capital); effective associations and business networks also play a role. Similarly, although it can be painful for programmes when a key champion leaves a partner organization, staff churn also seems to support the spread of innovations.

Conclusions

Looking back at the findings of the *Getting to Scale* paper, perhaps the most important lesson for practitioners is that programmes cannot lazily assume that the demonstration effect will work automatically. If programmes wish to use the demonstration effect as their strategy for scale, they need to think through carefully at the start of the intervention whether the three assumptions underpinning the demonstration effect are likely to hold. This means not just looking at whether there are sufficient first movers to partner with, but also who the second movers are likely to be and the capacity and incentives of these second movers, the visibility of the demonstration effect, and whether a knowledge transition mechanism exists. Although there will always be a high degree of learning-by-doing, thinking this through more carefully at the start of the intervention can help to avoid costly failures later. In many of the country and industry contexts in which development programmes work, the three assumptions often will not hold, requiring a different strategy to get to scale.

For donors, when designing programmes and setting milestones, funders should recognize that getting to scale takes time. This is especially true in thin markets. Five years appears to be the minimum length of time; for a full competitive response to emerge, seven or eight years may be required. If donors are unable to commit to this length of programming in one go, they should be prepared to commission successor programmes to fully consolidate the scaling process (contingent on good performance in the first phase). When designing programmes, donors should also avoid artificially limiting the flexibility of programmes. To reach scale requires a range of different strategies and tactics. Creating challenge funds, for example, that are limited to providing grants to first movers, are less likely to get to scale than M4P/MSD programmes that can adopt a range of scaling strategies depending on the country and industry context.

In arriving at these insights I owe a debt of gratitude to Alan, without whom I might not have even been asking the question of how programmes can get to scale, and certainly would not have had the wealth of programmatic evidence and lessons with which to formulate any answers.

Acknowledgement

This chapter is based on a longer paper published by Adam Smith International (Davies, 2016).

About the author

Gareth Davies is a Director of Tandem, a specialist monitoring, evaluation, and learning consultancy. Gareth has worked in market systems development since 2008. Gareth first met Alan Gibson at the Springfield M4P training course in Glasgow, and subsequently became a trainer on the course and worked alongside Alan on several projects.

References

Davies, G. (2016) *Getting to Scale: Lessons in Reaching Scale in Private Sector Development Programmes* [online], London: Adam Smith International <https://beamexchange.org/resources/785/> [accessed 12 October 2020].

Gibson, A. (2005) *Bringing Knowledge to Vegetable Farmers: Improving Embedded Information in the Distribution System*, Dhaka: KATALYST Bangladesh.

Gibson, A. (2016) *FSD Kenya: Ten Years of a Market Systems Approach in the Kenyan Finance Market*, Kenya: FSD Kenya and FSD Africa.

Lomax, J., Smith, K., and Taylor, B. (2016) *Katalyst's Contribution to Systemic Change: The Adopt, Adapt, Expand, Respond Cases*, Durham, UK: Springfield Centre.

PrOpCom Mai-Karfi (2014) *Education and Lasting Access to Fertiliser: How Nigerian Smallholders and Businesses Are Prospering Together*, Abuja, Nigeria: PrOpCom Mai-Karfi; Durham, UK: The Springfield Centre.

Ripley, M. and Major, A. (2015) *The BOSS Project in Timor-Leste: Thin Markets, Thick Impact?* Geneva: International Labour Organization.

CHAPTER 6

The art of market facilitation: Lessons from FSD Kenya

Joanna Ledgerwood

Abstract

Market facilitation is more of an art than a science, directed by principles and frameworks rather than lists of actions; this can make it difficult to translate theory into practice. This chapter explores the art of market facilitation based on synthesized learnings from Alan's review of the first 10 years of FSD Kenya's work facilitating the financial market system in Kenya to work better for the poor. It examines the wider lessons and challenges that emerge for organizations addressing the dilemmas of developing markets for the poor, and how they differ from other conventional approaches. By exploring in his review the things FSD Kenya got right and those it did not, Alan provided good practical lessons on how to effectively implement Making Markets Work for the Poor (M4P) for markets to become genuinely inclusive. This chapter consolidates these lessons to help build understanding around the M4P approach and to provide guidelines on key, practical questions facing facilitators. The overall lesson from these experiences is that the M4P approach provides operational disciplines and frameworks that work, but to effectively put market facilitation into practice, it is necessary to 'operationalize' M4P. And that is often easier said than done.

Keywords: financial inclusion, market analysis, monitoring and results measurement, real economy, facilitation, incentives, partnerships

One of the last seminal papers Alan wrote before his death was a 10-year review of Financial Sector Deepening (FSD) Kenya (Gibson, 2016). Building on the thinking that Alan pioneered, FSD Kenya seeks to make financial markets in Kenya work better for the poor. The case study shows that 'FSD Kenya's contribution to financial inclusion, while varying between individual activities, has been substantial in aggregate, and that, globally (beyond Kenya), there are important lessons emerging from this experience for development funding and facilitating organisations' (Gibson, 2016: vi). This chapter explores these lessons. Drawing heavily from his original text, it summarizes Alan's findings of FSD Kenya's experience operationalizing the Making Markets Work for the Poor (M4P) approach.[1]

http://dx.doi.org/10.3362/9781788531443.006

Basics for effective market facilitation

Making markets work for the poor is about creating the foundation for lasting change where the market system – its functions and players – is equipped to meet future challenges and to continue to meet the changing needs of the poor. The result is sustained impact, rather than short-lived or dependent on further injections of aid.

Facilitation good practice emphasizes action led by analysis, quid pro quo/transactional relationships building on partner incentives and ownership, technical credibility, closeness to the market, and developing an exit plan from the outset. Applying these principles allows facilitators to create momentum and catalyse change throughout the market system.

True sustainability requires wider system change

Ultimately, how a market performs (what happens in the core) is dependent on the supporting functions and rules (what's around the core). These functions are performed by a diverse range of public and private actors, formal and informal, all of whom are influenced by a wide range of contextual factors.

The M4P approach acknowledges that the lives and livelihoods of the poor are continually adapting to the changing environment around them, and that solutions are needed that adapt with them. It recognizes that achieving inclusion is more complicated than a straightforward equation of supply and demand; it involves many other functions – information, skills building, product and organizational development, advocacy, norms, regulations and policies – that determine behaviour and practices and influence transactions. From a market systems perspective, for intervention in the core to be valid it has to ensure that the underlying causes are addressed in supporting functions and rules. These *interconnected systems* are all systems in their own right. Interventions thus seek change in the wider market system which in turn catalyses further development in the core of the market. This means facilitators need to apply the same analytical framework to individual parts of the overall market system as the whole system. Viewing them through the same lens as that applied to the system as a whole requires a detailed analysis of sustainability. That is, if sustainability is not considered in the context of the system – the functions and players and 'who will do and who will pay' – sustainability analysis is not made real; a superficial, intuitive exercise rather than one that guides actions.

M-Pesa: Supporting a fairer market system

FSD Kenya has played a unique if often unrecognized role in the story of M-Pesa. Initially this focused on creating the regulatory space to allow M-Pesa to happen. But, over many years, it has engaged in other ways to mitigate M-Pesa's influence and shape a better, fairer market system for all players including the poor. The objective of FSD Kenya's intervention here has been to nudge the environment around M-Pesa – the information, regulations, coordination, and product development functions – so that the market system as a whole encourages more and better innovation and service quality.

Source: Gibson, 2016: 16

Understanding the market system

Market facilitation begins with market analysis – understanding how market systems are structured, identifying the main functions and rules as well as the different market players and how they fit within the market system.

> The diagnostic process begins by identifying the disadvantages the poor face in a market system (the 'symptoms') and iteratively proceeds into a detailed analysis that explains the continued existence of these disadvantages (the 'root causes'). Market systems are complex, so locating root causes can be difficult and time-consuming, but ceasing the diagnostic process too soon can result in programmes exerting their intervention efforts in the wrong places: dealing with symptoms but not their underlying causes. (Springfield, 2015: 7)

Good market analysis seeks to identify the underlying causes for why poorer consumer segments are excluded; that is, 'why market players behave the way they do'. Understanding how the market system encourages (or not) transactions for poor consumers and small businesses helps facilitators to determine where and how to intervene to catalyse improvements which will have the greatest and most durable impact on improving livelihoods.

This requires facilitators to answer basic M4P operational questions such as: What is stopping the supply-side from offering appropriate services? Why doesn't the demand-side use the services? What support functions need strengthening to support increased use of services by the poor? Do current policies and regulations support or hinder increased inclusion? How do informal rules affect market behaviour? How does the overall economic context affect inclusion?

Developing this knowledge takes time. However, facilitators cannot wait until they know everything; they need to start somewhere. I once asked Alan, 'How do you know when you're ready to intervene?' His response was simple: 'Do you know enough?' As with everything M4P, there are no hard and fast rules and building knowledge is an ongoing process; actively intervening in the market system, watching how players respond, checking if your assumptions hold, seeing what others are doing and how the market is changing, continually identifying constraints, new opportunities, and so on. Action led by analysis is at the heart of M4P.

A culture and practice of being close and engaged

Many of FSD Kenya's most important interventions have occurred when they have been responsive to an emerging situation (for example M-Pesa regulation and M-Shwari). This is more than serendipity. It is a function of developing the right relationships with stakeholders, of being sufficiently informed about specifics and the general situation in the market, and of knowing 'who' as well as 'what' in relation to market players. Facilitation always involves engaging with others; it can't be done by facilitators themselves.

Source: Gibson, 2016: 41

Strategic clarity is key

Having a clear vision of the future – not just of how individual parts will function but how the system as a whole will work and be funded – is key to lasting change.

Developing market systems takes a range of interventions aimed at addressing different constraints, each with their own vision (and thus exit plan), which are complementary in their effect and together result in a market system that works better for the poor. The portfolio of interventions undertaken by facilitators therefore has to fit with an overall future vision of the market system, and a future vision of the interconnected systems within. This vision must recognize that the role of facilitation (and facilitators) is not permanent; ultimately, the goal is for market players to change their behaviour resulting in increased transactions leading to scale. This requires regular review and challenge around the basic question: where do we envisage the market system x years from now? And what is our vision for individual parts of the system that will contribute to change? Without this discipline, market system development can end up being a multiple of separate activities, each with its own justification but which together miss the bigger strategic goal. Market facilitators thus have to set clear objectives for achieving systemic change and regularly review the consistency of their work in practice with the overall strategic vision.

An important part of developing a clear strategic vision is to consider the *feasibility* of achieving that vision – both at the wider market system level and for specific interventions. Will the intervention result in the desired market system changes which will result in increased use of services, which in turn, will result in improved livelihoods? And for the long term? An important M4P tool is to consider 'who-does-who-pays' in the current system and for those functions carried out by development actors (or missing functions), consider who *could* do and who *could* pay in the future. Of key importance here is to be both realistic and cognizant of market player incentives and capacities; they not only need to *share the vision*, they also need to have the incentives and capacity (or willingness to develop the capacity) to achieve that vision. Without this, interventions will not result in desired market change.

Developing a credit information system

In the 1990s, the Kenyan finance industry struggled with high levels of non-performing loans and bank failures. Credit information sharing (CIS) featured in regular but generally ineffectual discussions between the industry and Central Bank of Kenya (CBK). In 2007, a new law requiring negative information sharing was introduced but was not being followed and a Joint Task Force to advance progress on CIS was established but little had been achieved. FSD Kenya, seeing an opportunity and a need, took the initiative in proposing to coordinate the work of the Task Force. For the members, FSD Kenya represented a good choice – they were trusted, known, neutral, and involved.

FSD Kenya's intervention to develop the CIS has worked well, in part due to a relatively clear vision of the future – not just of how individual areas will function but how the system as a whole will work and be funded. It is doubtful if the existing level of progress would have been achieved otherwise. The level of stasis and dither around CIS meant that making progress here was not simply a matter of 'donor funds' but of active facilitation, coordinating tasks that are essentially one-off interventions. FSD Kenya has played the key technical and coordinating role thus far but the financial sector has incentive to make this work – and there are clear indicators in place to test this commitment.

Source: Gibson, 2016: 19

Facilitation, not direct delivery

Facilitation is central to achieving sustainability. Facilitators aim to stimulate market players to take on new (or adapted) functions and to 'crowd in' wider and lasting activity beyond the immediate partners/functions, while avoiding becoming an active market player. Facilitators are thus a 'third party'; standing outside the market system encouraging, influencing, supporting systemic change. Their primary role is to use resources to address constraints to allow the system to function more effectively and inclusively. Facilitation is therefore a public role (not commercial), it is temporary (time-bound), and it requires a deep understanding of the market system and the capacity to intervene with appropriate resources (financial, human, political).

A facilitator's role is explicitly catalytic – working towards a future vision of a market which does not require aid-funded support and ensuring that any intervention is guided by a clearly defined exit strategy. Without a clear vision of how the system will work in the future and how the intervention contributes to that vision, a void develops that allows 'direct delivery' to take precedence over facilitating others. The longer this continues, inevitably the more entrenched the facilitator becomes and the less the market develops. It is vital therefore for facilitators to signal clearly to stakeholders that their role is finite, and to ensure there are market players who are both willing and able to continue to provide services into the future. While this sometimes may require a compromise in terms of service quality as market players may not be as thorough or informed, it is absolutely necessary for sustainable change to occur.

This is not to say facilitators should never intervene directly in the market system, initially playing key technical and coordination roles. However, they must balance tactical opportunism with strategic direction. If delivery is the only activity undertaken or this is repeated (with the same or another partner) or there is little sign of impact beyond what is achieved directly, there is a danger that longer-term strategic goals (and ultimately the purpose of facilitation) are neglected. In the longer term, the strategic purpose of facilitation is *not* to have any continuing role in the system.

Although most facilitators realize they should not be doing 'direct delivery', this is often not as clear when facilitating the development of support functions. While direct subsidy for the delivery of services is generally disapproved of in official donor guidance, support services such as consulting and training have become one of the main areas of donor focus. For facilitators to successfully facilitate the development of service markets, support functions need to be seen as part of the market system and not a donor-supported activity. Without a clear vision and, particularly, when market capacity is thin, expectations on demand- and supply-sides are influenced, and it becomes more difficult for a market to develop.

Developing service markets

MicroSave was supported by FSD Kenya (and other donors) to enhance the capacity of the financial sector but to also develop providers of technical services to finance organizations. It did this through three related components: 1) working directly with providers (action research partners (ARPs)) to develop their systems and products; 2) using this experience to develop 'tool kits' which could then be applied to other ARPs and as a general resource; and 3) mentoring and training (and certifying) a number of service providers and individual consultants.

As a whole, MicroSave was seen to be very successful but this was mainly in relation to the direct positive impact on microfinance institutions/banks who were its partners. An external impact assessment of FSD Kenya in 2009 praised MicroSave for its 'hugely successful' work at the meso-level. But this was actually about the free direct delivery of technical assistance to banks; the review did not assess – because it was deemed too difficult – impact on the development of the services market. While doubtless funders can find justification in the 'need' of recipient organizations, this also reflects their own need to disburse 'support' – a fact of which stakeholders in Kenya, not least those in the financial sector, are completely aware. It is of note that MicroSave, a much bigger organization than in the past and with a strong reputation as a direct provider of services to financial service providers, is still donor-supported for most of its work.

Source: Gibson, 2016: 22

Characteristics of effective facilitators

A facilitator is able to intervene successfully if it is a known entity with an ongoing 'on the ground' presence, respected for knowledge and technical rigour, displays a 'low ego' to allow ownership, and is perceived as being independent, rather than a market player.

The M4P approach is about sustainably changing the underlying dynamics and structure of the market system to enable it to be more inclusive. Facilitators aim to change the mind-sets and practices of service providers, consumers, regulators, supervisors, and other market system players. However, market systems are not only complex, but also dynamic and unpredictable. To be an effective facilitator, organizations must:

- Be responsive – ensuring systems are in place for efficient planning and decision-making in order to react quickly when opportunities arise or to address roadblocks that other, less nimble organizations cannot.
- Be flexible – avoiding the need to define activities in advance; given the dynamic and unpredictable nature of market change, allowing freedom to adapt interventions in the light of new opportunities and experience.
- Focus on market system change and increased access – rather than focusing on prescribed activities and 'deliverables', accountability should focus on overall objectives with the means to achieving these kept open.
- Have a long-time horizon – recognizing the intractable nature of some market constraints and the importance of change processes being owned by local actors.
- Be credible and independent – drawing on sound technical competence, allowing close and influencing relationships to be formed with key organizations and individuals.
- Be efficient – allowing the greatest proportion of resources to be concentrated on resourcing the facilitation tasks of M4P.
- Be able to use a range of tools – supporting the ability to influence and engage in partnerships in a variety of ways depending on the need and circumstances of the constraint and market players involved.

Successful facilitation requires a good understanding of the M4P approach

The market systems approach requires a thorough understanding of the market system and the players within it as well as good knowledge of the M4P framework and tools. Learning the practicalities of applying the approach can almost only be learned through experience, and ideally, through sharing and mentoring from others that have successfully applied M4P. Weaknesses in the operationalization of the M4P approach can often be attributed to a lack of investment in staff's understanding and ownership of the approach.

While the basic M4P framework provides guidance on how to act, because M4P is highly contextual and intervention/partner specific, generally 'to-do' checklists cannot be provided. Importantly, the market systems approach challenges facilitators to make sense of the approach *in their own contexts*. It is ultimately spending time 'doing M4P' that develops the skills needed to do it.

The strengths and weaknesses of facilitating organizations are often personified in those of its director or CEO. The person leading the organization must have a deep understanding of, and know how to apply, M4P principles and tools and be willing to invest in internal processes for staff development (and their own) including mentoring and coaching as well as external training and support specific to understanding the approach. A strong leader needs to ensure staff are clear on the objectives and role of the facilitator and can effectively communicate and implement M4P. It is also important to ensure funders and others understand the approach and what it means in practice. When stakeholders such as funders, governance bodies, and new staff do not understand facilitation, implementing M4P can be undermined.

Successful facilitation requires technical rigour and credibility

Facilitation is a people-intensive task. It requires a range of attributes – including technical knowledge, market awareness, empathy, and enterprise. It is when a facilitator has developed technical competence, market knowledge, informed analysis, and independence, and shared this with the right audience, that intervention possibilities emerge.

Facilitators must be viewed as technically competent and bring something to market players they cannot do for themselves. This knowledge and competency builds over time by bringing a level of technical skills and continually assessing and understanding the market system and the players within it. This is done through participating in stakeholder forums, publishing research findings, and meeting with people and organizations able to influence. The combination of technical expertise and knowledge/information is instrumental in establishing and maintaining credibility. And although not commercial in their objectives, facilitators have to act in a business-like way and, like businesses, have to consider what they (and their brand) mean to different players.

While detailed analysis of the market system can lead to identification of a range of constraints that may be valid for intervention, analysis should only lead to intervention, especially in technically advanced areas, if facilitators have a realistic chance of providing – or accessing – sufficient knowledge and skills to intervene.

Developing the agriculture finance market

FSD Kenya's main intervention in the agriculture sector was aimed at the development of agriculture value chain finance (VCF) targeted at smallholder farmers. However, VCF requires rigorous quantified analysis of the value chain and the financial needs/flows within it, and this was an analytical approach that was relatively new.

The project, costing US$0.7 m, failed to gain traction and achieved limited learning. Why was this? Two issues undermined FSD Kenya's efforts. First, the project was seeking to 'establish a source of technical expertise' in an advanced research-oriented field, and therefore had to be technically led. But in practice it wasn't. External consultants were used but technical leadership from FSD Kenya was very thin. Its offer therefore – what it brought to the table, that is, more than simply the detail of written agreements but what was said and who was saying it – lacked credibility. Meanwhile the implementation arrangements with the external party who was to 'bring the expertise' collapsed as they shifted their focus to other activity. FSD Kenya committed to undertake a technically challenging task, and recognized this, but was left unable to deliver.

Source: Gibson, 2016: 24

Facilitators must be neutral, acting neither as market player nor donor

Stakeholders must perceive facilitators as neutral and trusted third party actors, with clear lines of communication with both private and public players. Although known to be funded by donors, facilitators must not be seen as 'another' donor project – but as an entity that is grounded in the local context.

Facilitators need to manage multiple relationships with different organizations and be perceived as acting in the national/developmental interest. This is what enables them to coordinate different (competing) players to cooperate for mutual/public interest, and to engage with different individual organizations on the basis of trust and confidentiality. Acquiring this status is a result of conscious effort – reinforcing the message of what the purpose of facilitation is and emphasizing that individual partnerships do not preclude other arrangements or imply 'being in the pocket' of a particular firm or government entity.

Funders, particularly those new to the M4P approach, need to understand the role facilitators play and not have misguided expectations. It is important facilitators are not seen as nor pressured to provide a short-term package of pre-defined activities; while not market players, they are also not donors or donor-funded 'projects' and cannot simply provide funding and wait for reports. Rather, facilitators must offer something of use beyond funding – information, advice, expertise, an understanding of constraints, relationships, what has worked elsewhere, and so on. It is this insight that allows facilitators to influence systemic change.

Facilitating a payments platform

FSD Kenya began discussions with Central Bank of Kenya (CBK) around payments in 2008–09 when the potential implications of M-Pesa were beginning to emerge and concern was growing that its first-mover advantage was shifting to a de facto monopoly position. FSD Kenya led a scenario development process to raise the industry's awareness of the significance of payments systems. This was followed by a study that recommended improved industry cooperation to allow economies of scale in payments. Working with the Kenya Banker's Association to consider options with respect to payments, FSD Kenya identified a strong business case for the industry to create an interoperable national retail payments system. The National Payments System Act of 2011 also made clear that CBK supported collaboration between providers in the development of payments systems.

FSD Kenya's credibility and neutrality allowed it to engage with different (competing) market players, its flexibility allowed it to adopt different activities, including placing a full-time project manager, and its longevity allowed it to stick with a, sometimes, frustrating process (over a period of 6–7 years) in a way that has allowed partner ownership to develop. As a consequence of these qualities, the impact of this intervention is likely to be significant.

Source: Gibson, 2016: 19, 39

Form follows function

The dynamic and unpredictable nature of market change means that being able to adapt quickly to new situations arising from the public or private sectors is important. This does not mean a 'blank page/open to all' position; rather it means allowing operational space within areas of strategic interest. Planning, budgeting, and decision-making structures require considerable flexibility, which a rigid project approach does not permit.

In general, traditional 'projects', implemented for a specific period of time with specific outputs, funded through 'accountable grants', are not conducive to effective market facilitation. Performance incentives based on achieving certain targets within a certain predetermined timeframe established at the beginning of the project make it difficult to be opportunistic and flexible in response to market realities. Further, timebound projects are likely to be branded as donor projects and be considered short-term, if generous, 'intruders' into a market.

Instead, a better form for an M4P programme is a special purpose vehicle (SPV), established as a local organization, funded by several donors through 'contributions' to a pooled fund. SPVs are grounded in the local milieu and embedded in the market context. This allows for credibility, expertise, and relationships to build, all important for successful facilitation.

Having a longer-term perspective and presence allows facilitators the flexibility to work with partners that may not move as quickly as originally believed, or when tackling an intractable issue that is long-term in nature, such as developing public institutions. This is, by its nature, a long way from the technical, short-term fix emphasis of many traditional development projects. While it could be argued that change could be achieved more quickly, pushing the pace of change risks undermining ownership and thus long-term success of facilitation. Longevity also allows new possibilities to emerge and to be pursued, and in complex/large-scale markets, creates the ability to address emerging challenges because earlier work has laid the foundation.

Local organizations also allow for increased efficiency and greater funding available for facilitation. And they may be attractive to donors who want to join other funders rather than fund a series of projects on their own. Furthermore, local organizations may be able to attract and develop strong staff by offering a platform (timeframe, opportunity, scope, rewards[2]) for 'good work' for 'good people' that is theoretically better than what is possible in standard projects.

However, form is not a panacea; it sometimes proves difficult to establish a local organization and to find the right staff, set up an appropriate governance structure with the right members. And as local organizations with local staff, there is a danger that facilitators established as SPVs do not see themselves as temporary and carry on long after the facilitation objectives have been met. But in the balance, a locally established organization has proven to be a better form for facilitation than timebound projects.

An appropriate form for facilitation

To a large degree, the original reasons for setting up FSD Kenya as an independent trust have been endorsed. The different hypotheses advanced, for example, in relation to benefits from programming flexibility, incentives alignment, longevity, and efficiency, have largely been realized in practice. And while it might have been possible to implement FSD Kenya's programme with a different structure, it would have been much more difficult than as a trust.

Source: Gibson, 2016: 41

Selecting the right partners and using the right tools

Facilitators do not simply provide 'donor funds' but must actively facilitate, coordinating tasks that are essentially one-off interventions. Facilitators can play the key technical and coordinating role initially, but market system players have to have the incentives to make it work and there must be clear indicators in place to test this commitment.

Facilitators partner with market system players to encourage and support them to, for example: develop and offer new or improved services; upgrade their capacity and performance; take on new roles in the system; change the way they relate to other actors; or change the way they formulate or enforce rules (both formal and informal).

Effective partnerships

Facilitators need to develop partnerships with organizations that have the ability to add value, whether through expertise, resources or motivation. Facilitators need to be flexible in developing an appropriate deal and changing the nature of the service being given (the 'offer') as a situation develops.

Selecting partners and being able to respond to opportunities as they arise is a function of developing the right relationships with stakeholders, of being sufficiently informed about specifics and the general situation in the system, and of knowing 'who' as well as 'what' in relation to market players. Working with multiple partners allows facilitators to test different solutions to common problems. This competitive element improves learning and increases options and ideas for what constitutes good practice.

Part of being an effective facilitator is being able to clearly articulate the 'offer', and in doing so, establish clear roles and recognize mutual benefits. It is also about having a 'low ego'; to effectively engage with different players and address different constraints, the facilitator's voice has to be considered and deliberate, shaped by its clear vision for how the market system might evolve. This helps to foster the right kind of productive, working relationships, tapping into wider motivations for each party: for partners, it is often the technical support and/or international endorsement and exposure; for the facilitator, it is the opportunity to learn from 'real-life' work with key providers which then informs and enables synergies in its work with other partners.

Particularly with commercial providers, it is always relevant to ask what is being given in return, even if it is simply a new idea or pilot project presented by the facilitator. Counterpart contribution is a vital test of commitment and a way of engendering ownership over the process and outcomes in the long term. Gauging the right level of contribution is a challenge, however. In a nascent industry, it can be argued that grant subsidy needs to be relatively high in the initial years, and then reduced over time, as the business case is proven and stakeholders' confidence and willingness to invest rises. However, if the relative level of subsidy is too high, or goes on for too long, it can have the opposite effect: it displaces stakeholders' willingness to invest and undermines the sustainability of key market functions.

Clarity of mutual purpose

M-Shwari is a combined savings and loan product launched in 2012 through a strategic partnership between the Commercial Bank of Africa (CBA) and Safaricom, Kenya's largest mobile network operator, which operates the M-Pesa money transfer and financial service. In 2015 it had more than 11 million accounts and, given its scale and originality, it created a significant disruption in the market.

FSD Kenya's approach to facilitating the development of M-Shwari was based on a temporary but close partnership, in which mutually compatible objectives were identified, where the distinctive, value-adding roles of each party were recognized and respected – and then reflected in how the partnership was structured and managed operationally. CBA had the opportunity and the resources to develop a banking product but had no prior retail banking experience or exposure to the types of clients relevant to the opportunity. FSD Kenya understood this market segment and could offer tangible value in helping CBA to bridge this knowledge gap.

FSD Kenya was transparent about what it wanted to achieve and had a clear vision. Its objectives, strategy, and anticipated impact pathways provided a guiding framework within which the M-Shwari collaboration emerged and was managed. Such clarity of mutual purpose was crucial to establishing the conditions within which genuine partnership discussions with CBA could take place. This understanding of each party's respective 'offer' allowed roles, responsibilities, and resources to be determined and delineated, as well mechanisms for jointly managing and directing implementation.

For CBA, M-Shwari has been broadly successful, and the collaboration with FSD Kenya has been central to this success. This can be attributed to a number of factors – both general and specific. In a general sense, FSD Kenya's flexibility ('the great thing is that they respond. If it's something they want to do, they'll do it quickly') and responsiveness encouraged a trusting 'cards on the table' relationship. Non-disclosure agreements were signed but, more than legal compliance, for CBA, aware that FSD Kenya worked with other competitor companies, it was FSD Kenya's credibility (manifested in key personnel and in a long record of previous work) that offered confidence. Part of this general attractiveness was also a practical modesty in FSD Kenya's approach; its instinct was, as much as possible, to keep in the background rather than intrude into the public view. In this way it hoped that the potential for distortion from the artificiality of foreign donor support could be reduced; noticeably, there is no mention of FSD Kenya in any of the CBA-Safaricom material on M-Shwari.

Source: Gibson, 2016: 12, 14

It's all about incentives

Interventions on 'how to change?' only work if they are consistent with 'why change?'. Misalignment between incentives of individual partners or the wider market, and the objectives of the facilitator can be problematic. Change must matter to partners; until they have incentive to change, change processes are likely to be someone else's (a government or a donor's) agenda.

Lasting systemic change requires that important market functions are embedded within the system. Using an M4P approach means facilitators encourage and support private and public sector players to take on new, or adapted, roles within the market system to make it more inclusive and of benefit to the poor. Key to sustainability are the *incentives* and the *capacity* of market players to continue to deliver the service in the long term without ongoing support. 'Incentives operate at various levels: for and between individuals, and within and between groups or organisations. They are shaped by attitudes towards risk and reward (e.g. losing or gaining money, status, reputation, opportunity, assets or resources)' (Springfield Centre, 2015: 16).

While capacities can (generally) be built, market players need to *want* to change. Understanding the incentives that shape behaviour in individuals and organizations is integral to understanding markets, to selecting partners, and to designing and managing interventions. Facilitators need to be careful not to be overly optimistic on partners' incentives, and must be aware of the extent to which donor funding seeps into incentives.

Understanding incentives in the SACCO sector

From 2006 to 2010 FSD Kenya invested $2.3 m in savings and credit cooperative (SACCO) capacity-building, but by 2010 recognized their interventions hadn't worked. Working with individual SACCOs at best produced isolated pockets of excellence but there was no spread beyond these. Despite regulation in 2008 providing tighter rules (particularly around capital adequacy and liquidity ratios and governance) SACCOs showed little inclination to change.

What lay behind poor performance in FSD Kenya's work with SACCOs was an incentives problem – SACCOs didn't want or see the need to change. This in turn was caused by, first, the traditions and values (informal rules) around SACCOs. As community-owned institutions and part of a 'movement', many SACCO members felt entitled to loans and resented external pressures to change. This view was promoted by the SACCOs' association and had powerful political backing. The second incentives issue related to the SACCO regulator, the SACCO Societies Regulatory Authority, which, in practice, did not have the resources or the political support to enforce the provisions of the 2008 Act.

In this context, even though it recognized the central incentives problem in SACCOs as early as 2010, FSD Kenya's analysis *under*estimated the strength of informal rules around SACCOs and *over*estimated the power of formal rules. With some exceptions, SACCOs still do not have the right incentives to change and therefore limited interest in investing in capacity. No matter the excellence of the technical assistance provided, FSD Kenya's capacity-building endeavours were never likely to be successful when they were battling against the prevailing incentives grain.

Source: Gibson, 2016: 13

Designing the right intervention

Facilitators undertake a series of interventions designed to catalyse lasting, widespread, transformational change in market systems.

Although Alan was reticent to provide 'how-to' guidance given that sustainable system change is dependent on context and requires a good understanding of local market systems and players, he did provide some useful questions facilitators can ask themselves when developing interventions to ensure they will result in systemic change:

1. Is the intervention consistent with the system analysis and vision? Does it 'fit' with the overall view of the constraints in the market system and the facilitator's role in addressing these?
2. Is this the right partner (organization and people)? In working with the partner is there the potential to exert wider change?
3. Is the relationship with the partner 'transactional'? Is the relationship one that tests partners' commitment and develops their ownership over the process and outcome?
4. Is the scale of resources appropriate? 'Enough' resources are required to catalyse new behaviour; if too much, then change processes can become artificial, 'bought', and not owned by market system players.

5. Is there a credible pathway to scaling-up and crowding-in? Is it clear how this intervention could lead or contribute to systemic change?
6. Does the offer fit with the incentives and capacities of the partner? Is the focus on the specific factors that are preventing change from happening now?
7. Is this a 'one-off' activity or a function that should be ongoing as part of the market system? Either could be legitimate but the answer here may guide how this is done and with whom.

No matter what the intervention, these questions are relevant. For example, in engaging with a private sector company considering a new product/service innovation, is this the best partner to deal with? Are they a market leader that will influence others? Is it clear why they do not innovate now and how our support would change this? Or, in relation to a government authority considering new regulations and enforcement mechanisms, how can the relationship be framed to assess and develop their buy-in and commitment? And to develop their capacity to do in the long-term after support ends?

Tools and activities for market facilitation

Facilitators require flexibility to respond appropriately to constraints revealed through analysis and should have few limits over what can be done with partners. They need the strategic and operational structure – the mandate, procedures, decision-making structures, and so on – to intervene in a range of ways, and to act quickly and flexibly. This is very difficult to determine in advance.

Facilitators draw on a range of different instruments, and in practice, interventions are likely to use more than one, tailored to specific partners, and may change as the intervention progresses and market systems change (or not) in response. Financial support is not the only way to stimulate systemic change. In fact, too much donor-fuelled support to push market players can, paradoxically, make providers more risk averse. There are other, less invasive options. Activities and/or funding instruments can include:

- *Technical assistance*: 'how to' advice on services and processes, among others, varying from short-term inputs to longer-term engagements to secondments to partner institutions. Targeted accurately, and of suitable quality, this can be effective, but the converse applies if lacking focus and insight.
- *Skills building*: the focus here is on knowledge and skills, with the same caveats as technical assistance. Skills building may be easier on a group basis to several potential partners. Training might also include exposure visits and awareness raising.
- *Information*: analysis to shed light on specific aspects of the market or particular issues, and made available to individual partners, groups or publicly. While facilitators need to invest in market analysis for their own purpose to effectively intervene, bringing that information and

knowledge *strategically* to partners and other stakeholders is of key importance. Often the challenge is to make this sufficiently specific to stimulate action and behavioural change.

- *Coordination*: an overarching, organizational role in bringing together different market players for a shared purpose such as common standards or information sharing. Requires detailed market knowledge, strategic vision, and credibility to be effective.
- *Events*: information, networking or knowledge development purposes can be served by organizing seminars or presentations, usually to complement another activity.
- *Grants*: direct financial support for agreed items/services, usually designed as a cost-share arrangement. This has the advantage of tangibility, but can be a blunt instrument, and in introducing funding into a relationship, there is greater potential for distortion to partner motivations and behaviour and to the wider signal communicated to the market.
- *Returnable grants*: an option when supporting commercial organizations. Similar to regular grants but agreement is made up-front that if the intervention results in a successful business opportunity and revenue to the organization, the grant is then repaid, normally without interest or return to the facilitator. The purpose of a returnable grant is to catalyse a business opportunity and share the risk while acknowledging that if it works, public funds will be returned.
- *Guarantees*: a commitment to share a portion of financial losses if incurred. The advantage of guarantees is the risk is shared and no funding is provided unless the innovation or pilot fails.
- *Service/organization set-up and provision*: this type of activist role is possible to justify but is unusual since it involves playing a market function often without a credible view of how this will be sustained; for example conducting research or delivering training programmes.

Going beyond grants

FSD Kenya's work with the CBA combined research and information provision with technical assistance and financial guarantees – the offer changed over time as the partner's capacities and incentives had changed. FSD Kenya's offer fitted the context; what it offered was not determined formulaically in advance. And it is evident that the value added by FSD Kenya was not really financial but rather took the form of insights and ideas.

Source: Elliott, 2016: 11; Gibson, 2016: 38

Monitoring market system change and responding effectively

Underpinning M4P, and explaining its difference from conventional approaches to development, is a different theory of change – that is, a different logic model of the change process that intervention should catalyse.

Market system change often occurs in an iterative, sequential manner rather than all at once. Facilitators need to be cognizant of the dynamic nature of markets and should adapt creatively to new realities. Rarely is the focus on only one intervention or one partner but rather facilitators continuously try multiple solutions with different market players and different innovations. Monitoring and assessing the results of multiple interventions and how markets, including interconnected markets, are changing allows facilitators to then act on that information to ensure successful facilitation. This is achieved through monitoring and results measurement (MRM).

A different theory of change

The M4P strategic framework provides a theory of change of hypothesized pathways from interventions to market system changes to increased access and usage, and, finally, to impact (reduced vulnerability, and/or poverty alleviation, and/or increased economic opportunities).[3] Results chains are used at the intervention level to detail the anticipated processes that will occur as a result of the intervention. Results chains are fundamental to designing interventions to check the logical flow before the intervention begins, and then for measuring progress and revising interventions along the way. Results chains support an iterative planning process by ensuring the link from one box to the next is logical and feasible and will eventually lead to impact. If not, then the results chain (and therefore the intervention) needs to be revised and/or assumptions adjusted.

Plausible pathway to impact

There was a clear, plausible pathway connecting support to M-Shwari with FSD Kenya's vision. At the outset, this impact pathway was supported by evidence about the economic impact of M-Pesa. The 'innovation' of building the M-Shwari banking product on to the M-Pesa platform reduces transaction costs, increasing access to formal savings and credit facilities, thereby enabling poor families to cope with shocks and reduce their vulnerability.

Source: Elliott, 2016: 9

Measuring systemic change and adaptive management

To be effective, MRM requires a culture and management style which promotes evidence-based decision-making. This requires asking the right questions and using the right tools to generate useful information, and then responding to that information.

Measuring and validating intervention results and tracking and verifying the link between interventions and inclusion objectives is achieved through the MRM system. MRM is an integral part of effective facilitation; it is continuous and ongoing and should be integrated with the programme team.

MRM and programme staff work together to design interventions (through jointly developing and refining results chains), agree on indicators, and monitor progress, continually checking assumptions and the causal links from interventions through to impact. As interventions are carried out, results are measured and monitored by tracking indicators for each box in the intervention results chain. This allows for two things: an assessment of the link from activities to market system change, increased access, and improved livelihoods (*proving* results); and the provision of timely information on market change that enables management to identify where change is or is not happening and then to adjust as necessary (*improving* results). 'Results chain indicators measure progress towards system-level, pro-poor growth or improved access and poverty reduction changes, as well as the sustainability of these changes' (Springfield, 2015: 39). MRM is thus an iterative process where feedback informs changes or modifications to interventions. It therefore has to be owned by the team, not relegated to a separate unit to simply satisfy donor reporting requirements. And it goes without saying, it is also important to monitor and measure change in the wider market system beyond the interventions.

This also means there is a need for strategic funding – funding that is highly flexible with longer time horizons. Funders need to agree to simplified and nuanced performance metrics, focused on market system players taking over rather than programmes simply achieving numbers on a predetermined schedule. This recognizes the reality that facilitators cannot force market players to behave within a certain timeframe or achieve specific targets. This places more complex responsibility on reporting than the conventional accountability model but creates an opportunity to combine accountability with learning. The result is shared responsibility, and increased and open communication and coordination between funders, facilitators, and other development actors.

Effects of a weak feedback system

The dynamic nature of markets underscores the need for rapid feedback loops. To remain relevant, interventions must be cognizant of changing context and able to respond accordingly. FSD Kenya's early experience in the SACCO sector demonstrated its capacity to respond and be flexible, yet the mechanisms through which feedback continues to inform decision-making appear weak. Disappointing results from work with SACCOs and consulting service providers has not been effectively used to inform and shape subsequent interventions or to adapt intervention strategy or tactics. In not routinely tracking and verifying the link between interventions and financial inclusion objectives, the ability of FSD Kenya to continue to support the sector in a way directly relevant to the financially excluded, remains constrained.

Source: Elliott, unpublished: 15

Balancing tensions and challenges

Market facilitators, like FSD Kenya, can only prod the different functions and players, with their different capacities and incentives, which make up a market and do so in a way which analysis suggests will lead to a better, more inclusive market system. Facilitators are not all-powerful social engineers; they push, cajole, inform, instigate, and stimulate; they don't control; not everything can work. So, this story needs to be balanced with recognition of limitations and failures.

Facilitating market system change is difficult and inevitably tensions and challenges arise that facilitators must address. In particular it is difficult to balance the need to get things done and show results, with the need to ensure market functions are embedded in the system. Equally challenging is the need to develop service markets or other support functions when capacity and incentives of market players are lacking.

Balancing pressure from funders to disburse, reach targets, and provide workplans in advance with the need to be flexible and opportunistic

Facilitating market system change requires facilitators to be flexible and able to take advantage of opportunities that arise or to change course or delay interventions until market players are prepared to act (or sometimes stop the intervention altogether). This requires a shift in culture to have a higher tolerance for experimentation and acceptance of higher risk for investments that may not perform as planned.

Facilitators experience a tension between 'waiting' for market players to respond to signals and incentives or directly kick-starting activity. Inevitably, the more a facilitator does, the less space and incentive there is for others. This is especially so when there is pressure to 'get things done'. In practice, this 'delivering-versus-facilitating/pragmatic-versus-principled' intervention dilemma is one that facilitators encounter frequently. Facilitators can only encourage the different functions and players, with their different capacities and incentives, so much. They do not control market systems actors, and not everything can work as expected. And even when things do work, it is not always in the timeframe as planned; facilitation frequently takes longer than expected.

Pressure from funders to disburse, or to stick to workplans or budgets agreed to in proposals, or to reach predefined targets by a certain time can result in facilitators using the wrong tools and instruments, such as 'buying numbers' through grants rather than facilitating market change; or intervening prematurely if there are no market players with real incentive to change. This pressure ultimately undermines facilitation and complicates market players' view and perception of the facilitator. Further, market facilitation seldom requires large amounts of funding disbursed in a short period of time. Funders need to balance the reality of this with the very real need to measure and report on facilitator performance, and their own pressure to disburse.

Establishing an SPV can address some of these issues. With SPVs, funders are inherently more removed from implementation – this is a key tenet of the rationale – and accept this position. This does not mean an abandonment of accountability, but it does mean less involvement and control and therefore greater trust in the senior management and an active role in governance.

Effective strategic oversight for M4P

FSD Kenya is a locally registered trust with a charitable purpose. It has a split governance structure with fiduciary responsibilities met by independent professional trustees (an accounting firm) and strategic and technical guidance provided by a separate Programme Investment Committee (PIC). The PIC comprises representatives from funders and other independent appointees selected for their insight into financial services. These governance arrangements provide more space and place more responsibility on the FSD Director to develop a programme of activity. This is a better fit than the more conventional arrangement of a donor-funded project implemented by contractors because:
- a non-profit trust offers a better alignment of incentives between implementer and funder around long-term development impact than the for-profit nature of a contracted-out model;
- a trust provides a practical, defined separation from official donor processes and the inevitable restrictions that accompany these – such as predefined components – and therefore offers more scope to respond to market change; and
- contractors with a more direct line of accountability to funders, especially if output-based aid, have less flexibility.

Source: Gibson, 2016: 7

Differentiating between the 'information' market function and the need for information and market knowledge for facilitation

Information is a key benefit that facilitators bring to influence behavioural and systemic market change. Knowledge and evidence generated, collected, analysed, and disseminated help catalyse the generation of new ideas and the adoption of improved offerings, technologies, and business models that have the greatest likelihood of systemic level impact. Similarly, activities that develop new knowledge and insights into different aspects of the market system feed into the overall development of the market and guide the facilitator's range of work.

Addressing fundamental information constraints is at the heart of the market development challenge and the facilitator's mission. Facilitators consciously play an active knowledge generation, management, and dissemination role through developing deliberate and proactive communication platforms to inform key stakeholders, solicit contributions to knowledge products and events, and disseminate featured resources. This engagement of a diverse spectrum of stakeholders provides opportunity for dialogue and learning that is essential for large-scale systems change and is central in defining the identity or 'brand' of the facilitator, and its offer as knowledgeable and independent, and as a thought-leader. This furthers facilitators' credibility as a preferred partner for interested stakeholders and is fundamental in supporting programme staff to influence market players to change their behaviour for the benefit of the poor.

At the same time, however, research and information are critical functions for an effective and inclusive market system and, in the long term, must be carried out by market players and not facilitators. Developing capacity in the system for this function is therefore an appropriate intervention for facilitators but is often difficult to do – in part because it is not always clear whose role it is (public, private or civil society) and who will pay for it, and in part because it is difficult to differentiate the internal 'knowledge management' function of a facilitator from the 'research and information' function in the market system.

Developing the research and information function

FSD Kenya recognized that developing an information and knowledge base through research was a key part of its task. This was necessary to raise stakeholders' awareness and understanding of financial inclusion – what it meant and what its implications were. But also, as a key tenet of its market systems approach, FSD Kenya's interventions had to be analysis-led, shaped by a knowledge of the underlying causes of market failure and exclusion. Knowledge is an essential part of what FSD Kenya 'brings' as a facilitator – what informs its offer – and research, in turn, is central to this.

However, notwithstanding the quality and value of the research undertaken, 10 years after initiating its first research activities, FSD Kenya (in its own words) is still 'playing a key role in the management (and funding) of FinAccess', and the same broadly applies to the wider research role. Self-evidently, FSD Kenya is the principal funder and provider of research. And, unlike the other roles it plays, there is no partner or set of partners for FSD Kenya in this research role. This is inconsistent with the facilitator ethos and also puts FSD Kenya in an anomalous position. While FSD Kenya's general instinct and practice is to stay relatively in the background and allow partners to be more prominent, it cannot do this here. But equally it is not comfortable with or oriented towards being an active, advocating voice in the market – this is not what facilitators are there to do – so it plays the research role in a relatively passive manner. If the task of facilitation is about doing but also critically about enabling others to do, FSD Kenya's research effort has been overwhelmingly focused on the former, de facto playing a public (if donor-funded) research role.

Source: Gibson, 2016: 28

How does a facilitator know when its work is done?

What is the 'future' of an organization such as FSD Kenya? As a local entity, does it continue to exist as long as there is funding? Or if it is truly a facilitator, how does it recognize when facilitation is no longer needed and therefore cease to exist? Or, like many other development initiatives, will one of the tacit priorities for the future be FSD Kenya's continuation – that is, FSD Kenya becomes a stakeholder; the means to an end is becoming the end.

Alan continually reminded us that the role of a facilitator is temporary. And while exit strategies may be developed and carried out for individual interventions, determining the exit strategy for a facilitator as a whole is more difficult. If a project, by definition the facilitator's work is timebound and may end before the intended market system change has occurred. Then what? Who continues facilitating change, if required? It is unlikely the need for facilitation would end conveniently at the same time as the project.

If an SPV, it would never make sense for a facilitating organization to hand over what it does to another organization. What it does, of course, should no longer be needed once 'markets are working better for the poor'. This presents a dilemma in terms of how to define success. If the goal of a facilitator is to reach full financial inclusion, how is financial inclusion defined? Is 'access for all' enough? How do we know when the system is sufficiently 'working'? When are supporting functions and rules 'good enough' to support inclusive market systems? When is inclusion truly reached and the work of a facilitator complete?

It may be relatively easy to measure success in the core of the market – that is, more transactions and increased access – but how does one measure the ability of the market system to take on key functions in supporting functions and rules such as research and information, capacity building, advocacy, market infrastructure, policy development, and implementation? What should the private sector be expected to do vs. the government; that is, what is a true public good? And without an active facilitating organization, will the quality and focus on the poor remain?

Alan once said to me the ultimate success of an M4P organization is to close its doors, to acknowledge the market system *is* working better for the poor and that facilitation is no longer required. However, we have seen very few examples of this. Instead, what often happens is a facilitator and/or its funders decide the best route is to become a service provider filling a market function. This may seem to make sense, especially if a facilitator has been 'doing' more than facilitating. However, it is often difficult to achieve true sustainability with this model and to allow the crowding-in of others, given the ongoing influence of donor funds, particularly, in service markets.

FinMark Trust (FMT) has been essential to the initiation, development of, and continuing conduct of FinScope in South Africa (and elsewhere). FinScope arose in response to the dearth of data on financial inclusion in South Africa and has effectively served to fill this information gap ever since. FMT's market analysis led it to understand that lack of information causes sub-optimal decision-making by policy makers, advocacy organizations, and financial service providers. However, it is less clear how well FMT understood the root causes inhibiting the emergence of this kind of information function within the industry. If information is so vital to a host of industry players, why hadn't a function emerged? Whose role is it to provide information within a market system – is it a 'public good'? Or a commercial function? Or both?

FMT was not established to become a global survey implementer; it was established to catalyse processes of change to lead to greater financial inclusion. This raises a question about what FMT's role should be now given that FinScope has become a global brand. On the one hand, there is risk that with diversion of resources into survey implementation, FMT might become less insightful about constraints to access or the quality of access, less able to engage in complex policy issues, and less effective as a change agent. On the other hand, there is a risk that FinScope's institutional home (FMT) is an entity largely funded by foreign aid, which might be a threat to its longevity and undermine the development of a permanent information or research function in the market system.

Source: Johnson, 2016: 9, 11

Inclusion, yes, but to what end?

While the headline results showed enormous progress had been made in expanding financial inclusion, deeper questions remained. Specifically, was the progress in financial inclusion translating into real developmental impact? Is the existing pattern of development and distribution of benefits projected into the future 'good enough'? The mainstreaming of financial inclusion as a concept allows for broad interpretation, so this might be seen primarily as a moral as much as a technical judgement. But certainly, a continuation of current trends does not match the original poverty-reducing ambition of FSD Kenya, or indeed of the M4P approach.

When Alan reviewed FSD Kenya's role and experience facilitating inclusive financial markets, he undertook a long-term perspective. While identifying where solid progress had been made – which in many ways vindicated the original conception behind the FSD model – the review led to questions regarding the role of finance in the economy and the ultimate impact of FSD Kenya's efforts to 'deepen' the financial sector.

> Kenya's finance market may well now be working slightly better for poor households and allowing them to manage their lives better. But it is clear that it is working even better for others – for middle-income consumers and, in particular, for the supply-side of the finance market which, with higher revenues and profits, has prospered throughout Kenya's 'inclusion years'. (Gibson, 2017)

Finance impacts on the lives of poor people in several ways. Most directly, poor households are consumers/users of financial services, and much of the effort in financial inclusion initiatives is aimed here. But finance also influences the lives of poor people in their capacity as employees/labourers and as entrepreneurs; as people in the 'real' economy. Financial services that work better for the poor must also work in this bigger economy; in particular, in the world of agriculture and business. Yet pressure to solve pressing short-term market constraints in a complex political economic environment can lead to a loss of rigour in pursuing sustainable solutions.

Consideration of these questions inevitably takes analysis into the domain of political economy. Political economy exists in every market context but in some the constraints emerging from this on developing the market for the benefit of the poor are particularly severe. Although some development practitioners may perceive that power/politics issues have less validity and relevance for them than technical issues – with which they are more comfortable – from an M4P perspective, following the approach does mean identifying the main constraints no matter their nature. And focusing on the poor – the 'P' in M4P – is often inherently political. The question is should facilitators seek to bring change to the political economy and the incentives that stem from this? The critical issue here, as with all interventions, is whether facilitators have the right mandate, skills, and organizational capacity to do so, and if they don't, can meaningful change be brought about by engaging solely on technical, capacity, information, and other non-political questions?

Reconsidering the social contract for the financial sector

Overall, in the last 10 years it is clear the Kenyan financial market has become relatively more inclusive, with more poor people accessing and using services. In this sense, it is a market which, in M4P parlance, is working more for the poor. But the benefits for poor people are primarily in terms of allowing them to manage their financial lives better rather than improving their opportunities. Improved financial access has helped people but it has not had the transformational impact that was once hoped – a finding in Kenya that mirrors global experience and which has prompted much debate on the role of finance in economies.[4] The biggest beneficiaries have been the customer group immediately above the poor, where choice and value has been expanded, and stakeholders on the supply-side (management, staff, and owners) whose rewards have grown substantially. Banks' sales have increased by 2.5 times and profits by 3.5 times, with profit margins also increased; the 'inclusion years' have undoubtedly been good years for the banks. However, the real economy is performing only moderately with moderate economic growth and low agriculture productivity. Poverty rates are still high. So, the financial market is working better for the poor – but it is working even better for others.

This apparent contrast between conspicuous supply-side success and a still-poor economy raises questions on the role of the financial sector. In particular, it begs questions on who/what it is there to serve, and on the incentives that drive behaviour. And in Kenya, is it realistic to expect financial markets to develop in a manner that has a significant effect on poor people's lives when the informal rules and incentives around them are so apparently driven by the compelling needs of the short term?

This situation is unlikely to change meaningfully unless there is a new, shared consensus – an implicit 'social contract' – on the role of the financial sector, and particularly of formal finance providers such as banks. And this should be to serve the needs of wider society and the real economy, including the needs of the poor, so that the financial sector is more genuinely inclusive. Such a change, manifested in the rules (formal and informal), would encourage a change in bank incentives and behaviour towards new, different services and reduced emphasis on financial returns.

This kind of change is not a matter of legislative diktat but is in the realms of the social and political, requiring debate and analysis among a broad set of stakeholders in the industry, government, the media, and civil society. Although discussion on the financial sector's social contract is not widespread currently, there are a number of converging voices and trends which make this an opportune moment for this discussion. Among these are moves to create a market conduct authority, banks' own (quiet) realization that their conspicuous growth and success (and high margins) do not sit comfortably in a still low-income/poor economy, and international concerns over 'financialization' – the role of finance in economies. The social contract on finance in Kenya is not an issue to be considered lightly and of course is challenging. Progress in addressing it would be neither quick nor easy.

Source: Gibson, 2016: vi, 34, 44

As a result of Alan's paper, FSD Kenya undertook a comprehensive exercise to retool – looking to achieve a deeper understanding and response to market development constraints and opportunities. But more fundamentally, Alan's review highlighted a limit to what could be achieved developmentally through financial inclusion as it was then being tackled. Alan's analysis pointed to the need to go beyond the problem of financial access to realizing financial solutions to real world problems. Addressing the needs of the real economy is today recognized as the core challenge for the wider FSD Network and many others involved in developing inclusive finance.

Conclusion

FSD Kenya's experience, while not universally successful but overall very positive, reaffirms the essential validity of the market systems approach. M4P provides an appropriate framework and guidance for intervention and sets a level of ambition (changing market systems) that matches the high ideals of international development. A narrower, more prescriptive, more delivery-oriented remit would have greatly reduced FSD Kenya's impact.

Alan was instrumental in influencing FSD Kenya, and the FSD Network as a whole, to become better market facilitators – to make a difference – and for that we owe him a great deal of gratitude.

Acknowledgement

This chapter is based on a paper published by FSD Africa (Ledgerwood, 2017) which synthesized learnings from Alan's study of FSD Kenya as well as six additional case studies written by the Springfield Centre on specific interventions of the FSD Network.

About the author

Joanna Ledgerwood is an independent consultant specializing in women's financial inclusion and market systems development. She is the author of numerous books and publications and is active on a number of boards and committees. Joanna first met Alan in September 2007 in Chiang Mai at a BDS seminar and they remained close until his death.

Notes

1. Much of this chapter is taken directly from Alan's case study; however, it has been reorganized from the 'mini-case study' structure into consolidated lessons.
2. With more resources available (less diverted to overhead costs), SPVs have the ability to offer higher rewards if required.
3. Many funders require facilitators to report on their outputs and outcomes (and sometimes impact) using logframes. To ensure interventions are designed to contribute to overall objectives, and to avoid creating a parallel monitoring system, results chains are often aligned with logframes and the M4P strategic framework as follows: activities = inputs; market system change = outputs; access/usage = outcomes; improved livelihoods = impact.
4. This conclusion and the implications stemming from it are at the heart of FSD Kenya's 2016–2020 strategy.

References

Elliott, D. (2016) *The Growth of M-Shwari in Kenya – A Market Development Story* [online], FSD Africa and Springfield Centre, UK <https://fsdkenya.org/publication/the-growth-of-m-shwari-in-kenya-a-market-development-story/> [accessed 1 November 2020].

Elliott, D. (unpublished) 'A technical solution to a political economy problem: round pegs and square holes', Durham, UK: Springfield Centre.

Gibson, A. (2016) *FSD Kenya: Ten Years of a Market Systems Approach in the Kenyan Finance Market* [online], Nairobi, Kenya: FSD Kenya; Durham, UK: Springfield Centre <http://fsdkenya.org/publication/fsd-kenya-ten-years-of-a-market-systems-approach-in-the-kenyan-finance-market/> [accessed 13 October 2020].

Gibson, A. (2017) 'Market facilitation is the way ahead, but it needs to do more', 27 March [blog], Washington, DC: CGAP <https://www.cgap.org/blog/market-facilitation-way-ahead-it-needs-do-more> [accessed 13 October 2020].

Johnson, D. (2016) *Using Information as a Driver of Change: Lessons from FinScope South Africa* [online], Springfield Centre, UK <https://www.fsdafrica.org/publication/using-information-as-a-driver-of-change-lessons-from-finscope-south-africa/> [accessed 1 November 2020].

Ledgerwood, J. (2017) *The Art of Market Facilitation: Learning from the Financial Sector Deepening Network* [online], Nairobi, Kenya: FSD Africa <https://www.fsdafrica.org/publication/the-art-of-market-facilitation-learning-from-the-financial-sector-deepening-network/> [accessed 13 October 2020].

Springfield Centre (2015) *The Operational Guide for the Making Markets Work for the Poor (M4P) Approach*, 2nd edition [online], funded by SDC & DFID, Durham, UK <http://www.springfieldcentre.com/wp-content/uploads/2015/11/2015-09-M4P-Op-Guide-Sept2015.pdf> [accessed 13 October 2020].

PART II

Expanding the application of M4P

CHAPTER 7

Making markets work for the poo-er: Water For People's pathway to market systems development

Kate Fogelberg

Abstract

Like most sustainable, systemic changes, changing the culture and practices of an international NGO is not a simple input–output model. Organizations need to be both motivated and able to change their practices. A blend of mutually reinforcing incentives and capacities – from leadership attitudes, information, staff skill sets, to resource allocations – all contribute to making markets work better for the poo-ers. This chapter reflects on the why, the how, and the so what of that journey.

Keywords: sanitation, M4P, MSD

'Can I see an old toilet?'

This became a familiar and oft-repeated request of mine for close to a decade, but in 2006, having just taken a job with Water For People, an international water and sanitation non-profit organization, I asked it for the very first time. It was my inaugural field visit, meeting colleagues, partners, and inspecting infrastructure that the institution had financed.

My request (this time) was not biological in nature. Rather, I was curious to see what happened to the toilets, taps, and handpumps that had been built by my employer years – or even months – ago. And even more curious about how people's lives had been impacted by having a toilet.

My colleague looked at me a bit strangely – nobody had ever asked to see old projects. Most visitors from headquarters would perform ad hoc supervisory visits of ongoing work. A project file was procured, complete with technical drawings of toilets, reports, receipts, photos, and names and phone numbers of the 25 beneficiaries. Nothing out of the ordinary, but as it was my inaugural Toilet Visit, I had heaps of questions:

> 'Are there only 25 households in this community?'
> *'No, but that's all that the subsidy was enough for'*
>
> 'So, who won the toilet lottery?'
> *'Oh, the people who said yes first. And who had the $25 co-payment ready.'*

http://dx.doi.org/10.3362/9781788531443.007

'Oh, how was the subsidy determined?'
'By how much donors gave us divided by how many people we could convince to have a toilet.'

As my cross-examination of the engineer responsible for the project continued, a plan was confirmed to visit some of these toilets – and their users – the next day. We drove to the outskirts of the city and pulled up to a three-storey brick house. Right, I thought, we're just leaving the car here before walking to a poorer area of the neighbourhood. Wrong. The inhabitants of the big beautiful house were among the recipients of the toilet lottery. I was confused – weren't subsidies supposed to go to poor people? Before chatting to the house owner about their beautiful bathroom, I discretely asked the engineer why these people needed support to build a toilet that was 1/50th the size of their home. The reply was that 'We had trouble finding anybody who wanted a toilet. This family was building their house and didn't have a toilet yet, so they were interested in getting a toilet from us.'

After a pleasant cup of coca tea, I had what would be the first of many toilet tours. It was a lovely toilet, but I was still confused about all of the decisions that led to me being in such a lovely toilet.

'Why did you pick this toilet design?'
'We didn't pick, it's what the engineers told us we got.'

'Why didn't you build this by yourselves?'
'It was in our plans, but then the NGO said they needed 25 people to take a toilet.'

'Do all of your neighbours have a toilet like this?'
'No, only some of us. The other ones didn't have the money to contribute or didn't want one.'

'So how do you think they'll get a toilet?'
'They'll have to wait until another institution wants to help.'

I've since poked my head in hundreds of toilets, mostly for business, but sometimes for pleasure. But that first visit still stands out to me because of how eye-opening it was to what was wrong with 'development-as-usual'. Questions that I would ask myself for many years to come were planted during that first visit:

- Is the lack of money the reason people don't currently have toilets?
- What happens when the toilet lottery stops? How can everybody access a toilet, forever?

Alan Gibson, a wiser, more eloquent Scot, summed up my frustrations with the development machine as 'the fairly familiar experience of an NGO realizing the challenges of scale and sustainability'. I didn't realize it at the time, but I would come to feel quite lucky to have found an institutional home in an organization that was open to learning from its past and willing to change, albeit at different speeds and to different degrees, across countries of operations.

Like most sustainable, systemic changes, changing the culture and practices of an international NGO is not a simple input–output model. Organizations need to be both motivated and able to change their practices. A blend of mutually reinforcing incentives and capacities – from leadership attitudes, information, staff skill sets, to resource allocations – all contribute to making markets work better for the poo-ers. This chapter reflects on the why, the how, and the so what of that journey.

Why change?

As George Bernard Shaw once said, 'those who can't change their minds can't change anything'. Wanting to change is the first step towards actually changing – as much for development workers themselves as the people whose behaviours they are often trying to change. Re-reading an old blog I wrote in 2010, I realized that the seeds of market systems development (MSD) were planted in my mind from the frontline challenges of achieving scale and sustainability, long before I'd ever heard the combination of M, S, and D:

> To me, a sustainable sanitation service, in very general terms, is one where everybody can get access to a toilet and associated toilet services (emptying, cleaning, upgrading) – of their choice – forever. A lofty goal, for sure, but one that sets in motion very different types of programs than a goal to give X Community a certain number of toilets at one point in time. This goal is shaping our sanitation work in Peru, which began with a sanitation market analysis in a region outside of Arequipa, in southern Peru, and implies working in a way that local systems – financial services, construction, ongoing maintenance – function without the not-so 'invisible hand' of an NGO. (Fogelberg, 2010)

My mind was ripe for the taking of ideas like MSD. So, imagine my joy, when two years later, I found myself seated in Alan's classroom in Bangkok and learned that this – a way of working in which sustainability and scale are truly at the core of an approach – was what others had been grappling with for years. But an open-minded, relatively junior staff member is not enough to catalyse institutional change.

What were the incentives for an international development organization to change? Incentives can be external, internal, or a combination of both. External incentives in this case mostly refer to changing funder or board priorities and the push that those can have on organizational strategies and priorities. Internal incentives refer to staff motivations to change the status quo, such as new leadership, a desire to be seen as different or innovative, and an intrinsic interest to learn and improve, among others.

In our case, the incentives were more internal than external. Although funding opportunities emerged that supported this new approach, responding to donor priorities was not the key driver of change. Rather, it was the convergence of new leadership with extensive field experience and an innovative, entrepreneurial attitude coupled with a growing evidence base – at both the sector and organizational level – of the challenges of sustainability and scale.

Leadership who wanted to do something different was fundamental to the institutional evolution. Without that, it is unlikely change would have happened, especially since this was not something that, at the time, was being pushed by donors. A big personality, who liked being seen as a disrupter and innovator, created an environment where staff at all levels were encouraged to try new things. We had a visionary and disruptive leader who set a high bar, but no clear instructions to get there. Figure out a way that everybody can access a toilet (and water) forever. The goalpost shifted from build 200 toilets this year to a much more complicated and interesting one. While this was attractive to curious folks like me, some of the more traditionalists in the field struggled, while others found it a good and necessary challenge.

Part of that enthusiasm to abandon the status quo came from a growing recognition that business as usual was not going to solve the global sanitation problem. Conventional sanitation programming, both at our organization and in the sector as a whole, could be succinctly described as the left-hand side of Figure 7.1. Simple solutions to seemingly simple problems. If a lack of a toilet is the problem, the solution is surely to provide one, right?

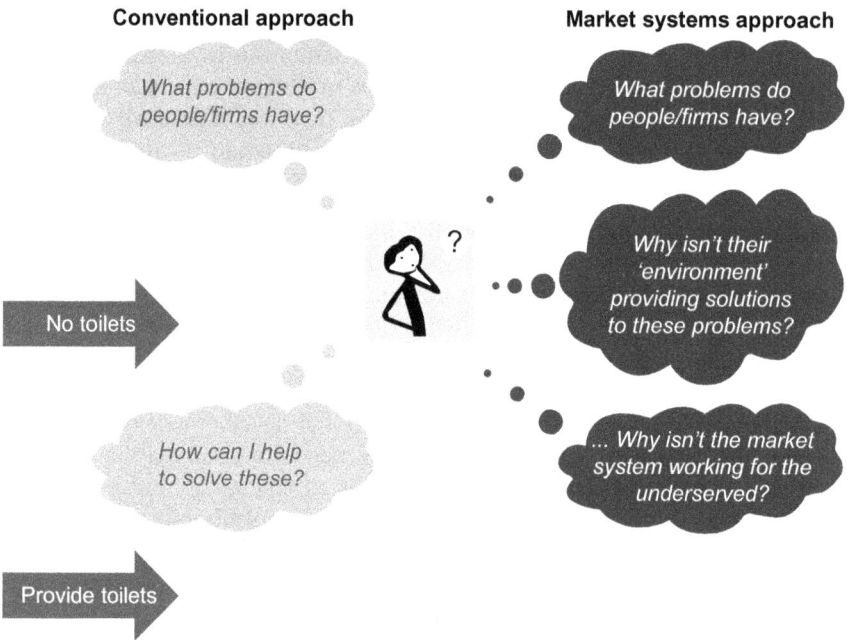

Figure 7.1 Conventional sanitation approach compared with market systems approach

As can be imagined, providing fully or partially subsidized toilets to some households was not having significant impact on the sanitation crisis. And by the early 2000s, a growing evidence base was showing that business as usual was not getting more people on the pot. Sanitation was the most off-track Millennium Development Goal, diarrhoea remained the second most frequent reason that kids under-five died, access was not keeping up with population growth, and what little post-construction research was done showed a mixed picture of infrastructure changing people's behaviours. This was coupled with a changing aid environment, with more calling for greater inquiry into development effectiveness and sustainability.

The sector was beginning to realize it had a problem. So, a few early adopters, Water For People included, took a long hard look at what they'd done in the past and began to change. There was something of a perfect storm – new leadership who wanted to do things differently, influenced by their own field experience, in a context of more critical analysis of the role of international development, and more honest inquiry into post-project sustainability.

Wanting to change is only one part of the process however.

How to change?

What capacities were needed for the organization to be able to change? Rather than a neatly planned process, a range of mutually reinforcing changes in learning, skill sets, and financial resources all contributed to the institutional shift. This section describes several of the shifts in capacities that facilitated the change towards more systemic development. And as no change process is without its own challenges, it closes with a reflection on some of the challenges along the way.

Learning and reflection

Although there was no roadmap at the time, looking back at the evolution, some steps do stand out. If you don't know what has happened with past projects, the default is to assume everything is fine. Developing a systematic process to assess post-project sustainability as an internal learning tool was the first trigger for change. Confronting our own assumptions about 1) what the problem was (causes not just symptoms); and what the solution was (facilitate don't deliver), was key.

An internal review of past work. As part of institutional commitment to better understand the sustainability challenges of both water and sanitation, we began by looking back to see if our assumptions held true. Like most NGOs at the time (and some still today), there was scant information on what happened once construction ended. It was assumed that with the training delivered and infrastructure in place, people would carry on using toilets as intended, and those who didn't benefit from the first or even second rounds of support, would eventually be inspired enough by their neighbours' toilets to build one themselves. Having led the methodological development of this process, I participated in many of the field trips to assess progress. It was eye-opening for many staff to see toilets being used as storage for potatoes, chicken coops, or simply having been dismantled and not used at all.

Asking different questions. Seeing first-hand the challenges of sustaining and expanding access was not usually enough to convince staff of the need to change our own behaviour. But gradually, with more and different types of evidence, attitudes started to change. For example, a market assessment for financial services for sanitation revealed that only 10 per cent of people, including the lowest income segment, felt they needed financing for a toilet, confronting one of our own major assumptions that financing was the problem. Another important piece of evidence came from an anthropological inquiry into people's motivations and triggers for deciding to build or not build a toilet. When asked to draw their 'dream home' hardly anybody included a toilet. When probed, it came out that the simple pit latrines that people saw as their only option did not tick the desirable box, thus were excluded from an aspirational home. People wanted 'city toilets' (i.e. flushing with water, tiled interiors, and a shower with hot water). This meant people would rather not invest at all in a 'good enough' solution, preferring to wait for something more permanent.

External reviews of current work. Complementing internal reviews of past performance, several times along this journey, we contracted outside firms with different expertise to review aspects of the organization's work. This included a review of our partnership models to provide business development services, experience working with financial institutions, and more. A review by the Springfield Centre provoked much-needed internal debate on the role of an NGO in paying for and providing business development services and providing seed capital to financial institutions. These practices, at the time, seemed 'better' than donating toilets, but in retrospect, were still providing key market functions that could have been provided by existing market actors.

Skills/human resources

More often than not, when I was out in the WASH world, people would comment how young, how female, and how non-engineery I was. Although this is changing, water and sanitation were historically staffed by people with engineering backgrounds. It is no surprise, then, that the solutions that emerge are technical in nature. Changing the skills sets of our own human resources was an important piece of the process.

Upskill your staff. Key staff members participated in market systems training, both formally and through on-the-job coaching. This included attendance at Springfield's Making Markets Work training, as well as regional training sessions that allowed for greater staff outreach. Several of us benefited directly from Alan's wisdom and wit during the two-week course and were all influenced by him. In addition to formal training, more informal, case-by-case mentoring was provided by both market systems and sanitation advisers.

Challenge your staff. Tucked away in a conference room in Blantyre, Malawi, pennies dropped as our teams revealed their analyses of 'Who Does, Who Pays' (Springfield Centre, 2014), a brilliantly simple and eloquent way to self-assess the sustainability of any development programme. Even as we got out of the core of the market – providing sanitation infrastructure directly – realizing we were still performing many of the necessary support functions for a sustainable sanitation system caused deeper reflection on where, how, and with whom to intervene.

Change your staff. Not everybody wants to do things differently or believes that things should be done differently. Institutions evolve, and it was necessary to let some people go who were not strategically aligned with the new direction.

Financial resources

It is all well and good if an organization wants to do better development, but if they do not have the resources do it, all that is left is good intentions. Some of the key capacity changes in this area included working with donors to change their minds, being creative with new opportunities, turning down restrictive funding, and expanding our unrestricted resources.

Change your donors' minds. Once a critical mass of staff within the organization believed this was the path to follow, it became easier to convince donors and others of the validity of the approach. Some donors are inherently less risk-adverse than others. Organizations that give money away are full of different people. We found that getting a champion within a funding organization was an effective way of resourcing and managing funding more flexibly. There will inevitably be challenges, but by building an open relationship with that champion it becomes easier to mitigate future programmatic challenges or communication complications.

Be creative. I was once in discussion with a donor that was quite interested in supporting a more systemic approach to sanitation – including analysis up-front to inform programme activities and avoiding committing to numbers of outputs. But being the sanitation sector, they still had a bee in their bonnet about a particular technology and wanted to promote it, as many donors often do. I convinced them to do a market assessment first to see if actual users of this type of toilet were as interested as those wanting to fund it.

Unsurprising to me, people were not interested in this type of dry toilet, and aspired to 'city toilets', with flushing water and a septic tank or sewer system. Informed by this analysis, we were able to proceed technologically neutrally and manage donor expectations accordingly.

Say no to the dough. As an organization that was not dependent on a single donor or project, sometimes we chose to say no to potential funders who didn't understand or accept a market systems approach to sanitation. NGOs, although technically not for profit, all operate on business models. They 'sell' the promise of outputs, outcomes, or even impact, to individuals, corporations, foundations, and governments interested to 'buy' that promise. As part of our transformative shift, some donors were lost along the way. These tended to be 'get your hands dirty' voluntourism types who either wanted to dig toilets themselves (although I'm not aware of any evidence that shows the lack of toilets the world round might be due to a lack of well-intentioned volunteers with time on their hands) or at the very least, wanted to know how many toilets were going to be built. But when one door closes, another door opens, and this was true of funding partners.

Grow your unrestricted funding base. It may sound contradictory, having just recommended declining some types of funding, but increasing the unrestricted funding base was also important. Organizations who have flexible funding can, in theory, act more flexibly and take advantage of opportunities. There are many fundraising strategies that allow for this, so an organization wanting to act more flexibly needs to be financed to do so.

Putting it into practice

Sanitation market systems development is now embedded in Water For People's strategy, choice of funding partners, interventions, and performance management. This was only possible because of the willingness and ability to change, but a few reflections below shed some light on how it was put into practice.

Say yes to the mess. A toilet pun this is not, but rather a recognition that changing people's behaviours along the sanitation value chain, from users, to suppliers, to government officials, to development actors and agencies is going to be complicated and non-linear. This is much easier said than done, especially when human resources are dominated by engineers. Being able to conduct broader systems analysis and understand incentives to change as well as managing partner and donor expectations became much more important competencies than designing a robust toilet.

Take advantage of opportunities. New programmes, new staff, and new donors were all opportunities to start from scratch. As new offices were opened, strategies could be developed from the beginning that adopted a more explicitly market systems approach. As new staff, especially leadership at headquarters and in the field, were hired, those were also key opportunities to message how the institution worked. As new donors were approached, or approached the organization, that too was a unique opportunity to position the institution's evolving approach to sanitation.

Learning by doing/failing fast. We took a tentative step out of the core of the market and stopped funding the direct construction of toilets themselves in some countries quicker than others. One of the first forays into 'market-based' sanitation was a competition for innovative business ideas funded by the World Bank. Recognizing that finite donor household construction subsidies for toilets were problematic, the 'innovation' was to subsidize masons to build simple ecological toilets. Ecological toilets, in theory, can produce liquid and solid fertilizer if managed well. The innovative business model in this case was gifts bags of cement plus a splash of training to a few masons, with the idea that masons – not an international NGO – would then market and build toilets for people without them. Cash-poor households would receive the toilet via supplier financing and repay the loan in fertilizer to the mason, who would then find a buyer. Nobody thought to understand the market for 'humanure' before embarking on this process, though, so it all came to a halt when large buyers could not be secured. Although not a success, useful learnings about how to intervene in a different way helped improve future programmes. Box 7.1 offers greater insights into what not to do when embracing market systems development.

Box 7.1 How not to change

A common misperception in MSD programmes is that the who is more important than the why or how. In embracing a more pluralistic approach to service delivery it is common to fall prey to overcorrecting and expecting private sector actors in and of themselves to be the solution. We had a steep learning curve of investing in individual businesses, paying for unsustainable business development services, and ultimately failing to do good market research.

Embrace diversity. Good market systems programmes rely on context-specific diagnosis and incorporate local opportunities into their interventions. Whereas past sanitation interventions were very supply-led, based on how much money could be raised, and typically included one type of technology with little consumer demand, adopting a market systems approach allowed programmes to be more context-specific. For example, in India, where self-help groups had long existed, early efforts there included seeding self-help groups to use rotating funds for sanitation construction. This later shifted

---

Box 7.2 Reference experience from elsewhere carefully

Early on in this transition, it was common for staff in Latin America to be challenged by headquarters and advisers to develop an extremely affordable safe sanitation option because that was what was happening in some Indian and African contexts. Friction ensued for several reasons:

- internal debates on who should develop new technologies – development agencies or private industry;
- feasibility factor given that the cost of materials and labour was much higher in the region;
- desirability factors – consumer research showed people would rather wait for a permanent, expensive solution than a radically affordable, but non-aspirational design.

From a change management point of view, these constant comparisons and pressure cost social capital that could have been used more effectively at building the case internally for change.

---

towards more mainstream sources of finance, but it leveraged existing institutions in a different way. See Box 7.2 for a cautionary tale of trying to export experiences from elsewhere.

Table 7.1 compares how some of the tactics changed as a result of the organizational evolution towards MSD. Although variations exist from country to country, overall, this transition meant that practically, partnerships broadened and tactics diversified.

Table 7.1 A shift in tactics

Traditional approach	MSD approach to sanitation
Engineers from the NGO drew standardized toilet designs – households had a single option	Sanitation enterprises decide which products and services to provide. Consumers decide which model they want.
Engineers from the NGO provided quality control by overseeing toilet construction	Technical assistance to sanitation enterprises to test more affordable, desirable, and/or appropriate technologies along the sanitation value chain
Social promoters from the NGO built demand for household sanitation directly	Public agencies and private providers both participate in creating demand – public agencies from a public health angle and private providers from an aspirational angle
HQ staff conducted fundraising for a limited number of toilets in specific communities	Brokering between micro entrepreneurs and lead firms producing sanitation inputs
HQ staff reported on numbers of toilets built with donated funds in specific communities	Providing information to financial institutions on the opportunity in sanitation financing (loans, leasing, etc)
	HQ began fundraising for sanitation service delivery initiatives

Challenges

Changing business as usual was not a linear, simple, or fast transition. Organizations have their own micro political economies with power dynamics between field offices and headquarter staff and individual attitudes and appetites affect the speed and extent of change. Some of the specific obstacles encountered on the pathway to market systems enlightenment included the following:

- *Human resources*. The sanitation field was, and in some places still is, dominated by technocrats. Unsurprisingly, this leads to an emphasis on engineering solutions to systemic problems.
- *Partner selection*. Partners – whether public, private, or civil society – were more often than not used to a traditional, transactional relationship. Moving to a more facilitative approach meant ending or modifying some partnerships, which can be complicated to manage in practice. Interestingly, second wave partners were often less expectant of donor goodies.
- *Philosophical and practical debates on the role of subsidy*. The role of subsidies in MSD programmes is a common debate and the sanitation sector is no exception. See Box 7.3 for further insights into one of the more emotional debates that emerged time and time again during the institutional change process.
- *Adopting new language without changing practices*. Change did not happen in every country at the same speed. Some of the slower to change adopted the language more quickly than changing their practices which then created additional challenges.
- *Cherry-picking pieces of the process*. Doing more robust diagnosis and analysis but falling back into familiar implementation tactics. For example, having a better understanding of reasons why households may or may

---

Box 7.3 Wrestling with the S-word

The sanitation sector more widely than any single institution continues to wrestle with the role of subsidies in the provision of universal sanitation services. There are public health arguments in favour of subsidizing parts of the sanitation value chain, most critically because of the externalities associated with sanitation practices. Recent research has shown that community or neighbourhood level coverage of sanitation facilities – and their correct and constant use – is more deterministic of health outcomes than individual access and use. Over time, external development subsidies for household toilet construction were removed, but in some cases, ongoing public subsidies have filled the gap. Recognizing that local authorities have political, as well as public health incentives, the programme in Bolivia persuaded the local water office to absorb a smaller, more targeted subsidy. This has included a local government post-construction incentive to households who build a toilet – similar to a scheme in many cities whereby utilities provide rebates when households upgrade their toilet facilities.

not purchase a toilet, but then providing that information directly, as opposed to working with and through a partner.
- *Mixed messages on resourcing.* Multiple times country programmes were attracted to additional finance that was not aligned with institutional strategic priorities.

In addition to the operational challenges encountered along the way, reconsidering the definition of, and approach to, sustainability was a substantial effort. Sustainability is as overused and underdelivered in the sanitation sector as in many others. As the institutional evolution process progressed, the focus on sustainability broadened from sustainability at the household level to sustainability of the system that allowed households to get a toilet. Figure 7.2 demonstrates three levels of sustainability – from sustaining the use of the infrastructure itself, to the agent providing the infrastructure, to all of the supporting services that need to be sustained for the service to continue being provided. It also visualizes how the programmatic emphasis changed with a shift from ensuring the sustainability of toilet use to the wider system that contributes to sustaining all of the functions needed to ensure future users could also access toilets.

Figure 7.2 Expanding the concept of sustainability

Measurement of sustainability has evolved. From counting outputs – how many toilets were built – to a more sophisticated reflection of progress in which interventions are annually reviewed, assessed, and either dropped, modified, or expanded.

An example of how the organization has evolved its tactics over time comes from Nicaragua. Initially, the organization co-financed a single type of household toilet. During this institutional evolution however, the focus first shifted to supporting sanitation enterprises with information, skills, and linkages. Recognizing that a skills gap is always going to be an issue for entrepreneurs, the organization began working in the skills support market by working with a technical training programme to provide the training to more people and long after the external intervention ended.

Because of the diversity of contexts in which the organization operates, after lengthy discussions of what 'scale' meant, the decision was made to focus on a qualitative description of scale, as opposed to numbers. The current sanitation strategy defines scale as the following:

> Many development agencies aspire to scale, but few define it well, if at all. Instead of focusing on a numerical target – as that would contribute to pursuing numbers over sustainable systemic change – and recognizing that 'scale' in rural Bolivia would be different from urban Kolkata, Water For People has defined scale in terms of characteristics of the sanitation system, not a large number. For Water For People, scale means:
>
> - Demand (for sanitation goods or services) increases without intensive promotion.
> - The product's or service's cost decreases due to market competition or mass production.
> - Supply chain growth occurs outside Water For People's facilitation activities.
> - Product or service delivery expands into new areas or all areas are covered.
> - The central regulating authority actively controls any public health risks related to the service. (Water For People, 2018)

It would be naive to suggest that this was a straightforward process with a few bumps in the road. But it would be equally disingenuous to suggest that organizational transformation is impossible. With entrepreneurial leaders at multiple levels and locations and ambitious and risk-taking donor partners, it is more than possible to change organizational behaviour for the better.

So what?

It is only fitting that this chapter close with a reflection on the 'So what?', a simple, yet powerful question that Alan often used. Why does it matter that a single, relatively small institution adopted a market systems approach?

A cynic may argue not much at all in the larger picture of international aid. But change in the aid sector is going to happen when a critical mass of donors and practitioners do things differently. While the focus of this chapter has been on an implementing organization, making the external case to donors and other implementers becomes easier from a position of strength – or at least a position of adoption and experimentation. Several donors have changed their funding practices to better align with sanitation systemic change programmes, in part because of how implementers have been able to demonstrate an alternative to providing toilets directly.

It's important to remember that institutions are not monolithic, static entities. They're made up of individuals, and for institutions to change, the people who operate within them must change. Good intentions aren't good enough. More people and more institutions need to want to, and be able to do the right thing. Doing the right thing in this case is simply using development resources to reach more poor people with sanitation services, more sustainably. It doesn't mean throwing all of your eggs into a private sector basket but using insights and analysis to add real value. In 2007, sanitation was voted the most important public health achievement since 1840 – over vaccines, anaesthesiology, and antibiotics. It clearly has an important role to play for individual and societal health and wealth. But how organizations choose to operate will determine how many people benefit and for how long. This chapter has shared the experience of one organization trying to do the right thing and here's hoping it inspires many more to do the same.

About the author

Kate Fogelberg works at the Springfield Centre. Before joining Springfield in 2016, Kate worked for Water For People, a non-profit organization that gradually adopted a systems approach to water and sanitation. She had the good fortune to be trained by Alan Gibson before getting the opportunity to work with him on several assignments at Springfield.

References

Fogelberg, K. (2010) 'Everybody. Choice. Forever: thoughts on a sustainable sanitation service', *Hot Donkey Milk*, 21 September [blog] <http://hotdonkey milk.blogspot.com/2010/09/everybody-choice-forever-thoughts-on.html> [accessed 19 December 2019].
The Springfield Centre (2014) *The Operational Guide for the Making Markets Work for the Poor (M4P) Approach*, 2nd edn, funded by SDC & DFID, Durham, UK: The Springfield Centre.
Water For People (2018) *Water For People Strategy 2017–2021* [pdf] <https://www.waterforpeople.org/wp-content/uploads/2019/09/WFP_StrategicPlan_English_Final_Web.pdf> [accessed 19 December 2019].

CHAPTER 8

Can M4P work everywhere? M4P in thin markets

Alexandra Miehlbradt

Abstract

Over the last 15 years, practitioners have increasingly applied making markets work for the poor (M4P) to sparser, newer, and more fragile markets. What have we learned from the experience of M4P in thin markets? Because there are many gaps in thin markets, it's critical to think in interconnected strategies, rather than only lead interventions. Tailoring M4P programmes to the causes of market thinness increases the chances of success. Working in thin markets requires using the principles of M4P creatively rather than sticking to a rigid 'rule book'. The field has more work to do to increase the effectiveness of M4P in thin markets, including developing additional frameworks, tracking market system change more effectively, and sharing experience more freely. Working in thin markets is set to become increasingly important in the coming years.

Keywords: making markets work for the poor, M4P, market systems development, private sector development, thin markets

Alan Gibson at his most succinct

Over the years I knew Alan Gibson, I often heard people ask him, 'Is M4P appropriate in all markets?' His answer, as often as not, was 'Compared to what?' He aimed to remind people that, if we want to reduce poverty sustainably and at scale, we have to consider the systems with which poor women and men interact in order to meet their daily needs. But his answer was also a reminder that making markets work for the poor (M4P) is not a rule book, but a way of thinking that can be applied in a wide range of contexts. The earliest M4P programmes were in relatively robust and dynamic markets such as agriculture in Bangladesh and financial services in Kenya. But over the last 15 years the field has increasingly applied 'market systems development' in sparser, newer, and more fragile markets. What have we learned about how to apply M4P to 'thin' markets?

http://dx.doi.org/10.3362/9781788531443.008

What are 'thin' markets and why are they thin?

According to the M4P Operational Guide, thin markets are those that 'are relatively uncompetitive in which there are few market players and/or a large number of 'absent' supporting functions and rules' (The Springfield Centre, 2015). Typically, thin markets have several or all of the following characteristics (Miehlbradt et al., 2018):

- small (with relatively few market actors and consumers);
- geographically dispersed with low density of market actors;
- few types of products available;
- limited specialization;
- weak information flows;
- limited coordination among market actors;
- a lack of supporting services, such as design, quality assurance, logistics, and finance;
- a lack of clear regulations and government practices;
- adverse informal rules and norms;
- poor connectivity, including both physical infrastructure and mechanisms for transacting at a distance;
- weak or non-existent civil society institutions, particularly associations; and
- limited mechanisms for managing risks.

The reasons why a market is thin vary. Based on experience to date, it is possible to start putting thin markets into rough categories. In some cases, thinness is caused by a number of the factors below.

Nascent markets are thin because they are new. Awareness of a new product or service is low and there has not yet been time for the development of supporting functions and rules.

Crisis-affected markets have been damaged by conflict or disasters. Conflict or crisis often breaks logistical and trust links among actors, weakens information flows, ruins assets, disrupts production, and/or reduces market buying power. A combination of these can reduce a market to a thin state, often for years.

Remote markets are far from economic growth centres. The combination of long logistical lines to growing consumer segments and often sparse populations frequently means there are few market actors and few types of products available. In remote areas, specialization in markets tends to be limited and market institutions are slow to emerge.

Markets dominated by socially excluded groups are often thin, sometimes because these populations are remote, but equally often because these populations are not considered as desirable partners in supply chains and market transactions. The exclusion translates into poor connections to growing markets, inputs, and/ or support services.

What have we learned about applying M4P in thin markets?

The increasingly diverse experience of M4P programmes in thin markets has yielded some useful lessons. In line with Alan's advice, the lessons are not about whether to apply M4P in a thin market, but how.

It's puzzles, not dominoes

Achieving change in thin markets almost always requires addressing multiple constraints, rather than just one or two critical constraints. This imperative requires that programmes think in strategies rather than individual interventions.

In more robust markets, change can be led by individual innovations. Much like a game of dominoes, single innovations can cause a chain reaction.

- first, one or two firms trial the innovation;
- the relevant consumer group responds with early adopters trying out the innovation;
- the firms adapt their business model to suit the context and maximize commercial viability;
- other firms see the success and crowd-in, expanding the reach of the innovation;
- then related firms, public bodies, and/or civil society organizations respond to the innovation with complementary or supporting products, services, programmes, and regulations, further expanding and diversifying the market and opening new avenues for innovation.

This sequence is laid out in the Springfield Centre's 'Adopt, Adapt, Expand, Respond' framework (Nippard et al., 2014).

However, in thin markets, one or two innovations usually fail to spark widespread market change because there are too many other constraints and gaps in supporting functions and rules. Instead, practitioners need to imagine a puzzle, where they are helping to put in place multiple interlocking pieces that support each other to foster wider change. The process is slow at first and it often seems like no coherent picture is emerging. However, as the pieces are put in place, a clearer picture begins to emerge. Helping to put pieces in place gets easier and it becomes more likely that others will fill the gaps with limited or no help.

Thus, in thin markets, it is critical that programmes have a clear understanding of the 'picture' or vision they are working towards (even though it may change over time) and the process of filling gaps to enable the vision to be achieved. This understanding typically manifests as a sector strategy or similar with a clear sector results chain and an understanding of how the market functions and norms are expected to support the core market to work effectively. From there, programmes determine which innovations must be developed together in order to work successfully and how these groups of innovations can, over time, support overall market development. While programmes in robust markets can try out one or two interventions at a time and sometimes see wider market changes as a result, programmes in thin markets must expect to implement numerous, complementary interventions before they begin to see coherence and evidence of wider market changes.

Getting the pieces – the innovations that interventions support – to interlock and support progress towards wider change depends on understanding the change processes required to build the market. These change processes include market actors' responses to incentives, market actors' adaptation of business models, the flow of information around the market, the coordination among market actors, and the adjustment of perceptions and norms. Programmes are finding that supporting these change processes encourages links among innovations. For example, while news of successful innovations may travel quickly in more robust markets, this often requires support in thin markets. Even when information about innovations is flowing, other businesses and institutions may not recognize opportunities to crowd-in or provide complementary products and services as there may still be too many missing functions in the market for easy entry. M4P programmes find that facilitating the flow of market information and connections among existing and potential innovators is critical to getting the 'puzzle pieces' to interlock. Programmes are, for example, working with partners to convene events or supporting the emergence of associations or value chain forums. See Box 8.1.

Box 8.1 Developing the horticultural inputs market in Fiji

In Fiji, the Market Development Facility (MDF) works in the horticultural sector, among others. There are approximately 70,000 farming households in Fiji spread over two main islands and many smaller ones. There is demand for Fijian produce overseas and approximately 25 exporters supply that demand, but they often struggle to fill orders. A lack of access and high prices for agricultural inputs is one of the constraints to the inclusive growth of the horticulture sector. Thus, one key change that MDF aims to facilitate is enabling more small farmers to use a variety of agri-inputs so that they improve their productivity and cultivate more commercially.

When MDF started in 2011 there was only one seed importer and one importer of crop care products. There were less than 20 retailers nationwide selling agri-inputs. They only offered a limited and expensive range of imported seeds, crop protection, and fertilizer. The retailers did not reach out to farmers or aim to understand different types of farmers; they only served a few pockets of larger horticulture farmers or focused on government contracts. There were a few seedling nurseries but most were donor supported and supplied development projects. Government conducted agricultural research but it was not benefiting small fruit and vegetable farmers. Government extension workers focused almost exclusively on male farmers.

Over five years, MDF implemented a dozen partnerships in agri-inputs. These first focused on agri-input producers and importers and included assisting:

- a large concrete manufacturer to produce agricultural lime locally, to improve soil quality;

- a seedling provider to expand and focus on commercial sales, particularly of export-oriented horticultural products;
- the first commercial tissue culture company in Fiji, to provide high quality planting materials;
- a second seed importer to import a greater variety of seeds for local farmers.

While these interventions increased the variety of inputs available in Fiji, distribution was still an issue. MDF linked two large hardware wholesalers with agri-input producers and importers and assisted them to add agri-inputs to their product mix. MDF also worked with a logistics company to develop a regular inter-island barge service to more efficiently and reliably distribute agricultural inputs and products around Fiji.

By 2017, the market was showing significant signs of development. More types of inputs were available to small farmers in all the major agricultural areas of Fiji. Some input companies were starting to specialize – for example targeting export-oriented farmers with appropriate vegetable seeds for export crops. One additional company had begun selling agri-inputs. Another, the largest hardware company in Fiji, was actively pursuing importation of seeds to add to its product mix. These companies were increasing the number of retailers in rural areas. Networks were beginning to form between distributors and input producers and importers. Additional barge services were starting. Companies and government were beginning to recognize the roles that women play and the decisions they make in farming households. The Ministry of Agriculture was helping to raise the awareness of small farmers about the availability and effectiveness of new inputs. Overall, input companies, logistics service providers, certification companies, banks, exporters and government agencies were starting to perceive small farmers as good customers and suppliers and to invest in growing the horticulture sector. Small farmers were increasing their use of inputs and improving their productivity. Women had increased access to inputs and information and were saving time.

What were some of the key features of market development in Fiji agri-inputs?

- Increasing access to one agri-input did not catalyse broader change; only when a number of companies invested in the provision of inputs did other market actors take notice.
- The availability of inputs did not automatically lead to the distribution of those inputs; MDF facilitated innovations in logistics to address this market gap.
- MDF played a strong role in sharing information with various market actors and facilitating links among market actors.
- Once a number of innovations were in place and functioning successfully, other companies began to crowd in to various market functions and networks began to form autonomously.
- Multiple demonstrations and sustained provision of information were necessary to changecompanies' and government's perception of small farmers and women.

Source: Miehlbradt et al., 2018

Tailoring is paramount

Tailoring is required in all M4P programmes. Experience is beginning to yield lessons on how to tailor M4P strategies and interventions to different thin market contexts.

Nascent markets. The lack of awareness of a new product or service coupled with limited supporting functions and rules increases the costs and required expertise of potential lead firms. An M4P programme can speed up the development of a nascent market by sharing risks with potential lead firms and facilitating the emergence of supporting functions and rules. For example, Élan RDC is supporting the development of the market for off-grid, renewable energy systems, such as solar systems, in the Democratic Republic of the Congo (DRC). Firms entering this market in DRC need to invest heavily in awareness raising, as well as develop new business models to address logistical, marketing, and financing challenges. There are virtually no formal policies or regulations governing the market. Élan is encouraging investment in the sector, sharing the costs of market research for interested firms, supporting the development of viable business models with lead firms, and connecting them with potential supporting functions such as payment systems. Recently, Élan began supporting the establishment of an industry association to advocate for sensible policies and regulations for the market (Saidi, 2019).

Crisis-affected markets. In markets disrupted by conflict or natural disasters, an M4P programme can help to restore or re-create market links and information flows, facilitate access to replacement assets and financing, and connect re-emerging producers with available market opportunities. For example, Timor Leste's agricultural markets were significantly damaged during the violent withdrawal of Indonesian forces after the vote for independence in 1999. In addition to the destruction of infrastructure and trauma to the population, many supporting agricultural market functions that were previously dominated by Indonesians, such as trading and inputs provision, were suddenly withdrawn. Combined with other factors, this crisis left many agricultural markets persistently thin. The Market Development Facility's (MDF) work in agriculture in Timor Leste focused on connecting or re-connecting small holder farmers with markets and encouraging the commercial provision of agricultural inputs and farming advice to small farmers throughout the country. MDF has particularly encouraged and supported input retailers to target women farmers with demanded agricultural inputs (Miehlbradt et al., 2018). A significant resource on work in crisis-affected markets is the *Minimum Economic Recovery Standards* developed by the SEEP Network (2017).

Remote markets. Identifying producers' competitive advantage in remote areas and getting business or consumer services out to those areas are common challenges. A number of M4P programmes are finding that remote producers can competitively serve growing markets for niche products when they receive appropriate services and the cost of connecting to growing markets is reduced. M4P programmes are helping local firms think through business models that overcome logistical challenges to reach and connect remote communities sustainably, for instance through ICT-based delivery channels or local agent distribution models. For example, Kenya Markets Trust (KMT) targets the livestock sector, among others. While the market as a whole is large and robust, a portion of the market comprises nomadic pastoralists scattered across relatively remote, semi-arid areas. KMT has been working to increase linkages between remote pastoralists and growing markets, to facilitate the adoption of sustainable rangeland management practices and land governance in semi-arid areas, to catalyse access to good quality and affordable animal health services, and to enable insurance companies to successfully introduce commercial, index-based livestock insurance (Kenya Markets Trust, n.d.).

Markets dominated by socially excluded groups. When markets are thin due to exclusion, M4P programmes must understand both the economic and social norms isolating target populations. Programmes have found that where there are economic incentives, it is possible to forge examples of successful economic partnerships between willing, typically more progressive, external actors and marginalized communities. At the same time, programmes have found that socially isolated communities may require mentoring and support to have both the confidence and the institutions to interact successfully with potential business partners from other communities. Examples of success on the ground can combine with the encouragement and leadership of key influencers to gradually change norms. For example, there are many ethnic minority communities in Viet Nam that rely on cinnamon cultivation for their livelihoods. Often these communities lack reliable connections to the processing facilities that form an essential link to growing and lucrative cinnamon markets, as well as technical assistance to improve cultivation practices and warehousing facilities. Cinnamon is one of the sectors in which the Gender Responsive Equitable Agriculture and Tourism (GREAT) programme in Viet Nam works. GREAT is connecting ethnic minority communities that grow cinnamon with more lucrative value chains through links to processing facilities that include the provision of services (Cowater Sogema et al., n.d.).

Adventurous programmes are working more and more in markets affected by several of the factors above, helping both to break down barriers constraining markets and to build up links and supporting functions and institutions that will help markets grow inclusively. For example, in Burkina Faso, Practical Action has trialled an M4P approach to developing the market for clean energy in the Goudoubo refugee camp and the surrounding host community through the Moving Energy Initiative (MEI). The camp opened in 2012 and is located in a remote, rural area. Previously, energy had been provided almost exclusively through non-market, donor-driven mechanisms. MEI worked with commercial energy providers to pilot solar businesses in the area in and around the refugee camp. The programme worked with a local training institute to develop a solar system training curriculum and to deliver it to field agents for the commercial energy providers. Other interventions included bringing actors together to address perceptions and networking constraints and a trade fair conducted by local government (Whitehouse, 2019).

A number of recommendations are emerging on how to tailor M4P programmes to thin market contexts more generally. These include:

Continually explore the context. It is not possible to sufficiently understand any market through research alone. The first few years of engaging with market actors provide invaluable insights about the hidden norms (informal rules) that underpin markets and about the real risks and opportunities that market actors at all levels face. Because there are many gaps in thin markets, an intimate understanding of these factors is fundamental to crafting an effective programme that gradually enables market actors to fill the gaps and develop a functioning and inclusive market system. Gaining the necessary understanding takes time and early work will necessarily be 'messy'. Early interventions are often exploratory. While this does not mean that they do not have a link to the strategic objectives, it does mean that the links and expectations may be somewhat vague at first. Because early stages of M4P programmes in thin markets are characterized by this exploration and learning, programmes must have strong systems in place for capturing information and insights as they come in and channelling them not only into the development of new interventions but also into the strategy for the sector and programme.

Take political economy issues into account. Particularly in small economies, politics tends to pervade business and be quite personalized. There may be some political economy issues that provide an incentive for change, while others act as a barrier to it. The most significant issues may come from the national, regional, or local levels. Recognizing these issues, taking the time to understand them throughout implementation, and feeding that understanding into pragmatic strategies and interventions will help to make programmes operating in thin markets more effective. USAID's Applied Political Economy Analysis is a useful resource (Menocal et al., 2018).

Be ready to take advantage of unexpected opportunities. Although it can be difficult to generate change in thin markets, the small size of some thin markets can mean that a new opportunity makes a big difference to the overall market. Emerging opportunities can provide new entry points in thin markets that may not have existed just weeks or months before. When operating in thin markets, programmes are finding that it is important to not only keep an eye out for rapid changes but also be ready to jump in with new initiatives to take advantage of opportunities when they arise.

It's about principles, not rules

As M4P has developed over the last two decades or so, it has sometimes been interpreted as a set of 'rules'. For example, some programmes adhere to a strict split in investment percentage between the project and a lead firm when supporting development and trial of an innovation. But as Alan reminded us often, M4P is a framework with a set of principles, not a rule book. Experience in thin markets bears that out; 'rules' tend not to be helpful. Instead, working effectively in thin markets requires teams to apply the principles of M4P creatively to encourage change based on the context, opportunities, and constraints in the specific market. Some of the lessons coming out of M4P programmes working in thin markets follow:

More intense and hands-on support is needed. Supporting innovation in thin markets requires longer and more intense support than in more robust markets. Thin markets are often not perceived as viable. So, programmes find they need to start by co-financing market research. Businesses in thin markets may be new, fragile, and/or risk averse and, therefore, may require significant mentoring to weather the inevitable challenges they will face. Even more capable firms are unlikely to be familiar with the market and therefore require more intense support to develop an appropriate business model to operate in the thin market effectively and sustainably.

Use of tactics (within a long-term strategy) can help to encourage change. Programmes working in thin markets are finding that they need to use creative 'tactics' to facilitate change. For example, prioritizing highly visible innovations early on can help to overcome the 'invisibility' of thin markets. MDF kick-started development of the tourism market in Timor Leste by working with multiple actors to better serve tourists from cruise ships (Miehlbradt et al., 2018). While a programme may have an ambitious long-term vision, it's helpful to keep initial interventions modest, to build trust and confidence in the change process. For example, the NU-TEC programme operating in agribusiness markets in isolated and conflict-affected northern Uganda often starts work in a sector by conducting action-research to develop business models together with market actors (Apuoyo, 2019). Being open to these types of tactics is essential to success in thin markets.

Creativity is required to find partners. The image of an ideal M4P lead firm is often a large and capable firm that has, to date, missed a particular market opportunity, but with a bit of a nudge, could not only trial an innovation but significantly expand it if the trial works. These firms usually do not exist in thin markets and, particularly initially, may not have any interest in getting involved in thin markets. Programmes have to be creative in finding appropriate partners. When markets are small, supporting functions often have to cater to multiple sectors to be commercially viable. Therefore, programmes may have to broaden their sector boundaries when working with actors filling gaps in support functions. Similarly, some of the best partners may be from outside a target sector with an interest in diversification. Programmes also have to consider any organization that is functioning sustainably in a thin market, including smaller firms, religious institutions, civil society organizations, community businesses, and local government agencies. Casting a wide net can turn up potential partners that a programme may have initially overlooked.

Be pragmatic based on the situation on the ground. The debate on whether M4P programmes should ever work directly with target populations is a fierce one and particularly relevant for thin markets, where market transactions are initially very limited. The argument 'for' is embodied in the 'push-pull' dialogue (Garloch, 2015). It argues that some disadvantaged populations are not sufficiently market ready to provide an attractive, or even commercially viable opportunity for businesses. Therefore, enabling communities to become market ready must be temporarily subsidized until businesses and the communities can reliably interact independently, allowing for reasonable profits. The argument 'against' M4P programmes working directly with target populations asserts that direct support treats symptoms rather than causes of market dysfunction. It also argues that it is easy to lose sight of a credible vision for a sustainable market system and direct support fails to take advantage of 'leverage points' where a firm or institution can reach a significant number of target group members efficiently. Effective programmes working in thin markets tend to be pragmatic in this regard. They gain a deep understanding of realistic commercial opportunities for disadvantaged producers or workers and what is required to change for disadvantaged populations to take advantage of those opportunities. They look for local partners that can fill the gaps in the provision of support functions and rules and carefully consider what could be 'one-off' support for a limited time until more gaps in the market are filled and what support functions will be required long term. Then, they craft a response around that analysis, working with local actors and monitoring the development of the overall system. For example, the Making Markets Work for the Chars programme in Bangladesh worked with local NGOs to organize communities on riverine islands to interact effectively with mainland businesses while simultaneously working with the businesses to develop viable models to sustainably source agricultural products from island populations (Rashid et al., 2019).

Fail fast and adapt. In thin markets, experimentation and failure is perhaps even more prevalent than in more robust markets. While failure is inevitable, drawn-out failures are not. There are a number of measures that M4P programmes can take to adapt or end interventions, rather than prolong efforts that are unlikely to show success. Working with market actors to test several prototypes of a new product or service and get rapid feedback can help to identify what is likely to work and what is not. This enables partner market actors to adapt products and services quickly and to discontinue efforts on those that show little promise. Strong early monitoring allows for catching problems quickly. This means not only getting information from partners but also working with partners to get early information from target producers, workers, consumers, and other market actors on a new business model. While this early monitoring is a cost, it saves time and money later in risky, thin markets by supporting early adaptation that makes innovations more likely to succeed. The growing body of information and evidence from USAID's Learning Lab on Collaboration, Learning and Adaptation (Learning Lab, n.d.) provides a wealth of guidance in this regard.

An M4P programme's response is shaped by key principles:

- an ever-deepening understanding of the root causes of market dysfunction;
- a focus on the system and a credible picture for how it could work more effectively and sustainably in the future;
- the search for pragmatic leverage points for intervention;
- and vigorous application of adaptive management based on results on the ground.

While 'rules' may not apply, these M4P principles have stood the test of time, including in thin markets.

What is the future of M4P in thin markets?

M4P has come a long way from its origins in large and dynamic agricultural markets. Alan was a consistent champion for applying M4P to varying contexts. For example, in a 2005 article he and Springfield colleagues published in *EDM* journal, they encouraged application of M4P to business services for the rural poor, a relatively rare endeavour at the time (Hitchins et al., 2005). Over the years, practitioners have learned to apply the principles of the M4P approach to newer, more fragile, and more isolated markets and there is emerging evidence of some success.

There is also more work to do. We need to develop additional or adapted frameworks that specifically speak to the 'puzzle' nature of thin markets, helping practitioners to think through which market gaps to help fill and how to get multiple innovations to support one another. We need to get better at tracking not only how an individual innovation influences a market system but also how a market system changes through multiple supporting innovations. We need better ways to understand and address the norms that underpin exclusion and the political economy issues that can prevent innovation in promising thin markets. Most of all, we need more sharing of experiences about progress and challenges in thin markets. Because the change process in thin markets tends to be less 'spectacular' than in more robust markets, progress in thin markets is less frequently the subject of case studies and conference presentations. We need to mainstream the conversation about thin markets in the M4P field so that we can more quickly build up a body of knowledge on effective approaches, lessons, and tips.

Working in thin markets, particularly those that are thin because they are dominated by excluded groups is going to become increasingly important in the future. When the M4P field began to develop in the early 2000s, the measure of poverty incidence globally (the proportion of people living on less than US$3.20 per day at constant 2011 PPP prices) stood at around 47 per cent. By 2015, it was about 26 per cent (Beltekian and Ortiz-Ospina, 2018). There is no doubt that markets have played an important role in reducing income poverty however there are areas and populations that markets have persistently not reached adequately and inclusively. As the development sector embarks on the 'leave no one behind' agenda, it will become increasingly important for the M4P community to creatively support the development of thin markets for the benefit of excluded women and men.

About the author

Alexandra Miehlbradt is a Director at Miehlbradt Consulting in New Zealand. She has worked in private sector development for over 25 years as an implementer, consultant, researcher, and trainer, with a focus on market systems development and results management. Aly met Alan Gibson in 2000 when they facilitated a conference session together and collaborated with the Springfield Centre on its M4P training course and several assignments.

References

Apuoyo, C. (2019) 'Achieving systemic change in shallow markets: case of northern Uganda', webinar on *Promoting Systemic Change in Shallow Markets – Lessons from Experience* [online], BEAM Exchange <https://beam exchange.org/community/webinar/systemic-change-in-shallow-markets/> [accessed 12 December 2019].

Beltekian, D. and Ortiz-Ospina, E. (2018) 'Extreme poverty is falling: How is poverty changing for higher poverty lines?' Our World in Data [website] <https://ourworldindata.org/poverty-at-higher-poverty-lines> [accessed 12 December 2019].

Cowater Sogema, Lao Cai & So'n La and Australian Government (no date) 'Aus4Equality Gender Responsive Equitable Agriculture and Tourism (GREAT) Program' [website] <http://equality.aus4vietnam.org> [accessed 12 December 2019].

Garloch, A. (2015) *A Framework for a Push/Pull Approach to Inclusive Market Systems Development* [pdf], Leveraging Economic Opportunities Brief, USAID <https://www.marketlinks.org/sites/marketlinks.org/files/resource/files/LEO_Framework_for_a_Push_Pull_Approach_to_Inclusive_Market_Systems_Devel....pdf> [accessed 12 December 2019].

Hitchins, R., Elliott, D. and Gibson, A. (2005) 'Making business service markets works for the rural poor: a review of experience', *Small Enterprise Development Journal* 16(2): 10–23 <https://doi.org/10.3362/0957-1329.2005.016>.

Kenya Markets Trust (no date) Kenya Markets Trust [website] <www.kenyamarkets.org> [accessed 12 December 2019].

Learning Lab (no date) USAID Learning Lab [website] <https://usaidlearning lab.org> [accessed 12 December 2019].

Market Development Facility (no date) Market Development Facility [website] <www.marketdevelopmentfacility.org> [accessed 12 December 2019].

Menocal, A., Cassidy, M., Swift, S., Jacobstein, D., Rothblum, C. and Tservil, I. (2018) *Thinking and Working Politically through Applied Political Economy Analysis (PEA): A Guide for Practitioners* [online], Washington, DC: Center of Excellence on Democracy, Human Rights and Governance, USAID <https://usaidlearninglab.org/library/thinking-and-working-politically-twp-through-applied-political-economy-analysis-pea-core> [accessed 16 December 2019].

Miehlbradt, A., Warner, B. and Swete Kelly, D. (2018) *Promoting Systemic Change in Shallow Markets* [pdf], Canberra, Australia: Market Development Facility <https://beamexchange.org/resources/1155/> [accessed 16 December 2019].

Nippard, D., Hitchins, R. and Elliott, D. (2014) *Adopt-Adapt-Expand-Respond: A Framework for Managing and Measuring Systemic Change Processes* [pdf], Durham, UK: The Springfield Centre <http://www.springfieldcentre.com/wp-content/uploads/2014/06/2014-03-Adopt-Adapt-Expand-Respond-Briefing-Paper1.pdf> [accessed 17 December 2019].

Rashid, S., Mahmuduzzaman, S., Chowdhury, J. and Bhowmik, A. (2019) 'M4C's experience of applying market systems', BEAM Grab the Mic webinar, 5 February 2019 [online] <https://beamexchange.org/community/webinar/m4c-applying-market-systems/> [accessed 12 December 2019].

The SEEP Network (2017) *Minimum Economic Recovery Standards*, 3rd edn [online], The SEEP Network <https://mershandbook.org> [accessed 12 December 2019].

Saidi, R. (2019) *The Last Frontier for Energy Access: The Renewable Energy Opportunity in the Democratic Republic of Congo* [pdf], Kinshasa, DRC: Élan RDC <https://static1.squarespace.com/static/5bc4882465019f632b2f8653/t/5caf6631e79c7023d6525a3d/1554998850604/22+-+DRC+Energy+Opportunity.pdf> [accessed 16 December 2019].

The Springfield Centre (2015) *The Operational Guide for the Making Markets Work for the Poor (M4P) Approach*, 2nd edn [pdf], funded by SDC & DFID, Durham, UK: The Springfield Centre <https://www.enterprise-development.org/wp-content/uploads/m4pguide2015.pdf> [accessed 17 December 2019].

Whitehouse, K. (2019) *Adopting a Market-based Approach to Boost Energy Access in Displaced Contexts* [pdf], Moving Energy Initiative, London: The Royal Institute of International Affairs <https://www.chathamhouse.org/sites/default/files/publications/research/2019-03-25-MEIWhitehouse.pdf> [accessed 16 December 2019].

CHAPTER 9

M4P and gender inclusion

Linda Jones and Joanna Ledgerwood

Abstract

Market systems development programming is often 'gender neutral' meaning that, based on the assumption that results will not be prejudiced by gender considerations, a gender lens is not applied. However, 'gender neutral' often means 'gender blind' particularly where market systems are male dominated (roles, power, flows of money). Without acknowledging that economies, sectors, business relationships, and communities have typically been male dominated, M4P programmes miss opportunities to ensure effective system change that benefits women. This chapter examines the need for proactive inclusion of gender and women's empowerment in market systems programmes. It draws on an earlier gender inclusion framework for market systems commissioned by the M4P Hub and published as a Springfield Paper in 2012 as well as an updated and expanded version of the framework published by the BEAM Exchange in 2016. The chapter provides a brief background on evolution of gender intentional inclusion in market systems programming, with the bulk of the chapter focused on providing practical guidance on how to incorporate gender into each step of the M4P project cycle. Addressing gender and other forms of social exclusion (disability, ethnicity, extreme poverty, etc.) is becoming a standard requirement of aid agencies and we would do well to make inclusion a standard in M4P programmes.

Keywords: women's economic empowerment, gender equality, inclusion, exclusion, strategic framework, project cycle

The Making Markets Work for the Poor (M4P) approach has greatly influenced how we tackle poverty – in economic, education, health, and other sectors – identifying systemic weaknesses that affect the lives of the poor. The approach, with its focus on facilitating increased access to markets and services, offers a powerful framework for addressing barriers faced by poor women and girls. This chapter examines how to integrate women's economic empowerment (WEE) with the M4P approach to contribute to gender equity and women's empowerment within economic systems. It draws on an earlier gender inclusion framework for market systems commissioned by the M4P Hub and published as a Springfield Paper in 2012 (Jones, 2012) as well as an updated and expanded version of the framework published by the BEAM Exchange in 2016 (Jones, 2016). It begins with a brief background on the M4P

http://dx.doi.org/10.3362/9781788531443.009

context for gender inclusion and explores the evolution of intentional gender inclusion in economic market systems programming. We then consider
how WEE efforts can be incorporated into each step of the M4P project cycle
to influence and facilitate market actor engagement to promote and support
market systems change that benefits women.

Background

The systems approach, as defined in the original M4P guidance documents
authored by Alan and his Springfield colleagues (Springfield Centre, 2008 a,
b, c), was criticized by some for not explicitly tackling social exclusion and
therefore paying insufficient attention to the systemic constraints faced by
marginalized people, especially women. However, this criticism is not founded
in Alan's conceptualization, as evidenced by the following quote from the
original guidance documents:

> M4P recognizes that conventional economic theory is not enough. That
> is, in conventional economics, markets are seen to operate under con-
> ditions of perfect competition and perfect information with rational
> market players ... This thinking does not take into consideration how
> people behave within market systems or market imperfections such as
> asymmetry and externalities. (Springfield Centre, 2008a: 12)

The guide goes on to further emphasize the importance of context and the
need to go beyond purely economic analysis to look at behaviour and other
dynamics in a market system, including 'informal rules'; that is, the M4P
approach explicitly seeks to understand who has control over resources, who
makes decisions, and how benefits are shared and used, ultimately leading to
addressing root causes and not simply treating superficial symptoms.

   While the M4P publication series in 2008 was ground-breaking, it did not
offer practical guidance on how to deal with gender exclusion. Since then, practitioners have experimented with methods for greater inclusion made possible
by the M4P lens. This has led to case studies and field experiences that offer
examples of how to address gender biases and barriers by working with private sector, government, and civil society partners to influence their attitudes
and behaviour. As a result of these contributions and a re-examination of the
approach and needed guidance, gender inclusion was more robustly addressed
in the updated and refined *Operational Guide* (Springfield Centre, 2015).

The evolution of more intentional gender inclusion in M4P programmes

'Inclusion' is a process that promotes the fair and equal participation of every
person in a market system, adapting that system as needed to allow all to
contribute and benefit, regardless of sex, age, ethnicity, religion, disability,
and so on. Gender inclusion emphasizes equal participation of women and

men across all dimensions of empowerment. This involves not only equal access to products, services, and opportunities, but also the agency needed for equal participation such as decision-making power, leadership roles, and balanced workloads. Ideally, inclusive change occurs at all levels and in all spheres of the system. While earlier the term *integration* was the goal of WEE programming, *inclusion* has now been adopted to connote a much deeper shift for gender equality and empowerment. That is, *integration* supported the adaptation of the individual to an existing system, while *inclusion* emphasizes changes in the system to meet the needs and situation of excluded groups (Jones and Bramm, 2019).

Around the world, women face a range of systemic constraints that prevent them from engaging equally in market systems: lower levels of education and literacy, entrenched biases and discriminatory social, norms, limited access to resources and opportunities, and disproportionate responsibility for unpaid care work at home and in the community. For market systems to be more inclusive, these root causes of unequal participation must be addressed directly and indirectly through shifts in the structures and functions of the system. In market systems development, we aim to empower women through activities that shift systems to be more favourable for women who are participating or who could/would participate in those market systems.

Including women's economic empowerment as an objective in M4P programmes is a development imperative: women are among the poor (and often poorer than men) thereby often making up a large part of the target population; women are important contributors to the development of market systems and removing barriers to their full participation contributes to growth; and women's economic empowerment is an important goal in itself, and increasingly recognized as such (Coffey, 2012). In fact, gender equality and women's empowerment are imperatives of the Sustainable Development Goals (SDGs); the aim of SDG 5 is to achieve gender equality and empower all women and girls (United Nations, n.d.).

The M4P WEE framework

Following the implementation of early M4P programmes, project teams shared concerns that they did not know how to incorporate gender considerations in a way that was both meaningful and compatible with the M4P approach. A framework document for M4P and women's economic empowerment (the 'M4P WEE Framework'; Jones, 2012) was therefore commissioned by the M4P Hub and published by the Springfield Centre as part of a multi-donor (DFID, SDC, Sida) effort to encourage dialogue and consensus-building on how to prioritize and operationalize women's economic empowerment within M4P initiatives.

The commissioned document married WEE and M4P in a single framework by:

- unpacking definitions of women's economic empowerment and identifying elements that are compatible with sustainable economic development;

- presenting definitions, principles, and an approach that are consistent with the basic tenets of market systems development;
- aligning women's economic empowerment methods with the facilitation role of market systems programmes; and
- Reinforcing the scalability and sustainability of M4P projects while taking women's economic empowerment into account (Jones, 2012, 2016).

Since its publication in 2012, the M4P WEE Framework has been widely adopted and adapted, demonstrating the potential for systems approaches to be compatible with gender inclusion and women's economic empowerment in some of the world's most challenging environments. Numerous experiences have been documented, many of which were summarized in an updated guidance document on M4P and WEE: *The WEAMS Framework – Women's Empowerment and Markets Systems: Concepts, Practical Guidance and Tools* (Jones, 2016) published by the BEAM Exchange.[1]

Basic dimensions of WEE in market systems development

The M4P WEE Framework, based on the M4P project cycle described below, concluded that to achieve greater gender inclusion in market systems programming, it was necessary to define women's economic empowerment and its main elements.

Common dimensions defining women's economic empowerment:

- economic advancement – increased income and return on labour.

Access dimensions:

- access to opportunities and life chances such as skills development or job openings;
- access to assets, services, and needed supports to advance economically.

Agency dimensions:

- decision-making authority in different spheres including household finances;
- control over manageable workloads.

These dimensions were further elaborated in the WEAMS Framework to create a more flexible tool that would allow for additional dimensions such as social issues that affect market engagement (e.g. gender-based violence), intersectional identities (e.g. minority women), and other factors relevant to the specific context and target initiative. Building on these identified dimensions of women's economic empowerment, market systems practitioners have developed valuable approaches to encourage the inclusion of women as viable actors in market systems. Women offer new markets for products and services; women can be excellent suppliers of raw materials to traders, processors, and other 'core' actors; women are often reliable and productive employees who expand labour pools; and, in the majority of households globally, women contribute to, or even control, buying decisions.

While many other factors are described below in designing inclusive M4P projects, it is important to comment on the overarching concept of 'gender neutral' programming. 'Gender neutral' in market systems means that a gender lens is not applied based on the assumption that the results will not be prejudiced by gender considerations. However, in the real world we know that 'gender neutral' often means 'gender blind' particularly where market systems are male dominated (roles, power, flows of money). Gender-neutral or gender-blind programming does not acknowledge that economies, sectors, business relationships, and communities have typically been male dominated; in order not to favour men nor further disadvantage women, programme activities must be gender inclusive and proactively address the gap, rather than widening the gender equality gap (Jones and Bramm, 2019). That is, what 'benefits' the market system from a supposed gender-neutral sense may not benefit women and indeed may marginalize them further.

Designing and implementing inclusive M4P projects

This section considers the five steps of the project cycle from the new M4P operational guide (Springfield Centre, 2015) and incorporates women's economic empowerment. This means WEE is considered as an integral part of the strategic framework from analysis and design through to monitoring and learning:

1. *Setting the strategic framework*: setting the initial strategy and selection of sectors, potential outcomes for women, men, and/or households.
2. *Understanding market systems*: analysis of market systems including functions and dynamics, female and male actors and their roles, the rules, potential for change, and the resulting outcomes for women and men.
3. *Defining sustainable outcomes*: designing and planning for market systems change, determining interventions.
4. *Facilitating systemic change*: interventions are implemented through partners with facilitation support.
5. *Assessing change*: defines the monitoring and results measurement (MRM) plan, indicators, and other aspects of the MRM process with guidance on sex disaggregation and gender indicators.

Setting the strategic framework

The strategic framework of an M4P programme sets out the vision and rationale – the basic theory of change – that guides the design, implementation, and monitoring of the programme. The first step is to determine the objectives of the programme and to select the sector(s) where the programme will work. Making WEE an integral and explicit part of the overall strategic

M4P strategic framework

Poverty reduction

↑

Pro-poor growth & improved access

↑

Market system change

△ Interventions

M4P WEE strategic framework

Poverty reduction & enhanced empowerment

↑

Improved access, agency & growth

↑

Gender responsive system level change

△ M4P-WEE interventions

Setting the poverty reduction goal
> Which group of women is being targeted and what is their economic profile?
> What is the anticipated final impact on the target group in terms of poverty reduction and empowerment? (More income? Higher return on labour? More time? Less unpaid work? Better quality of work? More decision-making authority?)

Setting growth and access objectives
> What are the most promising opportunities for women?
> How can women's position in the target market be improved?

Setting systemic change objectives
> How do service provision and enterprise practices need to change to best serve women in a sustainable manner?
> How do informal and formal rules have to change?

Defining the main thrust of systemic interventions
> Is there a need to target women specifically?
> What is the business case for women's participation in the market system change?

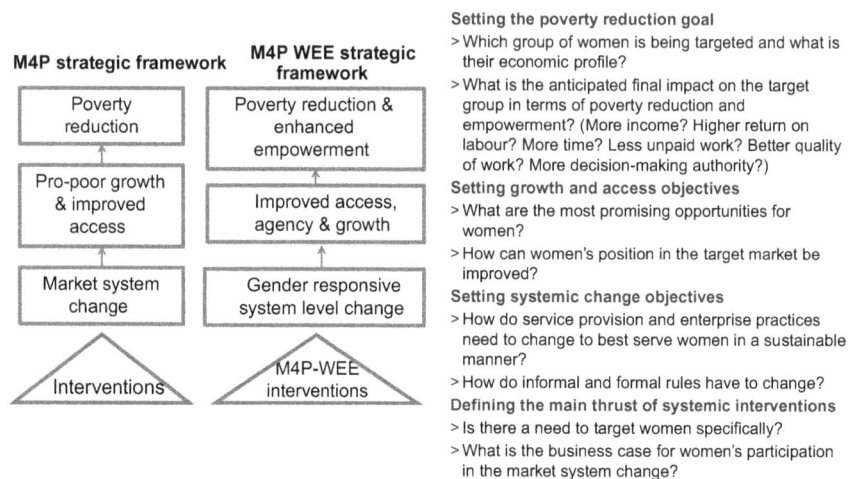

Figure 9.1 M4P WEE strategic framework
Source: Adapted from the SDC MSD-WEE strategic framework (SDC, n.d.).[2]

vision decreases the risk that gender is considered a separate 'component' and implemented by gender specialists. As a result, clear WEE objectives can be taken into account, articulated in each step of the process as outlined in Figure 9.1.

Understanding market systems

Gendered market systems analysis provides the necessary information for understanding and mainstreaming WEE into programme activities and outcomes. Gendered market systems analysis is most successful when: women are included in a range of research roles such as designers, field researchers, and analysts as well as respondents representing households and businesses; gendered differences are considered at every stage of research; and all information, whether qualitative or quantitative, is disaggregated by sex. In addition, a separate gender analysis of the overall context can be undertaken to provide broader insights into societal patterns regarding gendered norms and beliefs, assigned roles, and barriers and opportunities, recognizing that these affect the target market system as well as the wider system. Findings from the gender analysis should be included in the market analysis rather than just as a separate report to ensure gender is included in intervention design.

In conducting gendered market analysis, a number of principles need to be considered (Jones and Bramm, 2019):

The principle of *context and intersectionality* has long recognized that women are not a homogeneous group; they live in different socio-cultural contexts with varying political, business, and geographic environments.

Within a specific context, women are differentiated by class, caste, religion, race, and ethnicity, facing dissimilar barriers and unequal access to opportunities. Further, as intersectional analysis aims to reveal, the combining of multiple identities in an individual or group leads to distinct experiences.

Inclusion must be considered at all levels of the market system. Inclusive systems change should not only lead to greater empowerment for women in existing roles, but also result in the advancement of women as suppliers, buyers, service providers, business leaders, and consumers on their own terms. At the systems level, this means reducing or eliminating underlying formal and informal barriers to ensure equal access to resources and opportunities while building the agency of women so they can fully engage in market systems.

Constraints manifest differently for women and men. That is, the typical market constraints may be in the same areas: weak land tenure, insufficient productive knowledge and skills, limited access to technology, and lack of services, but how these manifest, and the nuances of the barriers, are a gendered phenomenon. This means the analysis of such constraints and opportunities must be gendered and programme design should be based on understanding the differences between women and men's underlying constraints. For example, a common assumption may be that certain farmers do not use improved fertilizers or irrigation technologies due to lack of access to these technologies. However, analysis of underlying causes might reveal, for example, that target farmers do not have clear title to the land that they cultivate, and they fear losing access to the land if they invest in its improvement. In the case of women farmers specifically, gendered analysis may further uncover that women not only have little or no access to land, but that their use of fertilizers is limited by socio-cultural norms that restrict their access to markets, finance, chemicals, or other needed supports and services.

M4P practitioners need to be aware of *trends and externalities* that impact contexts for gender inclusion in sometimes obvious and at other times more subtle ways. War, for example, places a huge burden on women and, in most extreme cases, the systematic abuse of women becomes a weapon of war. Perhaps in less dramatic ways, the creep of climate change and the exposure of millions or even billions of young people to social media worldwide are changing gendered norms, attitudes, and behaviours. In market systems programming, we cannot assume that the world of just a decade ago is the same as today. We need to look anew at contexts, be aware of trends, and understand externalities that may positively or negatively affect gender inclusion in market systems development.

The importance of rules – informal and formal. In market systems analysis, informal and formal rules affect women's participation and advancement in economic systems.

> Many projects focus on the core transactions and supporting functions of the market systems. This may in part be due to a bias in favour of

working with the private sector and the belief that transactions and services are easier to improve. However, legislation and its implementation, as well as informal rules, such as what is culturally acceptable for women and men to do, can have an enormous impact on large numbers of women and are an important field for M4P facilitation. (Coffey, 2012: 28)

When working to improve women's economic empowerment, it is particularly important to consider the gendered social norms that impact market systems including accepted business behaviour and attitudes of other market actors as well as laws and regulations that may restrict women from participating in economic opportunities. Questions to consider include:

- What are the gender roles relevant to the selected market systems, including division of labour and women's unpaid work?
- What access to and control over resources and supporting functions do women and men have and how are they different?
- How do formal rules (legislation, regulations) in the selected market systems affect women and men, and how is this different? (Coffey, 2012: 4)

Engaging a variety of stakeholders at multiple levels in the analysis helps to identify constraints based in rules that perpetuate gender disparity and limit economic opportunities.

Defining sustainable outcomes

In designing, market systems programme facilitators do not attempt to address all barriers present in the system for the target group. In gender-inclusive programming it is important to prioritize interventions based on the opportunity presented, the relevance to women, and feasibility for implementation, based on evidence that can lead to systemic change that benefits women.

Women, like all economic actors, engage in different spheres: individual, household/community, institutions, and economic sectors. Constraints and opportunities are different depending on the sphere of engagement, and success in one sphere may be thwarted by dynamics in another: for example, even if a woman comes from a progressive household where she is empowered, the workplace may not offer the same respect/opportunities, or vice versa. Programmes that mainstream WEE are often undecided about whether they can affect gender attitudes, values, and norms. Although some things are best considered a given, in many ways what a programme can influence depends on its resources and timeframe.

Interventions that contribute to WEE include those that target men and women, as well as those that specifically target women. The goal is equal opportunities in the market system, not equal treatment by the programme. Interventions that incentivize market actors to work with women while

---

Gender sensitized interventions

The Alliances Caucasus Programme (ALCP) focuses on developing *gender sensitized interventions (GSIs)* which reflects the fact that to impact both men and women, interventions must take into account that they perform different roles as market players, face different constraints, and are able to exploit different market opportunities. Each intervention results chain contains within it the steps (*'GSI boxes'*) necessary to ensure that an intervention is calibrated in a way to reach women as well as men and ensure equitable impact. Depending on the nature of the intervention it may mean as little as ensuring that women are targeted in advertising or that information dissemination reaches them, or in other cases, designing the intervention to take into account that finding the correct entry points with women will be pivotal to the success of the intervention: e.g. reaching women raw milk suppliers with specifically tailored information for the supply of quality milk.

Source: Bradbury, 2016: 14

---

strengthening their beneficial inclusion in the market system are best placed to increase WEE.

Kabeer (2009) proposed a range of interventions that can support women and redistribute unpaid labour: encourage public investment in infrastructure including water, roads, and electricity; promote women's participation in planning of infrastructure and other projects; facilitate growth in affordable child and elder care; and encourage men's involvement in unpaid household work.

Objectives – gender intentional vs. gender transformative. The Bill & Melinda Gates Foundation (n.d.) Gender Integration Criteria offer a useful articulation of the difference between gender intentional activities and gender transformative activities. Gender intentional activities aim to reduce gaps in access

---

Market Alliances against Poverty in Samtskhe-Javakheti and in Kvemo Kartli (Alliances SJ & KK) in Georgia aim to contribute to women's 'equal access to services, inputs and markets', specifically in the dairy, beef, and, for KK, in the sheep market. The projects' analysis shows that women have very little time available to expand their work in, for example, the dairy value chain. This is partly due to childcare responsibilities, and women have expressed the need for childcare facilities. In fact, work under the projects' governance theme has contributed to women advocating for this with local government, and one municipality has agreed to budget for a childcare centre. This success indicates that there may be opportunities for a more systemic approach to childcare; that is, developing the market system for this service in the project areas. Limitations on women's mobility, which are partly due to lack of transportation, and access to piped water are other constraints around which interventions leading to systemic change might be built.

Source: Coffey, 2012: 10

---

to resources, while gender transformative activities address power relations and gaps in agency. In the case of financial services, for example, products such as savings accounts, loans, and insurance might become available to women (gender intentional) but women's ability to access those resources on an equal footing with men may be more challenging to achieve (gender transformative).

Women's ability to make use of economic opportunities can be improved by considering interventions to address constraints rooted in women's reproductive, productive, and community roles beyond the selected market system. This includes, for example, their disproportionate role within the care economy of paid and unpaid work, inside and outside the household, which constitutes a special burden to women and a challenge to private sector development projects.

Facilitating systemic change

Working with partners across a range of organizations (private, public, and civil society), and at various levels, is critical in achieving long-term change in attitudes, beliefs, and norms around gender inclusion and women's economic empowerment. Selecting partners is based on their motivation and capacity to contribute to a desired systemic change. 'Partners can be specifically screened at the time of selection for their awareness of gender issues, their demonstrated willingness to address them in their own organisation, and their competence in implementing a gender-responsive approach' (SDC, n.d.). Moreover, gender-responsiveness can be influenced by the inclusion of women on boards and in management roles and on working committees.

Private sector partners (and even government) often need to be convinced of the 'business case' for engaging with women as consumers, suppliers, and employees. Why should they make special efforts to serve women? Considerations include the following:

- Do women represent a new market segment as consumers of products and services?
- Would working with women lead to increased efficiency or greater profitability by reducing costs or increasing revenues?
- Would engaging with women suppliers result in access to higher volumes of raw materials or improved quality?
- What are the challenges and risks for private sector partners to engage with women? What can the programme do to mitigate the challenges and risks?
- What opportunities can be leveraged? Are there social norms that will facilitate the intervention (e.g. women's current roles and social attitudes that support women's work in the sector)?

Facilitators also partner with public and civil society sector actors to facilitate inclusive market systems change. In partnering with government, for

---

Incentives to address 'practical gender needs'

In Bangladesh seed companies contract households to grow seeds. Katalyst used maintaining quality as the business case for seed companies to provide information and training to female members of such households. While women already played a major role in seed production, they were not targeted by the companies. Now a company organizes courtyard meetings for the wives of the male seed growers to educate them on post-harvest activities that ensure acceptable seed quality. Results indicated great success; contract growers' rejection rate has dropped to zero, contamination is reduced, and growers receive a higher price per kilogram of seed resulting in a 25% income increase. For women, the training allowed them to gain essential skills, and assist in improving the household income without breaking social barriers.

Source: Coffey, 2012: 12 (Shahnewaz Karim, SDC e-discussion, 22 March 2012)

---

example, facilitators can highlight incentives that speak to either economic or rights-based factors and outcomes, thereby influencing policies and legislation that incorporates provisions for gender equality. There are also a range of benefits from partnering with local civil society organizations. These organizations often have crucial knowledge of norms and attitudes, barriers, and even opportunities that are foundational to designing and delivering programming that shifts the norms and behaviours in market systems.

Consider rules and their implementation

Changes in legislation can offer an opportunity to work with the public sector in ways that affect WEE in and beyond a market system. The Market Alliances against Poverty projects in Georgia raise awareness at the level of local government on national level gender equality legislation that includes provisions for participation of women in local decision-making. While this is in an early stage, women's greater influence on local level planning and spending could result in, for instance, childcare facilities (one municipality agreed already) or better water supply (a key factor in increasing hygiene in milk production).

Source: Coffey, 2013: 29 (interviews with project staff, Georgia, 19/22 March 2012)

Assessing change

Assessing women's economic empowerment is a complex process in and of itself, but even more so when considering the complexity of market systems change (Markel et al., 2015). Building on the upfront analysis described above, it is necessary to design a monitoring and results measurement (MRM) system that incorporates: 1) sex disaggregated data; 2) gender specific indicators and questions; 3) a gendered viewpoint on systemic change; and 4) feedback loops that allow evidence to inform adaptive management and new approaches to programming.

In the same way that all analysis, planning, and design should incorporate gender and WEE as a matter of course, so should MRM tools and processes. The development of WEE indicators requires an understanding of what to measure, how to measure it, and how to report it. This requires a well-designed MRM system based on robust research and analysis, timely data collection, and sex disaggregation for all relevant data. WEE indicators must also go beyond sex disaggregation to include gender-specific indicators that measure, for example, access and agency dimensions such as impacts on workloads, mobility, and decision-making.

In order to assess changes that happen as a result of interventions, the following aspects are key to consider in the MRM system all along the project cycle:

- Develop intervention results chains that include expected results with associated indicators in terms of WEE explicitly.
- Establish sex-disaggregated baseline and set targets. Indicators should also cover unintended results where risks were identified during the analysis (e.g. risk that women will be harmed due to increased gender-based violence).
- Use gender-sensitive research methods to measure change in WEE.
- Ensure that findings on WEE are fed back into intervention design through gender-sensitive processes and revision (SDC, n.d.).

MRM and gender

Making gender meaningful in terms of programme implementation and monitoring and results measurement necessitates going beyond the collection of sex-disaggregated data alone. This requires both an understanding of gender equality influences and approaches, as well as sufficient programme resources.

The problem, however, with sex-disaggregated data is that it has varying levels of efficacy in providing *a true picture of the impact of an intervention on women*. This is particularly true when based solely on scalable quantitative indicators that cannot reflect the complexity of gender relations at the household and community level. It is essential therefore that this type of sex-disaggregated data be backed up by qualitative data that allows for an interpretation of the figures beyond face value.

The following examples highlight some of the issues found within the Alliances programme in Georgia which hinder sex-disaggregated data from showing the true level and nature of impact on women in relation to programme interventions. The programme response is in italics:

Scale: Presenting sex-disaggregated beneficiaries of programme interventions *actually* shows us the number of customers and suppliers of the programme-supported enterprises rather than who is really benefitting and how these benefits are distributed within the households. *Therefore, extra gender analysis is required to answer how the income is distributed within the family.*

Data collection: Women often sign their husband's name, i.e. the family or household name, when accessing services facilitated by the programme or supplying to programme-facilitated entities. *This leads the programme to have to devise ways of data collection which somehow shows the sex of the purchaser.*

Decision-making/end user: Men often do the marketing in town with women being left at home, yet women are for example in the case of veterinary medicine often responsible for diagnosing and requesting the drugs from the vet pharmacy which they will then administer. The data will show a prevalence of male customers although in many ways the decision-maker and end user is the woman in the household (HH) responsible for livestock husbandry in the home. *This issue therefore needs more emphasis on the development of indicators which will capture the complexity of decision-making and roles at the HH level and going beyond the issue of mobility.*

Income: Women are the main producers in the dairy value chain, responsible for livestock husbandry in the home and milking and processing. They are responsible for dealing with intermediaries from the home where they handle cash. However, payment from more formalized entities is conducted from the milk collection centre to which mostly men go and therefore again men's names are used and cash is handed to them. *The issue here is finding out what level of access and control women have to this income. When analysing data to find out whether women's livelihoods have been improved, sex-disaggregated data can present a bleak picture and tell us little, as often income becomes household income and the decision-making related to its use and control over its use is complex.*

Source: Bradbury, 2016: 17–18

Conclusion

Alan's thought leadership in international development left a mark on intellectuals and practitioners alike. And while gender inclusion was not a focus area of Alan's, like all great thinkers, his work is not static, but has opened the minds of many to explore new territory and build upon his work.

The industry's understanding of the characteristics of and the interplay between social and economic dimensions of inclusion has become much richer in recent years due to M4P foundational thinking and leadership. Policy makers and practitioners are better versed in the complexity of the challenges and are more equipped to design and implement innovative solutions. Today, addressing gender and other forms of social exclusion (disability, ethnicity, extreme poverty, etc.) is a standard requirement of aid agencies. There is no longer a need to shy away from inclusion in market systems programmes; in fact, it is incumbent upon us to take the opportunity and resources to contribute to much needed societal transformation around the globe.

About the authors

Dr Linda Jones is a thought leader in women's empowerment and inclusive market systems. She is Vice President of Inclusive Growth at Cowater International, and has contributed to the field in other senior management and consulting roles. She knew Alan Gibson from his incredible contribution to systems thinking but, sadly, admired him mainly from a distance.

Joanna Ledgerwood is an independent consultant specializing in women's financial inclusion and market systems development. She is the author of numerous books and publications and is active on a number of boards and committees. Joanna first met Alan Gibson in September 2007 in Chiang Mai at a BDS seminar and they remained close until his death.

Notes

1. The M4P WEE Framework, the WEAMS Framework, and *Women's Economic Empowerment in Development Practice: Creating Systemic Change* (Jones and Bramm, 2019) provided significant source material for this chapter.
2. Adapted from Markel (2014) and Coffey (2012).

References

Bill & Melinda Gates Foundation (no date) *Gender Integration Criteria* [online] <https://www.gatesgenderequalitytoolbox.org/wp-content/uploads/BMGF-Gender-Integration-Criteria.pdf> [accessed 13 October 2020].

Bradbury, H. (2016) *How to Put Gender and WEE into Practice in M4P: A Description of the Ethos, Systems and Tools Used in the Alliances Programme in Georgia* [pdf], Women's Economic Empowerment Working Group, DCED <https://www.enterprise-development.org/wp-content/uploads/DCED-WEE-into-Practice-2016.pdf> [accessed 13 October 2020].

Coffey International Development (2012) *M4P and Women's Economic Empowerment: Phase 2 Guidelines for Incorporating WEE into M4P Programmes* [pdf], M4P Hub and DFID <https://beamexchange.org/uploads/filer_public/46/04/4604fd7e-ee4b-48fa-9012-4cd48b564355/wee_m4p_guidelines.pdf> [accessed 13 October 2020].

Coffey International Development (2013) *Mainstreaming Women's Economic Empowerment in Market Systems Development: Practitioner Guidelines* [pdf], M4P Hub and DFID <https://beamexchange.org/uploads/filer_public/d3/5f/d35f410a-2064-46f9-8f04-7044a8a32c70/mainstreamingwomens economicdevelopment2013.pdf> [accessed 13 October 2020].

Jones, L. (2012) *Discussion Paper for an M4P WEE Framework: How Can the Making Markets Work for the Poor Framework Work for Poor* Women *and for Poor* Men? [pdf], Durham, UK: The Springfield Centre <http://www.springfieldcentre.com/wp-content/uploads/2012/11/M4P_WEE_Framework_Final.pdf> [accessed 13 October 2020].

Jones, L. (2016) *The WEAMS Framework: Women's Empowerment and Markets Systems: Concepts, Practical Guidance and Tools* [pdf], The BEAM Exchange <https://beamexchange.org/uploads/filer_public/0d/50/0d5009be-faea-4b8c-b191-c40c6bde5394/weams_framework.pdf> [accessed 13 October 2020].

Jones, L. and Bramm, A. (eds) (2019) *Women's Economic Empowerment: Transforming Systems through Development Practice*, Rugby, UK: Practical Action Publishing.

Kabeer, N. (2009) *Women's Economic Empowerment: Key Issues and Policy Options*, policy paper, Sida's Women's Economic Empowerment Series, Stockholm: Ministry of Foreign Affairs.

Markel, E. (2014) *Measuring Women's Economic Empowerment in Private Sector Development – Guidelines for Practitioners*, Donor Committee for Enterprise Development (DCED).

Markel, E., Hess, R., and Loftin, H. (2015) *Making the Business Case: Women's Economic Empowerment in Market Systems Development* [pdf], LEO Report No. 11, Washington, DC: USAID <https://www.marketlinks.org/sites/marketlinks.org/files/resource/files/Making_the_Business_Case_508_Compliant.pdf> [accessed 14 October 2020].

SDC (n.d.) *Mainstreaming Women's Economic Empowerment (WEE) in Market Systems Development*, MSD-WEE strategic framework.

Springfield Centre (2008a) *A Synthesis of the Making Markets Work for the Poor (M4P) Approach*, Bern: SDC/FDA (Federal Department of Foreign Affairs).

Springfield Centre (2008b) *Perspectives on the Making Markets Work for the Poor (M4P) Approach*, Bern: SDC/FDA.

Springfield Centre (2008c) *The Operational Guide for the Making Markets Work for the Poor (M4P) Approach*, London: DFID; Bern: SDC/FDA.

Springfield Centre (2015) *The Operational Guide for the Making Markets Work for the Poor (M4P) Approach*, 2nd edition [online], funded by SDC and DFID, Durham, UK <http://www.springfieldcentre.com/wp-content/uploads/2015/11/2015-09-M4P-Op-Guide-Sept2015.pdf> [accessed 13 October 2020].

United Nations (no date) 'Goal 5: Achieve gender equality and empower all women and girls' [online], Sustainable Development Goals <https://www.un.org/sustainabledevelopment/gender-equality/> [accessed 14 October 2020].

PART III

Reflections on making markets work for the poor

CHAPTER 10

Market systems thinking in inclusive finance: Influencing the influencers

Mayada El-Zoghbi

Abstract

The inclusive finance community is proud to have attracted private capital over the last decade. However, most funding is used to finance loans and minimal investment is made to understand the underlying causes of market failure and to address constraints that inhibit development of markets to benefit the poor. As the primary donor consortium for inclusive finance, CGAP set out to develop new guidelines for funders to support greater inclusion for the poor. Alan Gibson was instrumental in CGAP's decision to promote the market systems approach and continued to influence and support CGAP until his death. While many funders appear to support the approach, there has been limited progress and the current political economy of aid does not support good practice. For more funders to understand and adopt this approach we need to demonstrate and document success; use language that resonates with non-experts; and support capacity building of donor agency staff.

Keywords: market systems, financial inclusion

Once upon a time in Durham

The year was 2011. The financial inclusion field saw itself as more advanced than many fields because we were able to do what others in development had rarely been able to do, which was to achieve institutional sustainability for financial institutions serving poor people. We were proud to crowd-in so much private capital. CGAP's annual funding flows research identified over 90 microfinance investment vehicles (MIVs) and 61 public and private donors committing US$21.3 bn as of December 2009 (El-Zoghbi et al., 2011). While public funding still dominated funding flows with only 30 per cent of funding coming from private sources, the rate of growth of private capital was accelerating (ibid.).

At the same time, there was a sense of stagnation and some of the underlying dynamics did not correspond with our inflated sense of achievements. There were important questions about whether the funding from donors and public investors, which still mostly focused on expanding retail capacity through portfolio lending, was sufficient to address complex development

http://dx.doi.org/10.3362/9781788531443.010

constraints in different markets. Instead, stories around crowding out private capital (see, for example, von Stauffenberg and Rozas, 2011) and high concentration of funding into a few developed countries were frequent. Furthermore, after decades of support, there were very large numbers of poor people still excluded from the financial system – at least 2.5 billion as of 2010 (World Bank, 2011). Certainly the headlines about the negative impact of microcredit and suicides in India did not fit neatly into the success narrative.

For more than six years the Pink Book, or what is more formally known as 'The Good Practice Guidelines for Funders of Microfinance', had been the guiding principle for donors and public investors supporting the inclusive finance field. While the actual content of the Pink Book was not wrong, there was an overall sense that the material was outdated. We were uncertain of which direction to go. What should donors and public investors do differently to have more systemic impact on the lives of the poor?

It was then that my colleague and I took the train from Paris to Durham and met with Alan Gibson. This was a critical turning point in how CGAP decided to steer donor engagement within the financial inclusion community. Several very important messages resulted from this initial meeting. The first was Alan's clear delineation between market actors and those whose work was outside the market, including donors and development institutions. At the time, Alan drew a simple diagram (see Figure 10.1) that served as a key lens through which we at CGAP started to see and demarcate the role of donors and public investors who had a development mandate in inclusive finance.

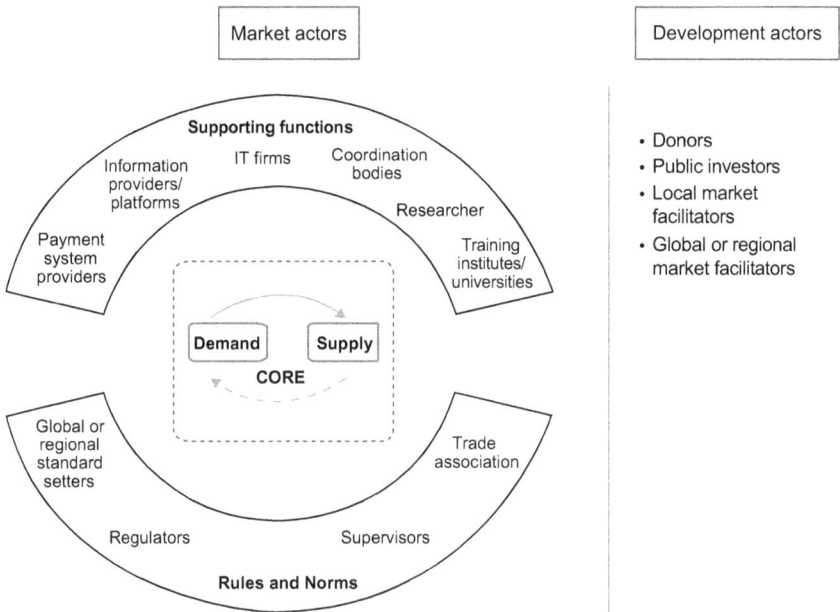

Figure 10.1 Actors inside and outside the financial market system

Another important message related to understanding why the inclusive finance community did not embrace market systems thinking from the onset. It was precisely because of our perceptions of 'success' that we did not feel the need to search for something better. We saw evidence of private capital flow into our field as sufficient proof that we were doing the right thing. Other fields which had struggled to achieve sustainable institutions were quicker to ask the big questions on the role of development assistance and the best way to influence market systems to achieve more lasting and systemic change. We noted that any shift we would need to make in our community was not going to be easy.

This first meeting with Alan Gibson was the beginning of a deeper engagement that continued until just a month before his accident. Throughout the years as my colleagues and I were grappling with how to influence both internally at CGAP and the wider donor and public investor community, we often turned to Alan and the Springfield Centre for guidance and clarity of thinking.

Looking back on progress so far

In 2015, CGAP released the updated Pink Book and the approach we took was both revolutionary and incremental at the same time. We took more than three years to influence and make the case for taking a market systems approach in our field. We held numerous funder consultations and events where we were nudging the community along. Alan featured in many of these. He authored one of the first signalling blogs (Gibson, 2017) that something new was coming. CGAP's messaging to donors and public investors and their evolving role was embedded in all of its work (see Figure 10.2).

When the guidelines were released, most CGAP members had bought into the need for a new way of working, which called for moving away from financing 'vanilla' loan capital where markets were already mature to diagnosing underlying causes of market failure, such as addressing information failures or facilitating policy and regulatory changes that influence incentives for market actors. The *New Funder Guidelines: Market Systems Approach to Financial Inclusion* (Burjorjee and Scola, 2015) was merely a testament to a shift that had already started happening. DFID, SIDA, and SDC were clear supporters of this approach and had been funding market facilitators in inclusive finance and many other sectors for years. Other donors such as Omidyar Network, USAID (O'Planick, 2015), MasterCard Foundation, and Agence Française de Développement (AFD) were also important contributors to work on market systems. Even JICA (Tsuji, 2015) was able to speak to the need for making a shift, albeit with a recognition that the organization would need a substantive mindset shift.

Now that five years have passed since the guidelines were released and nine years after our initial meeting with Alan, it is interesting to reflect on how much progress has been achieved. There are several high-level trends that are worth calling out.

	Traditional funding approach	Market systems approach
Focus of funder	Supply of services Focus on capacity building and funding of financial service providers	Facilitating of system Engage a range of market actors to change the way the market works
Aim of funder support	Direct Leverage public and private investment at the provider level	Catalytic Crowd-in local market actors to perform market functions
Sustainability	Organization level Focus on sustainability of financial service providers	System level Relevant market functions are provided by local market actors beyond the funder's intervention

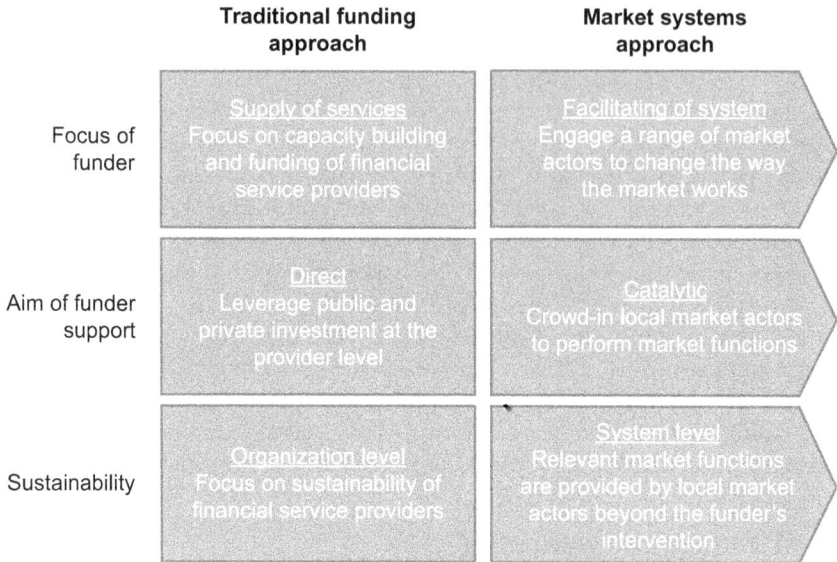

Figure 10.2 Excerpt from presentation to CGAP's governing body, February 2015

Broad, high-level buy-in, but limited progress operationally

There continues to be high-level buy-in and a conceptual understanding of what market systems thinking is. Increasingly donors are using the language of market systems thinking in their strategies. For example, AFD formulated its new strategy for 'Financial Systems', rather than 'Financial Institutions', and is looking at integrating the approach into its project identification tool-kit. BMZ's new strategy (which applies to all German implementing agencies) states that support has to enable markets to create solutions on their own, which is a core element of the market systems approach. IFAD explicitly commits to a market systems approach to inclusive rural financial services and provides guidance on specific aspects such as country-level policy engagement.

However, there has been little progress on operationalization of market systems approaches in financial inclusion programmes. In particular, there is very little difference in what donors and public investors are actually doing today from what they were doing a few years ago. For example, one senior member of the CGAP leadership team after reading the new donor guidelines said 'there is nothing new here'. The underlying assumption is that we are using new language but the way we operate is still the same; it also undergirds a misinterpretation of the meaning of market systems approach, equating it to a focus on commercial solutions. Data from CGAP's latest funder survey (2018) shows that the bulk of funding remains focused on retail providers (87 per cent) (CGAP Funder Explorer). On a positive note, the data showed that funders are allocating more than half of all funding to countries with less than 66 per cent account penetration, an indication that funders are seeking to direct resources to where they can add value. Meanwhile, funding for customer-focused projects (e.g. to build customers' financial capabilities) and market infrastructure (e.g. payments or information infrastructure) appears to remain the same at 5.6 per cent and 1 per cent of total commitments, respectively. This could suggest that they are using the market systems approach by addressing barriers beyond the supply side of the market, but what is being funded is only part of the equation. Market systems approaches are about how donor support is administered, not what is funded: funders need to address the underlying constraints and not just plug a hole with their funding. Ultimately, funders need to facilitate market actors to take on the functions that are missing in the market or not serving the poor, not replace that role by their interventions.

However, there are many donors and public investors that still offer very traditional 'direct delivery' solutions that are not leading to sustainable change. There are numerous cases of donors drafting regulations, subsidizing training, producing materials for financial literacy, or offering a 'payments in a box' solution. None of these interventions embeds an underlying understanding of the root causes of exclusion and the incentives that drive the behaviours of regulators, government officials, policymakers, the private sector, civil society, or poor people. They are fabulous ways to spend money however!

Current political economy of the aid business is stacked against good practice

Alan Gibson was well aware that development assistance is not motivated by nor driven by technical know-how alone. It has always been and will continue to be a very political endeavour. Politics requires donor agencies to continually renew their mandates by appealing to the public who are ultimately paying taxes and funding their budgets. The wave of right-wing governments taking over much of the western hemisphere are looking for ways to reduce their commitment to international aid; this has upped the ante for those in the aid business to speak the language of the right wing in order to stay in the aid business. Private sector engagement, public– private partnerships, and blended finance are all communications efforts to rebrand the way that aid is seen and to keep it relevant to the small government, and low taxation mindset. Yet doing good development work does not always require larger budgets. It requires flexibility, patience, and the ability to take risks, none of which is incentivized in the current political environment seeking quick wins.

Digging in a bit deeper into blended finance, a term defined by the OECD as the use of development finance to attract private capital towards development goals, it is apparent that this 'new' instrument is not about addressing market-level constraints, where capital is rarely the most pressing development constraint. It is about addressing donor problems in fundraising, coordination, and efficiency. Not only does this instrument help donors increase private sector engagement, it also helps them to 'sell' aid to their domestic audiences. Most importantly, blended finance helps donors spend large volumes while appearing to crowd-in capital; and doing this with few operational staff. In the financial inclusion sphere, blended finance is of course nothing new at all. Sophisticated financial structures that embed different types of actors with different risk and reward arrangements have been at the core of the MIVs and other intermediaries that have funded microfinance institutions for over 20 years.

Perhaps the most harmful impact of the changing political environment reshaping the aid business is the messianic efforts to cut operational budgets. Increasingly donors have fewer and fewer staff managing larger and larger programmes. Inevitably this leads to short-cuts in design and monitoring of programmes. It also leads to donors choosing high-volume initiatives over smaller and perhaps more meaningful interventions that can address a market constraint. There is also a trend of using large for-profit contractors who are able to absorb high-volumes and follow the direction of the donor. This trend is affecting many types of donors: multilateral agencies, bilateral agencies, and development finance institutions (DFIs). In a 2018 meeting with a team at the World Bank, it became apparent that loans to government under $500 m focused on financial sector reform, including inclusive financial systems, would not be prioritized in their Africa operations. It is no wonder then that credit lines continue to dominate in their operations, despite evidence that domestic markets have sufficient liquidity and that credit lines are not effective in changing the incentives of financial institutions.

Foundations do not have the same public-sector oversight. As such, they would at first glance appear to have the kind of resources and capacity to use a market systems approach in their grant making. Yet the evidence thus far is not promising. Many of the largest foundations supporting inclusive financial sector development are under pressure by their boards and founders to spend large sums to meet regulatory spending requirements and thus exhibit the same level of abandon as traditional donors when it comes to their market influence.

This political nature of aid begs the question: does good practice guidance even matter? For those of us who care about aid effectiveness, are we trying to influence the right actors? Perhaps our efforts should not target development institutions that can only do what they are mandated to do. Heads of these agencies will always seek ways to stay alive, irrespective of whether this is good for developing countries. Influence has to come at a much higher level; perhaps we need to influence the public who influence parliamentarians or congress, who tell aid agencies what to do. Of course, internal champions inside development agencies also matter, and work should also empower them to make change happen from within.

Anecdotal and limited evidence that the approach is effective

Part of the challenge in investing substantive resources into market systems-based approaches is that there is lack of evidence that these initiatives yield the kinds of results that demonstrate 'value for money' or where the impact can be plausibly attributed to the donor intervention. There is also an urgency for many donors to demonstrate quick results with their funding. Over the past several years, CGAP, FSD Africa and others have been working on improving measurement systems to improve metrics and processes to better define attribution. FSD Africa's work on impact-oriented measurement (FSD Africa, 2015), in which CGAP was a partner, was one of the first of these exercises to identify how monitoring tools, coupled with targeted impact research, could help to build the evidence and support a plausible impact narrative for financial sector deepening programmes that embed systems approaches. CGAP has built on this effort by developing a toolkit specifically for donors, public investors (Spaven and Broens Nielsen, 2017), and their implementing partners to effectively measure results of financial inclusion programmes that apply a systemic approach.

There are important case studies documenting country-level experience, including the review of FSD Kenya by Alan Gibson (2016). The case studies provide a plausible explanation of the role that organizations implementing the market systems approach, like FSD Kenya, have played in contributing to the development of enabling regulation, market innovation, infrastructure, and supporting institutions that deliver training and other capacity building services (see Ledgerwood, 2017 for a synthesis of the case studies). Beyond the work of in-country market facilitators, CGAP has also developed case studies that document how donors such as USAID (Nègre, 2017) and UN Capital Development Fund have used this approach in their operations.

Despite these efforts at documenting case studies, there is insufficient awareness around the effectiveness of market systems programmes. Most disturbingly, DFID, which has historically taken a leadership role in supporting a market systems approach in financial inclusion is increasingly retreating and introducing new instruments that undermine the neutrality and independence of the financial sector deepening trusts that they established to undertake market facilitation in local markets. Many bilateral agencies are now beginning to get into the business of 'returnable capital'. While lack of evidence may be one driver behind these decisions it is also driven by the need to demonstrate more direct results, nullifying the important and nuanced work that tries to measure the impact of market systems programmes. The drive for direct results leads us back to direct delivery programmes, thus a major set-back in progress.

Funders are still looking for the silver bullet

Most people recognize that we are living in an era where technological innovation is re-writing all the old ways of doing business. We are communicating differently using Twitter, WhatsApp and Facebook. We are buying differently – Amazon and Alipay. We are traveling differently – Uber and Lyft. So, it is nothing remarkable for those of us in inclusive finance to recognize and accept that technology is having profound effects on the financial services value chain. Yet despite the many examples of the failure of silver bullet thinking, we are still looking at technology as the next silver bullet.

Kentaro Toyama of the University of Michigan said it best at the CGAP annual meeting in May 2016, 'technology accentuates what already exists'. It does not fundamentally alter the DNA of the problem it aims to solve. If racism exists, technology will make it more pronounced. If women are harassed, technology will make harassment more efficient. Technology itself will not solve racism or eliminate harassment. Only people can do that. Development will never be about technology and it will always continue to be about people; even though we can use technology as a tool, of course.

The good news is that this silver bullet thinking has a predictable life span as most people will be looking for the next shiny object soon enough. But is there a way that markets systems thinking can influence this trajectory so that it minimizes the amount of harm done by such short-term mindsets? How can we speed up the learning curve for those who still believe direct delivery of products and services – this time through technology – will solve development problems?

The biggest concern is the level of damage that will be created in markets by donors who are pushing technology as the latest silver bullet. Damage is already evident, with many development institutions lured into taking funding to push agendas that are counter to market system building and getting into the business of direct delivery.

Moving forward: What more needs to happen?

Undeniably this is not an easy time for those of us working on financial services for the poor using a market systems lens. Not only have we lost one of the sharpest minds, but the headwinds from the broader aid trends and our own lack of progress on proving the effectiveness and operationalizing the approach are raising questions as to whether there is enough donor interest to keep moving forward.

There are several important priorities we need to achieve if we expect donors to continue to champion this approach. In essence, we need to make market systems thinking simple, easy, and fast. This is not how markets systems thinking is done. But it is the way of the new world we live in. It is the only way to communicate to the public. It is the only way to convince a busy philanthropist. It is the only way to get the attention of politicians. It is the only way to be heard in the here and now. So, we have to change. If we want to do market systems work, we have to make it simple, easy, and fast. That is the challenge before us. A few specific priorities stand out:

- *Demonstrate successes.* The onus is on us to document what is working and what is not. We need to push the frontiers of measurement practices so that we are using and building on the good work undertaken in the past several years to advance measurement practices. We need to bring in more people with the right skills in monitoring and evaluation and ensure that they can build on established good practices in measurement.

- *Use language that resonates with non-experts.* We need to speak in language that non-market systems people can understand. Even the term 'market systems' often generates the wrong understanding as people tend to see this as a focus on the demand and supply of the doughnut and hence only the commercial aspects of market development and assume it is only about private-sector development.
- *Make learning easier and faster.* Learning about market systems approaches is too time-consuming and still too niche to be of relevance. The approach needs to be embedded in technical content. Those working in financial services are only investing their limited spare time to learn about new trends and risks in our industry. We need to embed the market systems approach in the way to think about these new issues, not just requiring them to first learn the approach and then learn how to apply it in each and every new topic. But the approach itself is relevant for all kinds of development, not just inclusive financial systems. In the longer term, the approach should be integrated into core education and training for development professionals.
- *Support internal donor agency staff.* There are many internal champions in donor agencies that want to do development right by addressing root causes of market failures. They are working within agencies that are not structured to do market facilitation nor can they easily fund neutral, external market facilitators. Organizations like CGAP and others need to support the champions within donor agencies to simplify operational systems and instil a corporate culture that enables the use of a market systems approach. While this is a long-term goal, it is nonetheless essential as ultimately it is technical staff at donor agencies who will do the work.

I wish Alan were here to work with us to make this happen, but without him, we must be inspired by his ingenuity and figure out what he would do if he were in our place.

About the author

Mayada El-Zoghbi is Managing Director of the Centre for Financial Inclusion. Previously she led CGAP's strategy development and research on women's financial inclusion. While at CGAP, Mayada engaged Alan to support the development of new funder guidelines and to lead a strategic visioning exercise for MIX, where Mayada served as chair of the board for three years.

References

Burjorjee, D. and Scola, B. (2015) *New Funder Guidelines: Market Systems Approach to Financial Inclusion*, CGAP <https://www.cgap.org/research/publication/new-funder-guidelines-market-systems-approach-financial-inclusion> [accessed 28 January 2020].

El-Zoghbi, M., Lauer, K. and Scola, B. (2011) *Cross-Border Funding of Microfinance*, CGAP <http://www.cgap.org/research/publication/cross-border-funding-microfinance> [accessed 20 January 2020].

FSD Africa (2015) *Towards Impact-Oriented Measurement Systems for the FSD Network* [pdf] <https://beamexchange.org/uploads/filer_public/57/61/57610253-d9e1-439c-86eb-487c11c12afa/measurement-fsd.pdf> [accessed 20 January 2020].

Gibson, A. (2016) *FSD Kenya: Ten Years of a Market Systems Approach in the Kenyan Finance Market* [online], FSD Kenya <http://fsdkenya.org/publication/fsd-kenya-ten-years-of-a-market-systems-approach-in-the-kenyan-finance-market/> [accessed 20 January 2020].

Gibson, A. (2017) 'Market facilitation is the way ahead, but it needs to do more', 27 March [blog], CGAP <https://www.cgap.org/blog/market-facilitation-way-ahead-it-needs-do-more> [accessed 28 January 2020].

Ledgerwood, J. (2017) 'The art of market facilitation: learning from the financial sector deepening network' [online] <https://www.fsdafrica.org/publication/the-art-of-market-facilitation-learning-from-the-financial-sector-deepening-network/> [accessed 21 January 2020].

Nègre, A. (2017) *Market Facilitation to Advance Financial Inclusion* [online], CGAP <http://www.cgap.org/research/publication/market-facilitation-advance-financial-inclusion> [accessed 21 January 2020].

O'Planick, K. (2015) 'Shifting to market system facilitation approaches', 1 October [blog], CGAP <https://www.cgap.org/blog/shifting-market-system-facilitation-approaches> [accessed 28 January 2020].

Spaven, P. and Broens Nielsen, K. (2017) *Measuring Market Development* [online], CGAP <http://www.cgap.org/research/publication/measuring-market-development> [accessed 20 January 2020].

Tomilova, O. and Dashi, E. (2017) *Key Trends in International Funding for Financial Inclusion in 2016* [online], CGAP <http://www.cgap.org/research/publication/key-trends-international-funding-financial-inclusion-2016> [accessed 20 January 2020].

Tsuji, K. (2015) 'Do we need a financial inclusion paradigm shift?', 16 September [blog], CGAP <https://www.cgap.org/blog/do-we-need-financial-inclusion-paradigm-shift> [accessed 28 January 2020].

von Stauffenberg, D. and Rozas, D. (2011) *Role Reversal Revisited: Are Public Development Institutions Still Crowding out Private Investment in Microfinance?* [pdf], MicroRate <http://www.microrate.com/media/downloads/2012/10/MicroRate-Role-Reversal-Revisited.pdf> [accessed 20 January 2020].

World Bank (2011) 'Global Financial Inclusion (Global Findex) Database 2011' [online] <https://microdata.worldbank.org/index.php/catalog/1097/study-description> [accessed 20 January 2020].

CHAPTER 11

Just good development: Why did it take us so long to get there?

James Tomecko

Abstract

Several years ago, Rob Hitchins, Aly Miehlbradt, and I were running a small workshop on market development at a Swiss Development Corporation event in Nottwil, Switzerland organized by SDC's Income and Employment division. We were in the middle of a long-winded and complicated definition of our subject which, of course, included multiple diagrams of doughnuts, scale, sustainability, and impact, when a participant at the back of the room chirped up and said 'Isn't what you are talking about just good development?' And, indeed, it is! This chapter is about how this kind of enterprise development, since its genesis in the late 1990s, became 'good'. It touches on some of the early origins of enterprise support services and microfinance in the late 1980s and the recognition that the poor could pay market rates for loans or other key inputs, as long as these investments, however small, had clear impact and short-term returns.

Keywords: microfinance, markets, enterprise development, value chains

If there is one thing that I have learned in my five decades of working in development, it is that there is just not enough 'good development' to go around. When we consider the minimum requirements for this to happen: adequate funding, an engaged donor, a motivated and competent implementing agency, qualified and experienced personnel, a fertile and receptive local enabling environment (the list could go on), it is no small miracle when it does happen. This is not to say there have not also been some significant failures in market development, but perhaps the percentage of miracles, using the market development approach, is a bit higher. My aim in this chapter is to tell the story, from a personal perspective, of how what we now call market systems development morphed over the years to become what people simply call good development. But it was, because of the entrepreneurship, commitment, dedication, and honesty of practitioners like Alan Gibson that this happened. To underline the current value that this approach brings to the development table, it is worth looking back at what my field, enterprise promotion, was like before all of this.

http://dx.doi.org/10.3362/9781788531443.011

What was enterprise promotion like in the 1970s and 1980s?

When I first started working in development in 1970, as a regional planner in Tanzania, many of my colleagues, as well as myself, thought this venture into inter- national development would be a very short part of our careers. We would work ourselves out of a job and then find steady employment back in our own countries. Well, it did not work out that way, at least, for me!

At that time, Western economies made up by far the bulk of the global GDP and most of these countries were still experiencing a post-war boom that few thought would come to an end. Development aid was principally channelled through multilateral agencies and was directed mainly to institution building, budget support, and large physical infrastructure projects. In many developing countries there was so much aid, compared with national budgets, that donor agendas, however well meaning, simply overpowered local decision-making and priorities. Because there was more aid than absorptive and smart disbursement capacity, the penchant to conduct grand experiments with external technical assistance was rife. The grand experiment in which I personally participated, at the beginning of the decade in Tanzania was the promotion of 'Ujamaa' or villagization. The objective of villagization was to concentrate rural farmers in more economic units so that public services (water, health, education, etc.) could be delivered to them in a cost-effective manner. This ill-conceived programme was far too complex to implement for an embryonic public service and was clearly not an example of good development.

In post-independence Africa the national policy emphasis was on replacing foreign with local ownership in almost all spheres of the productive economy, and the core mantra for most international aid agencies was 'growth with equity'. In the enterprise sector these aspirations led to two complementary strategies: the creation of large, state-run corporations; and the promotion of small to mid-sized indigenously owned industries. The large corporations occupied the upper levels of industry (textiles, breweries, tobacco, and estate agriculture) while the promotion of smaller industries was meant to cater to what was called, by writers like Peter Kilby and Ian Little, the 'missing middle' (Kilby, 1971). Both of these strategies were strongly supported by virtually all development agencies.

Again, and partly because of the prevailing belief that capital transfers were the most important part of the solution to development, the incentives for both donors and recipients encouraged the promotion of large, expensive, state-run corporations. For example, multilateral institutions such as the World Bank financed a myriad of public enterprises; while bilateral donors provided the aid to complement these institutional investments. This aid consisted of either the personnel to establish these institutional systems or the equipment and technologies in sectors such as forestry, mining, manufacturing and agriculture that had once been productive but by then had become outmoded in their countries of origin. For developing countries, particularly in Africa, the concept of 'state enterprise' was a convenient answer to the scarcity of indigenous entrepreneurship while at the same time providing ample opportunity to employ an endless stream of university graduates and rural urban migrants needed by these large and growing public corporations. The evolution of this phenomenon of padding the state bureaucracy, sometimes called the 'economy of affection', is eloquently explained in Goran Hyden's book, *No Shortcuts to Development* (1983). Politically, these huge and very visible entities symbolized modernization, growth, and success.

For the promotion of the smaller indigenous enterprises the most prevalent model was the 'integrated approach'. Most pundits have attributed the origins of this approach to India where an enormous publicly funded apparatus had been set up in the 1960s to encourage the modernization of Indian industry (Staley and Morse, 1965). In brief, the model assumed that for the small or mid-sized entre- preneur to succeed a whole range of support services were needed, including: preferential access to raw materials, extension services, marketing support, technical training, infrastructure in the form of industrial estates or export processing zones, and subsidized credit, to name but a few. The replication of this approach spawned the creation in many developing economies of large, complex, state-owned enterprise promotion organizations and development finance institutions, the relics of which are often still evident today in some form or other. In the 1970s and 1980s, India was the focal point for entrepreneurship development most notably EDI in Ahmedabad; while for training in extension services and industrial estates SIET in Hyderabad was preeminent. India was also the key source for the expertise needed to establish and run these enterprise support institutions. I recall when I was working in the mid-1970s for Tanzania's Small Industries Development Organization, that if Ernst Schumacher's Indian-inspired book *Small is Beautiful*, a treatise on 'economics as if people mattered' (1973), was not prominently displayed on your bookshelf, you simply did not rate as a practitioner. Promoting small-scale production and/or intermediate technologies almost became an end in itself.

How enterprise development began to change in the 1990s

After more than a generation of multi- and bi-lateral funding for an orthodox and often formulaic approach to support these small enterprise promotion organiza- tions, there was a growing recognition that these institutions were harder to keep going and stay relevant than originally envisaged. Erratic public priorities, high turnover of staff, poor institutional memory, and limited capacity to process lessons, all contributed to disappointing results.

By the late 1980s, most of the development finance institutions, set up to fund the mid-sized 'missing middle', were on their second or third restructuring, mainly because of unsupportable loan losses. What, of course, had been ignored were the millions of microentrepreneurs at the bottom of the income pyramid. To some, however, they had not gone unnoticed and experiments in South Asia (Grameen Bank in Bangladesh), South-east Asia (BRI in Indonesia), and Latin America (Banco Sol in Bolivia) in microcredit were showing that not only could these target groups be reached at scale with institutional investment, but they could also afford to pay what eventually became known as a 'market rate' (cost plus) of interest; a price for credit that enabled microfinance institutions to become financially viable and for some, to reach scale. This was the Holy Grail of development. The late 1980s and the 1990s were the decades of microfinance.

Their business model was conceptually simple but difficult to get right: if you could efficiently lend to a large number of relatively stable and existing small businesses at high enough interest rates to provide a modest profit, you could then attract more capital, thereby reaching even greater scale. Loans were 'securitized' through instruments like peer group guarantees and loan approval processes that built on the Nobel Laureate, Joseph Stiglitz's message that a lender could substitute borrower information (credit history) for hard collateral (Haldar and Stiglitz, 2016). On closer inspection, interest costs were relatively small and affordable for these small clients, especially when compared with the costs of other inputs such as raw materials, labour, and overheads. This confirmed that *availability or access* to credit was far more important than the *price*.

This new crop of financial institutions grew by: supplying a product in demand; pricing it at market rates; and delivering it principally through non-governmental institutions that could both retain qualified and committed people and have the organizational independence to practically adapt their operations to diverse conditions.

As we move into the new millennium, markets begin to make sense

The stark contrast between these dynamic microfinance organizations and the rather conservative low-impact, state-run enterprise promotion agencies became even greater by the late 1990s. Many donors asked themselves the question, 'If microfinance organizations can sustainably deliver credit to low income enterprises, could we not aim for this to happen with other support services?' Bear in mind that the prevailing conventional wisdom up to this point had been that the poor could *not* pay market rates for loans or other inputs, and yet, here was the microfinance sector growing from strength to strength while charging market rates. Development analysts started to turn their heads from the expensive and clumsy integrated approach and began to speak more of 'minimalism' where organizations became specialized in one or two specific products rather than trying to supply a whole range of services, poorly. After all, these new microfinance organizations clearly seemed to demonstrate the validity of specialization.

Led by key members of an informal network of stakeholders, the Donor Committee for Small Enterprise Development (later to be renamed the DCED) a wholesale re-think was commissioned of how donors could achieve greater sustainability and more impact through *non-financial* enterprise programmes such as management and technical training, extension services, support for embryonic chambers and business associations, etc. Enter Alan Gibson in 1997 who, at the behest of the Donor Committee, conducted a relatively comprehensive assessment of the plethora of donor-funded projects. This was a painful exercise because in the plain light of day, virtually all of these programmes were ill-conceived, supply oriented, of short duration with limited developmental impact and for only a small fraction of the intended target groups. In effect, they were for the most part a collection of hastily contrived solutions looking for a problem, but dressed up in 'logframes' to give them respectability!

After this review, a set of themes began to emerge that were to form the embryo of guidelines later published in 2001 as the 'Blue Book'. These themes explicitly stated that projects: should be demand led and behave in a business-like manner; have an explicit approach to sustainability with a credible exit strategy; be strategic and focused rather than trying to supply everything to every enterprise; build local ownership as quickly as possible; specifically plan to reach scale; use the principle of 'subsidiarity' for determining which organization was best placed to deliver which service; and finally, place a tight focus on performance measurement. Does this start to sound like good development?

Central elements of this 'New Approach' can be seen in Figure 11.1. Note that the 'Old Approach', presented in the lower half of the figure, illustrates that donors and governments were delivering services directly to enterprises themselves. Whereas, in the 'New Approach', services go through a *facilitator* which then supports a larger number of private providers to deliver a wider range of 'demand driven' services to a large number of enterprises. The principle of *subsidiarity* was used to determine which service should be delivered by which provider and to which enterprises.

Demand driven soon became a much bigger part of the development vocabulary and donors started to ask questions like, 'if a service is actually in demand and is recognized by the small entrepreneur as a key ingredient of their success, shouldn't they also be prepared to pay at least a portion of this cost?'. Moreover, if payments by the entrepreneur are a recognition of real needs then surely payments for these services are a proxy indicator for impact. The challenge now, was for development agencies to understand 'real needs' and to create commercial awareness or demand of these needs from these enterprises. This was, however, made even harder when similar kinds of low quality services like training were still given away by public institutions for free. The effect of these 'give aways' was to suppress or, at the very least, confuse demand from the small enterprise sector. Convincing previously donor-funded public organizations in developing nations to cut back on free service delivery when their institutional status within their governments was often derived from the substantial budgets allocated to give these services away was a 'big ask'!

While this hard-hitting message, something Alan Gibson was well suited to deliver, may have rung true with many of the donors and practitioners in the

A. New approach: Facilitate market development

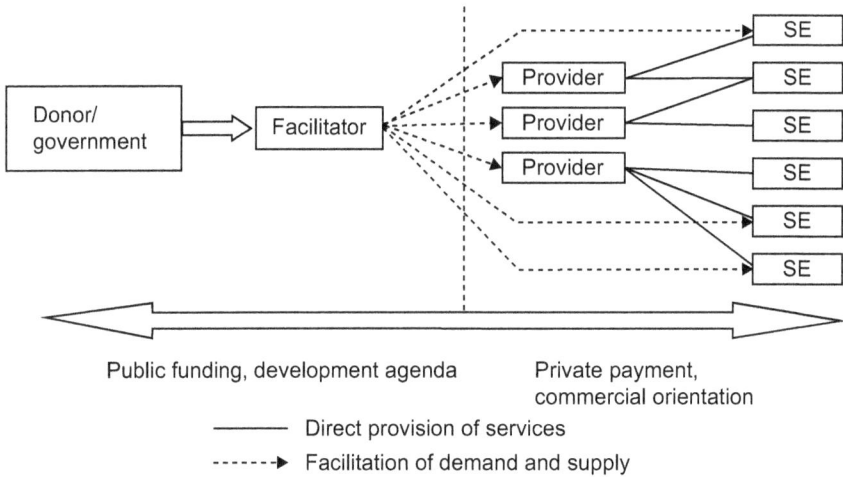

Public funding, development agenda   Private payment,
                                            commercial orientation

———— Direct provision of services
------► Facilitation of demand and supply

B. Old approach: Substitute for the market

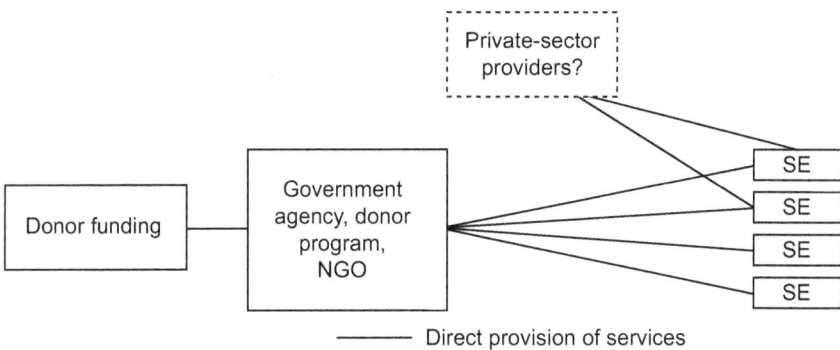

———— Direct provision of services

Figure 11.1 Actors and their roles
Source: DCED, 2001

field, the whole machinery of donors was still geared to direct delivery of sub-sidized services. It was simply easier to design these kinds of projects and tout them to host governments who could then use them to augment their own development budgets while 'doling out' sub-standard services to seemingly grateful local enterprises. Even though everyone knows the story of 'teaching a man to fish ... etc., etc.', giving away more fish just seemed to attract more interest, attention, and headlines.

So, even in the face of sound developmental guidelines many donors chose to take the path of least resistance. Keep in mind however, that these organiza-tions are not the 'monoliths' that we might imagine. The funding, design, and commissioning of many projects were actually carried out by a large number of capable and moral professionals, both in their HQs and in the field; so there was still some space for good development. Recognizing this fact, the Donor

Committee embarked on popularizing and disseminating the market development message by convening a number of conferences on several continents.

For project designers interested in following this approach, understanding
and piloting use of these services became the core elements of their project
strategies.

Pilots were initiated in various counties such as Bangladesh, Nepal with
the explicit mandate to create greater access to and use of business development services or BDS for greater numbers of economically active small
business target groups, including smallholder farmers. Initially, attention was
directed to business services already in the market and supplied to larger and
mid-sized businesses including market information, finance and taxation
advice, product design and standards, new production systems, improved
technology, and business planning. Existing or new service providers were
now sought who could adapt, scale down, or develop new, lighter and less
expensive products and services that could be commercially sold to smaller
businesses. This, however, proved harder than imagined and on closer
inspection it was found that many of these services were actually already
being 'minimalistically' delivered to small entrepreneurs and farmers within
the many transactions they had with either their suppliers or buyers. For
example, technology advice and basic technical training was available from
suppliers of new equipment or the agents that serviced their existing equipment; productivity information came from raw material input suppliers;
market information came in the form of product specifications from buyers
and these buyers often provided the minimum production standards needed
to upgrade the quality of production; and lastly, basic business planning was
often an integral part of microfinance.

These services came, in some form or other, from the existing relationships that every small business or smallholder farmer had in their key supply
chains. The term 'embedded services' was popularly introduced to describe
these value-adding services that were available, but not always optimized
within existing transactions. Here was where we could find the elusive service
providers that could be animated to improve and scale up their offer to a wide
range of small businesses and farmers. If a small enterprise owner or farmer
had a market transaction, however small, with an input supplier or a buyer,
here was the opportunity to restructure the transaction so more value could
be created for both the buyer and the seller.

The orientation in project design shifted from product/service access and
demand stimulation to 1) identifying the growth constraints of your target
group; 2) assessing whether these constraints could be addressed by new information, services, and inputs, etc; 3) finding market actors who could sustainably provide these bits of information or services; and 4) constructing a project
initiative to support these market actors to scale up delivery of these services/
inputs to an increasing number of the target group in a commercially sustainable way. These types of projects were slower to get off the ground but had
the potential to have more sustained impact over time. They were frequently

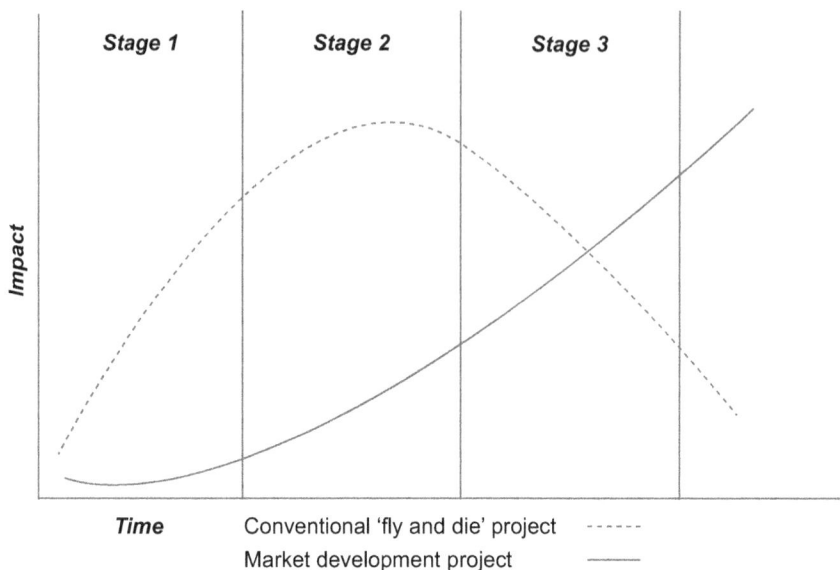

Figure 11.2 Project impact over time

contrasted with the 'fly and die' projects that generated direct impact for a short while but stopped when the funding ended as depicted in Figure 11.2.

Over time, and with increasing emphasis by donors on reaching greater numbers and on poverty alleviation, attention began to shift from an exclusive focus on small enterprise to include small farmers and agricultural value chains where the number of beneficiaries is large and poverty is great.

Value chains and market development

People often assume that market systems development projects and value chain development projects are the same thing, and indeed one does often find value chains in market systems development projects. But the term 'value chain' was originally made popular by the American competitiveness guru Michael Porter, in 1985, to describe the complex process through which a firm adds value to its products or services (see Figure 11.3).

In the international development community however, the term is more or less synonymous with a sub-sector, for example, furniture, where small furniture manufacturers are intricately connected with a whole host of upstream suppliers (wood, metal, equipment, finance, etc.) and with downstream buyers (wholesalers, retailers, and direct consumers). The aim is typically to focus on that part of the value chain which is likely to have the greatest potential impact on poverty reduction.

Value chain analysis is frequently used by development practitioners to assess the overall competitiveness of a value chain and to break it down into

Primary activities:

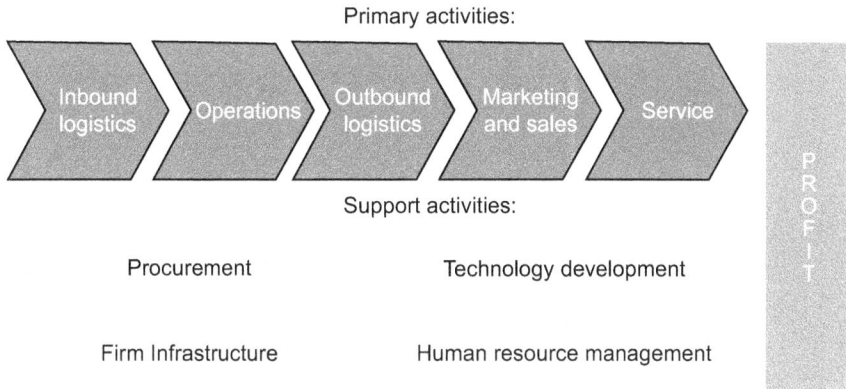

Support activities:

Procurement   Technology development

Firm Infrastructure   Human resource management

Figure 11.3 Porter's value chain model

its constituent parts to see where improvements can be made. A key part of the diagnosis is based on benchmarking the productivity in these constituent parts with other international or national competitors. While value chain analysis may identify core competitiveness issues and is often part of the *analysis* when designing a market systems development intervention, the important addition of market systems development is in the identification of sustainable and potentially system-changing *solutions* that leaves the value chain more productive and enriched.

The competitiveness of the Thai palm oil sector may, for example, be constrained by the scarcity of feed stock (oil palm fruit) for its mills, forcing them to operate inefficiently. While a value chain project may work directly on feed stock supply constraints, the market solution may involve working with palm oil crushing mills to deliver a variety of low-cost services to small farmers, the impact of which is to increase their productivity to meet the unfulfilled demand for fresh oil palm fruit (see Figure 11.4). In summary and perhaps to oversimplify, value chain analysis is used to identify problems and in some cases, provide short-term solutions directly, while the market systems approach is employed to supply sustainable solutions over the mid and even long term.

Results measurement

Partly out of the necessity to prove to practitioners, donors, and governments that something was actually happening in market systems development, early market development project managers, in the first decade of the millennium, put a lot of emphasis on measurement. The dominant tool for designing and measuring most market systems development projects, as for most donor-financed projects, was the logframe with its four well-defined levels of goal, purpose, outputs, and activities. In the hands of a good designer, the logframe is a useful tool to conceptualize and explain a project to funding agencies, but during implementation there were frequently big gaps between the core

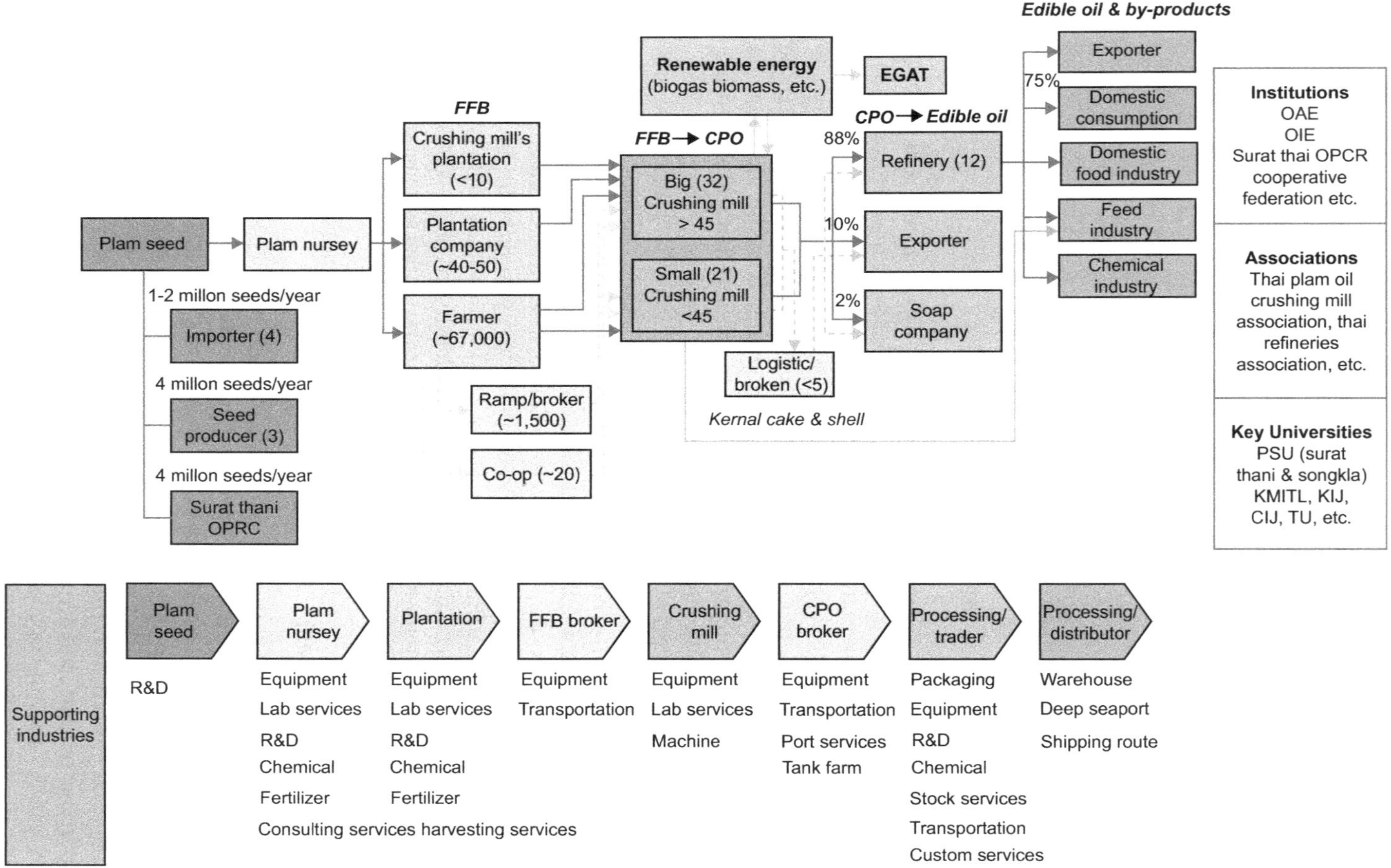

Figure 11.4 Thai palm oil sector map

project logic and what actually happened on the ground. This lack of clarity contributed to 'mission drift' during implementation and then eventually, when a request was formulated for a monitoring and evaluation specialist to fix this, it was often far too late to reorient project implementation.

While the logframe and its variations was a particularly useful discipline for working through a project's logic, formulating its indicators of success and critical assumptions, it was best suited to project situations that were broadly predictable. It worked well for institution-building projects in which there was a single institution, a range of fixed problems, and a predetermined set of activities to address these problems. This was, however, not the situation confronted by most market systems development projects, which frequently had multiple partners with different problems, several target groups each with different needs, different geographic conditions, etc. This produced a lot of uncertainty with the high probability that some project activity might yield no impact whatsoever. This meant that even though project design could define the overall targets in terms of outreach and impact, implementers needed the flexibility to find multiple solutions during implementation and not only at the project's start; a very uncomfortable situation for most donors and one that needed a leap of faith in what was, until that point, a very untested approach.

The practical answer to this was the emergence of the 'intervention'. An intervention could fit into a logframe but its attribution to impact was more clearly defined. An intervention consists of:

- a target group described by its location, income, sub-sector, size, gender etc.;
- a set of target group constraints and a set of probable pathways to improvements;
- strategies for how these improvements/changes can be accomplished;
- identified intermediaries that have the incentives to address these changes sustainably;
- an initial 'offer' to these intermediaries to enhance their delivery speed, scale, and efficiency of the changes;
- pilot activities enabling measurability of the change process so that modifications can be quickly made before deciding to abandon or adapt it;
- the eventual use of this experience to achieve scale through systemic change.

In a project context, interventions could be clustered by target group, geography, sector, solution typology, or even partner. Because interventions take place in real time and theoretically respond to market opportunities they often cannot be determined when the overall project is being designed. Based on past experience, estimates can be made of the anticipated number and type of interventions in a project. Depending on the budget and duration, a mid-sized market systems development project may have, for example, 20–50 interventions over a five-year phase. Larger projects such as AIP-Rural in Indonesia or Katalyst in Bangladesh, while still having logframes, have had hundreds of interventions in 15 to 20 sub-sectors or value chains. Like many venture capital initiatives, between 25 and 35 per cent of these are likely to fail, another 35 to 40 per cent will represent good value for money, while the rest should make up a project's flagship interventions.

Within the framework of the intervention, specific and tailor-made causal models or *results chains* could then be constructed to work out in greater detail what changes are desired, what changes can be attributed to which actions, and how the changes and their effects can be measured. This means that large, broad, and sometimes unfocused baselines at the start of projects are avoided, giving way to conducting many smaller and more precise and cost-effective baselines for each intervention; baselines which are then carried out as and when it is clear that some change is likely to have happened. Without the results chain and a standard for measuring results, the claims of most market systems projects would seem hollow. But without a 'measurement standard' to compare interven- tions, discussions on an intervention's 'value for money' were baseless.

The idea of developing such a measurement standard was mooted when a group of practitioners met at an ILO conference on 'Developing Service Markets and Value Chains' in Chiang Mai, Thailand in 2007. The argument was that without a commonly accepted standard for practitioners to use in measuring impact it was impossible to estimate what worked and what did not, not to mention creating value for money. To provide 'teeth' to the stan- dard, independent auditors would be certified to assess and score whether a project was or was not using credible method- ologies for measuring its impact.

The introduction of: 1) the *intervention* as the main building block of the project; 2) the use of *results chains* to help think through project attribution to impact; and 3) a workable *standard* for measuring this impact, when taken together represented a breakthrough not only in project design but also in project measurement. Up to that point most projects claimed there was a the-oretical 'attribution gap' between their outputs and outcomes, a gap for which they were *not* responsible. Accountability for impact could be sidestepped by implementers as long as they delivered all of their outputs on time and to the specification of the funder. In these cases if no impact occurred it was the fault of the designer and not the implementer; a rather static construct with little room for adaptation during implementation. Now, with tighter interventions and results chains to provide parameters for more accountability for impact during project implementation and a results measurement standard that could deal with credible indicators and attribution to outcomes, the orientation to 'predetermined' outputs became irrelevant; each intervention became a slice of the overall project's theory of change, from activity to impact; a project's impact was simply an aggregation of intervention results.

This standardized system of results measurement also meant that each new project did not need to reinvent the wheel in developing their monitoring and evaluation system, since the nuts and bolts of this were well-defined in the standard and simply needed to be adapted to the nature of the project. Through a coalition of willing donors, project managers, highly qualified consultants, and the DCED, the contents of the standard were field tested between 2008 and 2010 in four projects (Thailand, Kyrgyzstan, Bangladesh, and Cambodia.) These results were eventually published as an early version of the *DCED Standard for Results Measurement*.

Nowadays there are not many market development projects that do not use this standard in some form or other. Providing the standard is well implemented in a project, it provides project managers with up-to-date information to feed into their portfolio reviews so they can allocate and reallocate project resources on a regular basis to maximize value for money. Funders, moreover, are provided with credible impact numbers that can be used as inputs to compare their portfolios across countries and sectors.

Conclusion

While others in this book will no doubt present more up-to-date accounts of market systems development projects and their impacts I think we can safely say in 2021 that, since its genesis in the late 1990s, the market systems development approach has been successful even if we only take the number and size of projects as an indicator. Early protagonists like Alan Gibson stimulated a major re-think in project delivery and sustainability; they opened the door for new ways of designing and measuring projects with applicability to a wide range of low-income target groups in a wider range of economic sectors such as finance, health, social protection, and education. In my view the key reasons for this success are outlined below.

A strong network of experienced professionals

This network emerged from the active training and use of experienced professionals from different disciplines (enterprise development, results measurement, agriculture, inclusive finance, value chain development, poverty alleviation) supported by the long-term institutional infrastructure of organizations such as the Springfield Centre for capacity building, and the DCED/ BEAM platform for knowledge management. External observers that sometimes participate in market development events often comment on the *unique quality* of professionalism and camaraderie evident on these occasions.

The Springfield Centre's semi-annual training events have continuously refreshed this pool of expertise with a blend of energy and experience while moving forward and continuously adapting training modules based on research and lessons from the field. For those that, for some reason, cannot make it to a Springfield event, the donor community has supported a high-quality repository of papers, studies, and reports (DCED/BEAM) that document both theory and practice in the application of the market systems development approach over the last two decades. If the currency for networks is ideas and if the growth of a network is measured in the volume of transactions related to these ideas, then the market systems development network is doing very well; there are over 170,000 page-views per annum (most of which are for the results measurement standard).

A principled conviction to good development

The conviction that good development provides sustainable and cost-effective impact for the poor at scale was frequently confronted with demands for 'taking the easier path' or for following a more commercially acceptable alternative. This confrontation inspired the evolution of: 1) strong theoretical frameworks, adapted over the years, to explain why and how markets can work for the poor; 2) the development and publication of many practical guidelines for dealing with partners, measuring systemic change, building HR capacity, and fine tuning the information systems needed to analyse results; and 3) a readiness to abandon approaches and terminologies that are not consistent with these core principles.

Optimizing a few key flagship projects

A few key flagship projects (such as the ones mentioned above) were optimized in the early years of the evolution of market systems development. These projects had the funds and opportunities to experiment and apply critical thinking and acted like magnets for some of the best minds in market systems development to further enhance the approach; they are the 'lighthouses' pointing the way. Katalyst was one of the first of these projects; it helped to define impact, tested some of the first methods of measuring direct and indirect outreach, provided the donor community with credibility for the approach, and ultimately incubated a new generation of competent practitioners that have made significant contributions to market development projects all over the world.

Another example is the large-scale AIP-Rural project in Indonesia, now in its second five-year phase. This project has routinized high-quality counterfactual impact assessments (6–10 a month) on its interventions with short feedback loops to improve outreach and impact; crafted a monitoring and results measurement system that continuously measures a wide range of value for money indicators; developed inclusiveness and gender strategies that are more consistent with a market approach and with greater appeal to partners; published many detailed 'how to' notes on issues such as measuring behaviour change in partners; and created guidelines on deal-making and partnerships, personnel strategies on recruitment, retention, and staff capacity building.

Projects like these are crucibles for innovation and excellence and generate even greater expectations to deliver results within budgets and to contribute to the development of solutions that have implications for other projects. It takes years to embed this concept in the institutional memory of the development communities (foreign and local); for this reason, large, long-term, and success-ful projects can create their own inertia and attract the attention of public and private agencies to think about the usefulness of the approach in other sectors such as rural development, social protection, health, and education.

Future challenges of applying the market development approach to enterprise promotion

A more proactive role for governments

While it is well recognized that there are functions within the market sys-tem that are indeed the role of government, the task for the government, beyond creating a conducive enabling environment to facilitate private sector engagement is still 'ill defined' and requires a level of nuanced understanding difficult to reach in most countries.

A more sophisticated engagement of the private sector in development

At various times and at various events, the private sector has stepped up to the development plate, but without direct donor support its success stories are still few and far between. Participation at conferences on responsible/inclusive business or corporate social responsibility (CSR) can easily lead one to the conclusion that many global players are still 'greenwashing' dubious practices with CSR band-aids and glossy presentations that all too easily garner praise from bodies like the World Economic Forum and major donors. While the rise of private philanthropy is welcome and the emergence of large-scale foun-dations such as those of Gates, Soros and some of the smaller actors such as Sainsbury and Mastercard provide a good foil for the more traditional public sector, just because a programme is supported by the private sector does not necessarily make what they do good development. We all too frequently see the same mistakes made over and over again by these new donors; simply changing the source of funding from public to private is not the solution.

The private sector has more than 'efficiency' to offer; it has scale and sustainability built into its delivery model. The challenge is how to persuade this sector that achieving impact is completely compatible, in many instances, with its bottom line and that whatever funds it has for its CSR budget (typi-cally an add-on to its public relations effort) should be directed to piloting how development impact can be incorporated into its core business model. This is after all the essence of market systems development. While some of these actors may already be motivated, for a wide variety of reasons, to do so, public support and finance to recycle the lessons of market systems develop-ment will be an essential part of this success.

In this chapter I have tried to illustrate the evolution of thinking and practice of enterprise promotion and how it spearheaded the reshaping of many fields in international development. Through thoughtful project design, rigorous delivery systems that measure impact and value for money, and the cross-fertilization of the lessons of many initiatives in many countries, all of which were facilitated by 'thought leaders' like Alan Gibson, the balance of projects exhibiting 'good development' has been tilted to the more positive side of the scale.

About the author

James Tomecko is semi-retired after a career of 48 years in Africa, Asia, and Europe in the areas of micro and SME finance, entrepreneurship, enterprise policy/strategy formulation, value chains, and market systems development. He first met Alan Gibson in 1994 when Alan was working with one of Jim's favourite experts in this field, Allan Gibb at the Durham University Business School.

References

DCED (Donor Committee for Enterprise Development) (2001) *Business Development Services: Guiding Principles for Donor Intervention in Business Development Services* [online] <https://www.enterprise-development.org/dced-guidance/business-development-services-dced-guiding-principles> [accessed 21 January 2020].

Haldar, A. and Stiglitz, J. (2016) 'Group lending, joint liability and social capital: insights from the Indian microfinance crisis', *Politics and Society* 44(4): 459–97 <https://doi.org/10.1177%2F0032329216674001>.

Hyden, G. (1983) *No Shortcuts to Progress: African Development Management in Perspective*, Los Angeles: University of California Press.

Kilby, P. (1971) 'Hunting the Heffalump', *Entrepreneurship and Economic Development* 1–40.

Porter, M. (1985) *Competitive Advantage: Creating and Sustaining Superior Performance*, New York: Simon & Schuster.

Schumacher, E. (1973) *Small Is Beautiful*, London: Blond and Briggs.

Staley, E. and Morse, R. (1965) *Modern Small Industry for Developing Countries*, New York: McGraw-Hill.

CHAPTER 12

Shame on you! A soteriology of making markets work for the poor

Julian Hamilton-Peach

Abstract

This short story tells how to effect long-lasting and large-scale economic change. It is a tale of worry and struggle, of continuously seeking and checking that the way ahead is good and that the market is responding to our work. Ultimately, it is a tale of success. This is the story of the changing fortunes of a DFID-funded programme in Nigeria from 2008 to 2012, known as PrOpCom. It is also a record of the influence Alan Gibson had on the author.

Keywords: M4P, economics, perseverance, humour, poverty, MSD, market systems, Nigeria, Africa, agriculture, inclusive business

Introduction

This short story tells how to effect long-lasting and large-scale economic change. It is a tale of worry and struggle, of continuously seeking and checking that the way ahead is right and that the market is responding well. While we may encounter good fortune along the way, the main reason we succeed is because of our nagging doubts, which stimulate resurgent bouts of enquiry, analysis, and high-stakes strategy.

This is the story of the changing fortunes of a DFID-funded programme in Nigeria from 2008 to 2012 known as PrOpCom (Pro-poor Opportunities for Commodity and Service Markets), or as people would say at traffic hold-ups on seeing the programme sticker attached to the side of the vehicle, 'Hey, Popcorn! How de dey?!' I quite liked the moniker 'Popcorn' as it gave the impression of 'from little comes much'; a simple almost magical transformation process from hard kernels to sweet-smelling, fluffed balls, and the change is irreversible. If only market systems development, or making markets work for the poor (M4P), was as easy as making popcorn.

In the beginning, before M4P

The programme started with good intentions and the excellent backing of one of the world's largest development consulting firms. Though the circumstances were difficult, there was a strong commitment to do well. What do I

http://dx.doi.org/10.3362/9781788531443.012

mean by difficult circumstances? Nigerian businesses seek short-term, large profits – by any means possible. They do this because tomorrow may never come, and because if others can, why can't I? The outlook is 'end-of-month' and, at best, about getting a larger slice of the existing pie. Meanwhile, donors, keen to see results and anxious about failure, often provide far more funding than is needed to stimulate a change process; and they want results quickly and an exit after a few years. As a result, economic development programmes are suckers for businesses that take a grant; aid equals grants to most businesses. Government presents its own problems. Another difficulty as Adam Smith told us, markets require good governance if they are to be healthy. The record of Nigerian governments at the state and federal level is to tax business, to patronize it for political ends, but to do little to provide incentives for efficiency or growth. So, programmes trying to improve the way a market works are definitely inconsistent.

In the beginning, based on years of experience, the implementing contractor analysed value chains identifying what worked well and where the problems were. In one instance, a lot of effort was made to understand the rice market in the south-western states of Nigeria. Large meetings were held on an annual basis with stakeholders in the value chain – almost like large assemblies with rice marketers, millers, traders, leaders of organizations that claimed to represent farmers' interests, state government officials, agronomic researchers – the whole caboodle. As understanding of the value chain grew, the programme found itself only slightly closer to achieving large-scale, systemic change. This was partly because a farmer organization manoeuvred the programme to focus on their relatively small volume, niche rice variety. It was also caused by the inevitable lack of consensus on what to do first. Everybody wanted their problem solved first: millers wanted the programme to teach farmers to grow rice properly and to supply clean paddy to the mill at reasonable prices; traders wanted credit with which to buy paddy from farmers; farmers wanted credit with which to buy inputs and they wanted government to arrange irrigation so they could farm in the dry season too. This led the programme to lots of stakeholder meetings to discuss what should happen in the market system. This was slowing the programme down and not adding much new knowledge or force for change. Further, it was alienating the businesses who saw the programme as an aid initiative that was pandering to government and being naively caught by local vested interests.

With such intense work happening in several markets, the programme was advancing on the analysis front but was not leveraging business change based on incentives. The default response became a grant to pilot an initiative. With delays due to agricultural seasons, progress was slow. By the time of the mid-term review in 2008, despite considerable and professional endeavours in very difficult circumstances, the programme had not achieved all that DFID had hoped. A change was required and DFID and the contractor were keen to bring it about. The Springfield Centre was called in to suggest a way forward. It recommended a more thorough application of the strategic framework that is central to the M4P approach, and to use the knowledge gained from value chain analysis to catalyse lasting change based on incentives. The implementing contractor also decided to refresh the programme leadership and picked me for the job.

Before turning up for work in Abuja, it was suggested I attend the highly celebrated Springfield M4P training fortnight in Glasgow. So, off I went to the dark city where many kirks have been re-tooled as bistro pubs; and that is where I first met Alan. He was my tutor for the core part of the course. I was interested, but with him at the front it became interesting. He took us on a tour of provocative wonder, to places we had worked in and things we had done that we thought nobody else knew about since we had locked them in a dark cupboard. I well remember his aporetic 'Really?', in response to an assertion, delivered long and slow with a sideways grin, cocked head and sense of 'are you sure, Jimmy?' joking menace. I turned up early for class and stayed late. Alan never held back from my eager-beaver questions. The essence of his message was that there is a doctrine and a faith, both of which must be thoroughly, deeply understood, but progress can only come from boldness, bravery, struggle, curiosity, anxiety, and worry.

Over those two weeks, I moved my understanding from the advanced boundaries of the sustainable livelihoods approach in the company of Dorward et al. (2003) in their critique of that approach for not fully considering markets, into the new, green foothills of M4P. So charged, like a can of Irn-Bru, I left for Abuja to boost the fortunes of PrOpCom.

Deliverance through M4P

This is not the place to recount the details, but rather the main points of what we all did to make the programme work better. We put M4P doctrine to work in the faith it would work.

Kultur

It has been said that Nigeria's biggest problem is that there are too many entrepreneurs: short-term, high margin, low investment types. This is true, and I met lots of them. Another aspect of Nigeria is the dominance of government. When considering solutions 'government should do dis or dat' is the usual refrain; rarely is it about 'business should', for business and government are mainly in the game of ripping each other off. Coming to understand Nigerian business cultures – and there are many, many widely varying cultures – getting to know the key characters and their interconnections, and working out which ones were potential allies or villains in the struggle to change the way a particular market works was key. It frequently felt like 'crossing the river by feeling the stones' as Deng Xiaoping described managing the economy. We had little idea how wide or deep the river was and it was night-time. All of us in the programme pooled our knowledge, networks, gossip, and experience.

Homework

Living and breathing questions and worries about market failures leads to understanding what might be and how to get there. Alan had encouraged me to be absorbed by the work by saying, 'Well Julian, you'll just have to see'. Immersing myself in culture by joining a choir helped me to relate and better understand how business worked or didn't and what our role might be. I was seen to do other things as well: lots of walking around markets scratching my head, standing and staring and asking folk questions in order to understand. Over time, more of the team were doing the same. We spent a lot of time trying to figure things out in the market. It became normal to say 'I don't know' to each other. And that's how we came to know.

Shock therapy

A lot of time during the first half of the programme had been spent understanding the market, writing and re-writing problem trees. Using this strong foundation, I pushed the team out to meet businesspeople, farmers, politicians – anybody of influence, ideas, and networks. We all worked hard on the road, and we started to have business and market knowledge at our finger tips. We knew more about what motivated the status quo and what might change it. An important step in this process was inviting a team of market systems old hands from Bangladesh. For two weeks, we all toured the country, debating and arguing, postulating and predicting. It became shockingly clear that the visitors were better than we were at understanding our home turf. And this was because they had been groomed by Alan many years before: worry, probe, analyse, ask and ask again, are you sure, what are the numbers, opinions, facts? This tour helped wake up the team to the reality that unless they knew the markets by being in the markets, all their efforts to portray the markets in conceptual terms and in visual constructs like problem trees were for naught. We needed to know the prevailing prices, the terms for raw and processed materials, the distributors and the routes they used, the amount of roadside 'tax' charged by police, margins along the value chain for every step, and the scams with government that were attracting entrepreneurs like magnets while preventing innovation.

Aids to thinking

Understanding value chains as a flow of goods, services, and money is very helpful, but not sufficient to determine what to do. We were keen to use M4P to help us get results. One analytical framework often used in M4P is to ask who does an activity and who pays for it: 'who does/who pays?' It is a simple, powerful way of understanding what is going on and whether there is a mismatch that undermines sustainability. It can be used to posit future scenarios to see if changes might be made to create a market founded on sustainable relationships: that is, effort is rewarded, and benefits paid for. For example, a programme may consider piloting with a business to advise smallholder farmers about a new product the business is selling. If the programme pays those providing the advice in order to get the pilot going, then there is a problem with sustainability and scale. If the programme is paying the business to advise farmers, how is this going to be scaled? The obvious conclusion is that the programme should help the business to realize the advantage it will gain: sales revenue from a new market, market information about customer preferences and willingness to try a new product, the knowledge about costs of advising customers in different ways. The profitability analysis can be made with different assumptions on sales volumes to determine potential profits. Yes, the conclusion may be that some form of subsidy or other assistance is required from the programme to get the business to pilot, but the nature and extent of that support will be considerably changed, and the chances of enduring success enhanced by the analysis.

Just do it!

An important part of working out an intervention strategy is identifying potential partners. If we could not find a partner that was willing to innovate or invest and was merely waiting for a cash handout from us, then we moved on, seeking a real partner. This became a continual activity and as a result we got to know more about the market, and the relative share each business had. This occasionally led us to find the underdog business looking to usurp the incumbent. Or the wannabe top branch manager who wanted to shine bright from within a murky, vast national bank. These partners were the champions of change and benefited for it. They also tilted the table causing other businesses to change or lose out.

Many pots on the fire

The convention of PrOpCom had been to identify a large market, say, rice, and then do something to resolve the many blockages in the value chain. All perfectly reasonable and normal in most circumstances aided by good engagement with stakeholders. But, in Nigeria, where finding a motivated business partner was difficult, government was a menace to free enterprise, and the risks of failure were high, I could not maintain this convention. We needed a broader, more opportunistic programme strategy which recognized that some of our activities would fail, and some succeed. I developed a portfolio of interventions balanced to meet the interests of the funder, and each in its own way touching certain points of success: quick but small impact, large but slow, women-centred and so on. The portfolio was flexibly managed. I moved resources as opportunities or obstacles arose. Each intervention had to prove itself or get closed or iced. While we were close to our work, no intervention was so precious that it had a reserved spot in the portfolio: interventions had to be working to continue. In formal reports to the funder, the portfolio was described and justified; as it matured, the prospects of impact were considered and estimated and aggregated. But, I also kept a part of the portfolio 'off balance sheet'. It was here that we did some of our best work, developing ideas, exploring relationships with more willing politicians or powerful businesspeople, gaining confidence eventually to bring some items onto the balance sheet to be shown more formally. Alan had encouraged me to take risks but to be clever with the donor, not to show or tell everything about our work.

Help!

I had been asked to attend an M4P training event run by the Springfield Centre in Nairobi. Alan was there and in a quiet moment I presented him with a problem I had encountered, a boring managerial problem for which I sought a clean, professional, orthodox solution from the Durham temple of M4P. When does an intervention that encompasses many aspects of a market system get so complicated and large that it should be split into two interventions? He was quick and short in his reply. 'Well, that would be a managerial decision, Julian.' I was not expecting his reply. What Alan was reminding me was that it was up to me to figure out the organization and that there were really no hard and fast rules with M4P. The organization was ours to create. And so we did. It was this wily, entrepreneurial approach that Alan encouraged in me.

Strategy safari

When professionals describe a value chain or an economic sector, they do so in either sweeping general statements that attempt to summarize the complexity built up over history, or speak at length giving the details elicited from close research. To either of these forms of rendition, Alan would patiently listen, leaning to one side, looking at you, saying, 'Uh-huh, uh-huh'. You knew that it was building up to the, 'and what are you going to do?' denouement that you feared, because it was then that his focus on the basis of your strategy would be unleashed. He emphasized that strategy was a choice: you chose not to do as much as to do, and he wanted to know the basis for that choice. You prayed it was rational, based on evidence that you could assemble and present and that the deductions were sound. For if they were not, you would hear the beginnings of his judgement with a drawn-out, 'Well ...'.

We turned PrOpCom from a programme that understood value chains to one that put M4P into action. We put the foundation of knowledge into a strategy for changing the market system. How was this market going to grow, how might poor people be part of that, and what role might we play as facilitators? We took risks to present a vision for the future to businesses or politicians, looking to excite them into action.

Building skills and attitudes

A programme is delivered by a team of people. It was clear that some people were looking to collect a wage, while others were motivated to improve their skills and contribute to building a better Nigeria. My job became moving the first lot towards the second, and deciding who should leave. I positioned my desk facing the route to the front door of the office, and close to the entrance to the kitchen. I was at work early and often the last to leave. It soon became clear who was last in/first out, taking longest tea breaks and out of the office in town for unexplained reasons. If I had been out of the office travelling all week, on my return I would greet such people and enthusiastically ask 'What have you achieved this week?' And if the response was waffle and process, I would make it clear that I expected more. They would have to send me their plan for the following week and find me joining them in their meetings. Some sensed that PrOpCom was no place to coast and chose to leave. Some rose to the occasion and have gone on to achieve great things for their country and move into international consulting. I recall one occasion when I invited a colleague for a walk. He was failing to get partners to seize the opportunity we perceived in the market. What irked me was that he did not seem upset by the lack of progress and remained loyal to his market analysis that showed there was a demand from farmers and a profit to be made by importing and selling rice threshers either directly to farmers or to entrepreneurs who could offer the threshing service to farmers. During the walk, I said I understood that he would like to resign and go into the machinery import business as clearly it was so profitable. Shocked, he admitted that he was at a loss as to why the intervention was not progressing as envisaged and suggested two very plausible reasons that he had not previously mentioned: the short season of business, and an existing traditional system of manual threshing by chronically impoverished people arranged through religious institutions as a means of social care by farmers. OK, now we were getting at the truth.

It was clear that having an MBA was not sufficient for success as an intervention manager. It also required interpersonal and political economy skills. I hired new people with knowledge from the regions, with networks of business titans and politicians, and where I could, kept them at work in their regions rather than bringing them into the Abuja office. This strengthened the programme's ability to understand the market and to engage with people of influence. That was a key advantage that soon paid off.

To help find the right new people to join the programme, I borrowed a competency framework from Engineers without Borders in Zambia, adding a category of skills on political economy. This framework covering communicator, relationship builder, entrepreneur, coach, innovator, and political economist, resting on a foundation of core attitudes and capacities such as determination, curiosity, data analysis, and self-awareness, helped us to assess candidates and more clearly communicate what we wanted in terms of performance. I also introduced a simple test for creativity as part of our recruitment.

I was determined not to hire anyone who failed that part of the recruitment process; what we needed most of all was ideas and the passion to help others reach greater heights. We needed to lose Excel and get out the painting easels, music scores, and dancing shoes. And so we did.

Stand and pause together

Another initiative on managing people and teams was the introduction of after-action reviews. This method, used by the US Marines Corps, was designed to be done immediately after action by those involved, standing on the ground they had gained or lost, talking to each other. The questions are simple: what did we intend to achieve, what happened, what's the difference, and what can we learn? I asked one person in each team to consult with colleagues and write their after-action review before the end of work on Friday. It was sent to their team colleagues and to me. It was a stimulus to honesty and accountability and I hoped it sowed the seeds for some reflection over the weekend of what could be achieved in the coming week. Every quarter or thereabouts, we gathered in Abuja for a review. Intervention managers had their moment to stand in front of their peers and explain their strategy and progress and to ask for help. Over time, this review format became a mainstay of establishing intellectual honesty within the programme. I made sure there was no grandstanding or modesty. Discussion allowed wider options and consideration of new approaches. We soon became more used to the question, 'how else could this be done?' It was also a safe environment to practise the elevator pitches that were so essential in getting the attention of influential people in business or government.

Fortune favours the bold

We had tried to influence the main incumbents in the fertilizer market and failed badly. However, there was hope. A new company was being established that would manufacture urea and blend other products. To gain a better understanding and to show some commitment, we had an opportunity to shape how this company viewed the market but it would require an initial visit to their office. The only problem was that their office was in the Delta region which was in the midst of significant civil unrest with large-scale suppression from the Joint Task Force. Time to be brave and take a chance. To boost our chances of showing we had some ideas; we invited the founder of the inputs promotion NGO in Kenya to meet us at the main airport in the Delta. We did not tell him about the high levels of insecurity. I had heard that the company had a reputation for hiring bright, sharp, young businesspeople. So, I pulled my faithful, blue, indestructible polyester jacket from the cupboard and headed south. After a hectic chase from the airport in an armoured, escorted convoy, which involved occasionally clipping the edges of other vehicles to get them out the way, and at one point looking back to see an armoured personnel carrier with some sort of big gun on top right behind us, we arrived at the walled residential compound adjacent to the fertilizer plant. Pleasantries were exchanged over dinner and we got ready for the following day's tour of the plant and business meetings. Why was this necessary? If we were to influence these people, we needed to earn their respect by bravely visiting them when nobody else would, and we needed to check out whether there was any substance to the rumours that this company had big ambitions to overturn the fertilizer sector. The meetings led to an agreement to pilot demos to farmers in the north of the country, which quickly led to a commitment from the chief marketing officer to a sales target of 10 per cent of total sales to be small packs. Alan would have been proud of us. He had told us the facilitator's role involved risk and bravery. We had to step out and call for change. And that's what we did.

Get lucky

There were definitely times when we got lucky, and milked it. And why not, we were desperate! Someone sent me the CV of an excellent results measurement specialist and asked me to forward it to another project that had asked for help. I read the CV and realized I had just got lucky. An ex-Katalyst results measurement specialist who had been at school in Nigeria and wanted to return? This mail was not going to be forwarded! Or how about the day a colleague met an old friend now working for a new, striving major agribusiness. Bingo! One breakfast meeting later, we were in with a chance of a new partner that was reaching out to smallholders with vast amounts of ambition and cash. Or, my favourite example: I had been asked to meet a major businessman in the north to discuss an offer he had received from government to open a string of one-stop-shops for farmers. I did not know much about the businessman, what his family had done, or what he did now. We met in his office, which appeared to have a travel agency in the front part. We got lucky because the previous meeting over-ran, which meant we were stuck waiting in reception, and, as usual, I roamed around to see what this place was about. I discovered a wall display of vintage cigarette packets. I asked my colleague and was told that the businessman was the latest in a long line of self-made entrepreneurs with strong links to the UK, and that his father had been an importer of cigarettes. It was a proud history. So what was he doing taking free milk from government, I thought. And did he not realize that he would never get paid? In the meeting, I started nice, but took a chance. I felt lucky and tore into him, shaming him for denying the legacy that he had inherited. He pushed back his chair, tilted his cap, and asked me, 'So, what should I do?' Now we had someone with whom we could work!

Whiteboards can be useful

M4P appears at first, and in some sorry circumstances even forever, to be all about analysis, writing on whiteboards in rooms over-filled with sagging chairs, sparring in a jargoned foreign language, with colleagues about root causes or parts of a doughnut. This leads to strategic frameworks, theories of change, and eventually to a giant multi-tabbed Excel workbook called an intervention guide. This is deadly boring stuff. Even those who naturally speak reductive reasoning start to grow weary. The first few years of PrOpCom trying to uncover the mysteries and complexities of agri-Nigeria had been a little too faithful to analysis, and had left us with lots of theories but not a lot of certainty of where to go next, what to do. I determined that we would start to learn by doing. I introduced a short, sharp concept note system forcing those with ideas to be clearer. Those that made the grade were backed with small amounts of money to gain short-term answers. I backed the concepts in person, visiting the markets, businesses and farmers to show I was interested as well as invested. Progress helped us tell stories about what we did which built confidence in our business partners and funder. But most important of all, and to our great surprise, it drove us eagerly back to the whiteboard to work out our ideas better, with more urgency and greater intellectual honesty. Absurd analysis and sparring were out; reality was in. And, amazingly, we even accepted the yoke of the intervention guide, that painful account of what we intend to help bring about and the record of whether we did.

Get out of here

All the programme staff were in an old house parked on a bend of Mississippi Street in Abuja. While this enabled us to interact and share information with each other, and to liaise with DFID, it made us less able to learn about the markets, to build trust with businesspeople in social settings, to measure our progress and modify our activities, and to design appropriate new interventions. If we could find good people to work in posts in the north and the south-west, and even in Lagos, then the centre would start to become the 'outpost', away from the action, and those that worked there would feel the need to lean on and learn from their new colleagues closer to the action. I was determined not to create mini offices in each location, and I wanted to hire people with initiative and connections. I ran the interviews to hire the first person in the north. Of all the candidates with exemplary résumés of years working in development projects, I ended up picking the least-obvious candidate: someone with a natural science degree (with the rigour of scientific method), who had worked his way through university (hustle and grit), who answered each question quickly and correctly with least waffle (communication skills), and who was not afraid to challenge me (how much Hausa do you speak?). He turned into a key asset; one that Alan would admire because people in-post helped us to answer those doubts about whether we really knew what we were talking about. One of the side-effects of having colleagues in the market was that more of us were willing to join them for short visits to observe, participate, enquire, and hopefully understand how the market was working and how other markets affected it, and thus how we might intervene.

Our colleagues opened doors, introduced us to people, made our time more productive. And, thankfully, found better places for us to wash, eat, and sleep.

Friends in court

Donors frequently get a hard time, and whether or not you think this is justified, just remember they have pressures and accountabilities, rules and procedures, and they are paying your wages. I always tried to 'serve' the client as best I could by providing short reports, verbal briefings, clear communication, and tangible evidence of progress; and by solving their problems instead of asking for help to solve ours. I would also stay in touch with senior leadership to ensure the official responsible for the programme was protected by showing clearly how the programme was meeting the donor's national objectives. And I encouraged DFID advisers to join us travelling in the country. This was not always easy to arrange as they already had much on their agenda. The few trips in the country that we did were important for building confidence. As a result of looking after the client, we were given a lot of space and flexibility to experiment with interventions which helped us to learn and so make greater progress.

The people on the bus

Some programme staff are more important than we realize at first sight. Our cook and cleaner was on a casual wage contract. We formalized the employment and encouraged her, while taking a wage, to charge for the food she made. She deserved stability of employment for caring for our workplace, but also the flexibility to run a business. The range of food types increased and the quality and speed of service was rewarded. Young professionals that we had hired, unable to prepare their own breakfasts at home, would come to work early and dine at Chez Vero's. The kitchen became the engine room and I let her run it. It was in the middle of the office. The dried fish, *egusi*, pounded yam, *ogbono*, and Indomie with boiled egg sustained us. Many of our informal meetings, which produced good ideas or dealt with our more silly ones, were around the kitchen table. I knew the health of the programme was in the bounce of people going into the kitchen, the welcome they received from colleagues already around the table, and their satisfaction on leaving, fired up to do better.

Another frequently overlooked part of a programme team are the drivers. Why they are overlooked is a mystery to me. These people have your life in their hands; they know where you are going when you don't; they take you to the markets where they observe and wait while you sit in meetings. They also have an amazing network. We had a driver who had previously worked for the UN-FAO in a regional position. He could have driven me from Abuja to Dakar without a map. We recognized the drivers' role by setting new standards of performance with the help of one of the best trainers I have ever met; and we rewarded them with increased basic pay and equal field allowances. Staff meetings did not start until drivers were around the table. I even asked them to help with field surveys occasionally as they knew better than many of our degree-holding staff how to relate to rural traditional leaders. The bus cannot leave until all the people are on board, and the journey will not be a happy one unless the people on the bus have a role, do it well, and are appreciated.

So what? Success and otherwise

PrOpCom ended with an external summary review. DFID picked two reviewers of towering intellect and experience. Their report published in April 2014 remains on DFID's website noting, '1.26 million people reached; 17,000 jobs created; net income of £41 million generated; and an estimated £4.9 million invested by private companies'. But did this last?

For a while, the work on fertilizer became well-known. But, during a period of political love-making, DFID naively agreed with the new, star Federal Minister of Agriculture to pay for the costs of deploying a voucher subsidy scheme for farm inputs. This drew business attention towards the new subsidy scheme and away from seeking innovations to reach the millions of farmers that were a potential market segment. Fortunately, the voucher scheme eventually closed and normal business resumed. There are now three big fertilizer companies vying for small farmers' attention.

Our work on stimulating an agricultural mechanization service market failed and succeeded. Farmers continue to thresh rice by hand in most of the country thereby losing part of the harvest and lowering its market price due to admixture. The efficiency and quality gains of machines are not as attractive as the social gains of employing the poorest to manually harvest and thresh. The roots of this choice are in social exchange (informal rules) rather than economics. The majority of Nigerian farmers still dig the soil with implements that can be found in a museum of anthropology; machines have barely arrived on the scene. Despite a long legacy of government giving out tractors to curry political favour, we were able to broker the start of a movement for change. It started with one brave bank manager, an enterprising tractor company, and about 20 tractors. This movement has now expanded to a network centred on the Tractor Owners and Hiring Facilities Association of Nigeria. Five banks and three tractor companies are providing finance and technical support so that new, small mechanization service businesses can prosper. About 1,000 tractors are at large working with over 200,000 farmers.

Finale

So what have I learned?

- There is no easy road to systemic change, no quick fix; the journey is washed in sweat and worry and you should pay a penance for arrogantly thinking you could make markets work better for the poor, for it is not you that makes the change happen. The penance you will pay is more sweat and worry and you deserve it. Never forget that you are just making it easier for others to succeed.

- The way to the light is through analysis of cause and symptom: there is no quick fix that lasts. And your friend on the way is an attitude of diligent, unending, fervent enquiry. Curiosity is a delight that is never satisfied, enjoy it with friends and it will be your saviour on the road to redemption, taking you towards the light.
- Donors just do not have much interest in what matters to you. They have their own concerns. Deal with them as you must but do not make them your master. Contractors are even worse: fickle, flittering butterflies lured by the next opportunity to tender their assistance to the donor. It is the bereft, head-scratching, sky-gazing, optimistic, risk-breaking, market players that are your sole masters.
- The team is A+. God bless 'em! Nurture your colleagues with discipline and cream.
- Shame on you, for doing any less than you should!

About the author

Julian Hamilton-Peach works with DAI. He led DFID PrOpCom and its successor in Nigeria from 2008 and has since mentored people in the practical aspects of facilitating change. Alan Gibson was his first M4P teacher and formenter.

Reference

Dorward, A., Poole, N., Morrisson, J., Kydde, J. and Urey, I. (2003) 'Markets, institutions and technology: missing links in livelihoods analysis', *Development Policy Review* 21(3): 319–32 <https://doi.org/10.1111/1467-7679.00213>.

PART IV

Alan Gibson on aid, why development fails, and other matters

Introduction

Rob Hitchins

The late Nico Colchester, of *The Economist* and the *Financial Times*, once made the distinction between things that were soggy and things that were crunchy. He characterized sogginess as 'comfortable uncertainty': actions that are defined by compromise, half-truths, fence-sitting, and face-saving. Crunchiness, on the other hand, leaves you in no doubt where you stand, for better or worse: actions that are defined by clarity, evidence, commitment, and conviction.

Alan was crunchy. He tried to do the right thing. He tried to make a difference.

One of Alan's distinctive attributes was his perseverance. His diligence and determination. Get the job done, to the highest standard, meet the deadline. 'On, on' was his mantra in the face of difficult circumstances, often with little regard for personal cost, comfort or self preservation. The easiest route isn't necessarily the right one. On, on.

Another attribute often associated with Alan is fearlessness. One long-standing colleague suggested that Alan 'bet the firm' on challenging the status quo. This got me thinking. Was Alan really that brave? Tenacious, yes. Direct, certainly. Prepared to confront uncomfortable truths, unquestionably. But does that count as brave? It hardly puts him or anyone who works in international development in the same category of courage as a combat soldier or a firefighter. In our work, doing the right thing shouldn't require bravery. If the status quo isn't working for millions of disadvantaged people, then the status quo needs to be challenged. That was Alan's job. That's our job. We don't praise a surgeon for not being squeamish. It's a prerequisite. When convention isn't working it is incumbent on us to try something different.

The following blogs by Alan convey his 'crunchiness'. They also convey his criticism of the international development programmes of DFID and of the Scottish government, among others. There is much here that makes uncomfortable reading for many supporters of international aid, but the intention is not so much to attack 'sacred cows' but to propose a better way forward.

http://dx.doi.org/10.3362/9781788531443.013

So why does development fail? Here's why ...

'Why does development fail?' To a familiar and fundamental question arrives insight from an unusual source with, potentially, far-reaching significance.

Rory Stewart is an unusual politician – far too cerebral for a start – and someone able to bring a diverse pre-politics perspective to bear. Stewart chose his speech in the parliamentary debate on the tenth anniversary of the Iraq war (13 June 2013) to reflect on his learning from his time as a provincial governor from 2003 to 2005. His analysis deals not with the decision to go to war per se (arguments all heard before) but, having made that decision, with why the UK's post-war development efforts were such *a failure and scandal'*. (It's worth ten minutes of your time: click http://www.bbc.co.uk/democracylive/house-of-commons-22891120 and fast forward to 1hr 30min 27 sec).

Although a speech about the specifics of Iraq, it is the implications of this beyond Iraq – to the UK's engagement with low-income countries through international development efforts – which are revelatory and worthy of consideration by anyone with an interest in development.

Stewart outlined a number of underlying reasons why the UK's intervention failed. Among the most important being (paraphrasing):

- Inappropriate incentives: officials not having the right incentives to understand and address key issues *('The entire structure of our organisations, their incentives, their promotions, recruitment, the way they interact with policy-makers ... does not help us to acknowledge failure')*.
- Weak capacities: poor knowledge and skills in how to deal with the complexity of a different environment and in developing the right *'relationships with the local reality'*.
- Ineffective and misleading reporting processes: monitoring procedures which allow a picture of progress to be painted while reality moves in a profoundly different direction *('every week I claimed great success')*.
- Lack of in-depth analysis: among officials and observers (such as the media) an absence of critical reflection on performance *('it isn't helped by the way we talk about it')*.
- Lack of moral courage: a reluctance to openly articulate informed criticism of policy and practice *('it is not good enough that not a single senior diplomat formally recorded their opposition to what was going on')*.

What all this adds up is that we do not *'acknowledge failure'* because, as a country, *'at some level, we're not serious'*.

The analysis is damning and, I'm sure, correct. But how does this have any relevance beyond the historical and specific context of the UK's miserable record in Iraq? Well, taking the above factors – I'll call them the Stewart Framework – and applying them to the UK's wider development efforts channelled through DFID, presents a revealing picture.

Inappropriate incentives: For a DFID civil servant, say a technical adviser, typically posted for three years in-country, career incentives encourage you to:

- Be hyper-critical ('tough') of any projects or contractors that you inherit (after all, they're not yours).
- Develop new projects and (crucially) get these approved. Projects don't have to be 'good' (in the sense of dealing with underlying causes) but need to be consistent with formal and informal compliance signals from DFID management. Don't worry overly about how do-able projects are. Once these begin to get going – these will take eighteen months or so to set up – and their performance scrutinised, you will be on your way to a different posting, and no one will connect bad performance with you.

Incentives have all to be seen in a context of DFID – with a rising budget and higher profile – as a more political entity than in the past. This is a process that started under the last government and has continued in this one. Decision making takes place in a political space in which what matters is looking good (scalable images) and sounding credible (sound bites). The technicalities of 'how to' are inexorably squeezed out, piffling concerns in the context of the bigger picture. There is a basic misalignment between personal and organisational incentives and genuine development goals.

Weak capacities: When DFID and its predecessor (ODA) had a smaller budget it had a reputation (in relative terms) for competent technical know-how. By common consent (including – if quietly – from within DFID) its technical cupboard is increasingly bare, with know-how such as contractor and budget management and internal procedures emphasised. Most of all, in an era when high budgets are its distinguishing feature and its biggest problem (how on earth to spend all that money?), the capacity to deliver projects that spend large amounts is highly prized. How/how well matters less.

Ineffective and misleading reporting processes: The furious on-going overhaul of DFID processes – epitomised by the tortuous new 'business case' format – has resulted in: (a) new levels of bureaucracy; and (b) an emphasis on delivering and reporting on (easily-measured) direct deliverables, rather than on underlying changes in the real world affecting poor people. More broadly, the larger DFID's budget and profile has grown – and the more frantic its efforts to demonstrate its toughness with suppliers – the more invasive and crippling the bureaucratic burden has become.

Lack of in-depth analysis: With little incentive to go beyond the superficial, DFID's own analysis seldom reaches the underlying reasons why intervention fails. In doing so, officials are safe in the knowledge that conventional media coverage scarcely moves beyond clichéd partisanship, with its familiar characterizations:

- Aid bad: *The Daily Mail* and the bovver-boy, 'Hate Johnny Foreigner!' – right
- Aid good: *The Guardian* and the querulous, hand-wringing, 'You just don't care!' – left.

The essential dysfunctionality of the UK aid machine – how and why it is the way that it is – remains unexamined.

Lack of moral courage: I am not privy to the innermost debates of DFID but there is not much evidence of deeper thought about underlying efficacy when targets have to be met (with bonuses dependent on these) and the wider rules governing behaviour – 'spend big, act tough, look good' – apply. And from the wider aid community – contractors, academics and NGOs – there is the usual noise but few question the validity of the aid machine itself (of which they are, of course, a paid-up, dependant part). No-one prominent from the aid world has stated publicly that the large and expanding size of the DFID budget is a hindrance to achievement. And so this territory is left to less considered voices, and the usual ping-pong of 'aid good-aid bad' starts again. Nuanced, thoughtful views are scarcely heard.

What all this boils down to is that there is a close parallel between the factors behind the failure in Iraq – incentives, capacities, processes, scrutiny – and those which characterize the UK's wider development effort now. Like Iraq, development is not something we are serious about. Rather it's a game for DFID and other development actors where laudable aspiration is confused conveniently with achievement, and where failure cannot be acknowledged.

Of course, some may say 'surely some mistake here. Iraq may not have been our finest hour, but even if there is a passing likeness between the factors impacting on Iraq's post-war rehabilitation and current DFID development endeavours, DFID's wider development work achieves and excels. The processes may be similar but outcomes are completely different, aren't they?'

Really?

The Iraq experience is unique in terms of its blazing prominence and the scale and consequences of its failure. But anyone thoughtful and engaged in development for a period of time – and able to detach their own self-interest from their analysis – will acknowledge the development industry's 'emperor's new clothes' secret. Namely, in terms of the underlying essence (failure), DFID's experience (with rare exceptions) is many small, diluted Iraqs. How many? Forty? Fifty? Hundreds? I don't know, but it is widespread, and probably close to the norm. Without the notoriety and drama of Iraq, much of our broader development experience is a series of mediocrities and disappointments that constitute collectively a similar level of failure and of scandal. Believing that the same underlying set of causal factors applying to both can produce different results is untenable and is disingenuous.

In the light of the above, what can be done? This is not the forum to set out an agenda for reform. But, as a starting point, with the Stewart Framework as its guide and externally shaped and driven, there needs to be an urgent, independent review of DFID's performance and structure, including its incentives, capacities and processes and the level of scrutiny around it. And from this, perhaps, an agenda for a better and smaller DFID may emerge.

And if you still doubt the links between the Iraq experience and DFID now, take a look at the political noises guiding both. David Cameron expresses his pride in the UK's aid spending – *'it makes me proud to be British'* – in much the same, blind self-righteous way that Tony Blair speaks of the UK's role in Iraq – *'we can look back with an immense sense of pride'*. Such hubris did not serve the cause of development in Iraq – and it doesn't serve the cause of international development now.

Why DFID's proposed new Start Up! programme is bunkum and should be ditched

When a donor issues a proposal of dubious development worth, the usual practice of contractors is to keep schtum, hiding any concerns beneath their commercially self-interested 'the client knows best' default position. Or not bid. However, the Start Up! programme, for which DFID has now stated that it intends to offer an invitation to tender, merits a break with traditional practice (and we at Springfield are never knowingly traditional).

Aimed at *'improving the in-country support for start-up companies in DFID focus countries'* and with an indicative value of £40–70 m, the Start Up! proposal is a farrago of inaccurate analyses, regurgitation of failed 'solutions' and expedient misreading of recent development history. It will not – cannot – address the core problems which it purports to be concerned with. Indeed, it may well worsen them.

Start Up! – and yes, the exclamation mark is part of the title – is concerned with a recognized, hardly new, issue: how to develop an environment that will stimulate more and successful business start-ups and the dynamism and economic and social benefits that come from these. It proposes a range of financial and non-financial activities. These include grants for early-stage businesses, grants for investors, grants for workspace provision, training, coaching and mentoring for entrepreneurs, and networking and coordination between investors and small businesses. What's wrong with all this? Here are eight reasons.[1]

1. Start Up! ignores history: the analysis and proposed solutions are a throwback to a different era, the UK in the 1980s and early 1990s when business start-up was seen to be a major problem and a bewildering variety of government schemes offered direct support (financial and non-financial) to small firms. An enterprise development industry emerged – based around local enterprise councils – focused on the individual firm, and underpinned by models of the small business development process. The UK's early forays (through the ODA, DFID's predecessor) into private sector development were essentially transfers of this experience into other countries. For example, the South African government's 1995 White Paper on Small Business was based on the UK experience, written by British consultants and supported by the ODA. All this is largely seen to have failed. Its main value is as an experience from which we can learn and improve – not to which we should return.

2. Start Up!'s view of DFID's experience is revisionist: in the above context, the claim that *'there is little or no experience of development agencies such as DFID seeking to nurture early-stage investor networks and make them work better for enterprises'* is simply incorrect. This was a key focus of much work in Eastern Europe, Latin America, and many other locations across Africa including in Ghana, where research for Start-Up! took place – where Empretec, for example, was for many years engaged in this kind of work, with DFID support.

3. Start-Up! misunderstands and misrepresents development agency learning: the proposal states that *'the BDS approach favoured by many in the development community in the 1980s and 1990s struggled to create financially sustainable services'*. BDS (business development services) as a term was actually only coined in the late 1990s. There was never a 'BDS approach' per se; the prevailing approach to non-financial services in the 1980s and 1990s was (as above) direct donor-supported delivery. And it failed. What emerged from that experience was an approach that focused first on: (a) BDS market development, and would eventually lead to some agencies seeing their wider role as focusing on the development of specific market systems (whether in finance, agriculture etc); and (b) BDS not as generic services (business training, mentoring, advice, consulting) – too abstract to be meaningful – but as business services within other markets (finance, agriculture etc). There has been a continuous if sometimes wavering line of logical learning and development – but this is lost here. Start Up!'s hazy rationale displays a depressing lack of DFID institutional memory.

4. Start Up!'s analysis is thin and confused: the level of analysis around Start Up! is, at times, startlingly shallow. Firms complain (in a survey they know is for a donor agency, remember) that they can't get external financing, ergo there is a finance problem (businesses complaining about banks … surely not?). Start-ups say, of course, that they need more specialised advice, ergo it's something that should be provided. This is 'research' as the thoughtless generation of entrepreneur wish-lists; research which sticks at symptoms, with little attempt to get to underlying causes.

5. Start Up! confuses a conducive business environment with a welfare state for business: the ethos of the programme appears to be that DFID should be providing everything, lifetime *'support'* (a word used 49 times in the proposal). Wherever there is a gap, DFID's job is to fill it directly – allowing firms to start, develop and grow in a warm bath of subsidized training and advice, in subsidized premises, supported by subsidized finance before graduating to receive DFID challenge funds. DFID, throughout, as generous giver, ironically in much the same way as the dysfunctional, government-run small business agencies of most African countries aspire to behave.

6. Start Up! has no genuine systemic ambition: Start Up! sticks to the familiar ground of small business needs – what problems do firms have? – but

does not ask, let alone answer, the more important systemic question: what are the constraints that are preventing the effective functioning of the systems around businesses – information, finance, services and workspace – that could address firms' problems? Instead we have repeated (9) references to an entrepreneurial *'ecosystem'*, which certainly sounds a good and wholesome thing but, without any analytical underpinning, is largely meaningless.

7. Start Up! is a collection of diverse grants and directly-funded services that add up to ... what exactly? Start Up! – with money to burn, no fears over the spoiling effects of too much direct support and only the vaguest sense of the *'ecosystem'* it is trying to develop – is, and will be seen to be, another DFID grant factory. Dispensing goodies, distorting expectations and incentives, and undermining other genuine (and whisper it, sometimes successful) attempts to catalyse markets.

8. Start Up!'s rationale is to fit with DFID's realpolitik goals: ultimately the only sense of Start Up! is that it feeds into an increasingly politicized DFID's bigger purpose: looking good, looking business-like, spending (big sums of) money. The easy froth of appearance is what matters, not the difficult substance of facilitating change. And for contractors, what could be easier than setting up more grant gravy trains and taking a healthy margin in the process?

Not justified by credible analysis, unconcerned with lessons learned, with no coherent vision, this is Start Up! If DFID were true to its Evidence Based Value For Money mantra it would ditch it forthwith. Start up? Perhaps Shut Up! would be more appropriate.

Note

1. This draws on *'Start Up! – a proposed new DFID programme'* prepared for the programme's market engagement exercise.

If we want better development, cut the UK aid budget

The UK government, like its predecessor, is pursuing a policy of increasing the foreign aid budget. Aid this year is scheduled to be £11.3 bn, almost three times (in real terms) its level in 2000. At a time when most other areas of public expenditure are being cut, it is an extraordinary increase. It will also mean that the 0.7 per cent aid/national income target set by the UN has been reached (it was 0.31 per cent in 2000). This growth trend and this 'achievement' have been widely praised – 'historic', 'landmark' – from within the development world. And any criticism from outside that world has been decried variously as 'out-of-touch', 'insulting' and 'misguided'.

Noticeably, there have been few if any voices from within the development world which have publicly questioned the wisdom of this budget increase, let alone advocated for a budget cut. In that context, and as someone who has spent their working life within the development sphere, here are four reasons why the cause of international development will best be served not by an increase in UK aid but by the opposite: a substantial reduction.

Reason 1: The 0.7 per cent target is based on a false premise

Almost lost in the mists of time, the original rationale for this target stemmed (loosely) from the financing gap model, in which growth was seen simply as a function of investment levels with the role of agencies being essentially to plug the gap between actual and desired investment. Even if one assumes this had some validity five decades ago, it is now widely seen as lacking any relevance to a vastly changed modern world. Moreover, the notion that what developing countries 'need' can be represented as a simple formula related to rich country economies is flawed. Indeed, Michael Clemens and Todd Moss (2005), in their comprehensive demolition of the validity of the 0.7 per cent aid target, calculate that applying the same method used to arrive at the 0.7 per cent figure to conditions now yields an aid goal of a paltry 0.01 per cent of rich country income. A slightly different picture.

Although propagated as though it represents a deep truth arrived at through precise scientific calculation, the 0.7 per cent target has no credible intellectual underpinning to suggest that it is the 'correct' amount of aid to make a decisive lasting difference to poverty. It is essentially made up – an arbitrary figure emerging from a political judgement arrived at in 1970 in the UN which has mysteriously gathered trappings of moral certainty. There is no tangible, technical reasoning at its heart; it's a convenient number for aid advocates and politicians to quote. If the 0.7 per cent target was simply that – well-intentioned but harmless fluff – it would matter little. But in practice it looms large over aid debates and policies, and its effect on the functionality of aid is damaging and significant.

Reason 2: The focus on aid amounts (how much) perpetuates the myth that more is better

Running through discussion on aid is the tacit opinion that a higher UK aid budget is, inherently, a good thing, which is, in turn, based around two flawed views of the nature of development.

Development as charity: Development is seen as a 'good cause', a slightly more complicated, institutionalised way of extending a whip-round for the needy and unfortunate, where the kindest and best people, organisations and countries give the most. This is development as a continuing fund-raising bash. What use is made of this giving, whether it makes a significant difference or only acts as a short-term palliative, matters less. The point is to give. The more you give the better. This trumps any other concern. Seeing development in this way essentially relegates it to a do-good endeavour and to the mix of objectives associated with this: wishing to make a lasting effective difference, yes, but also being seen to help and feeling good about ourselves for offering to help. The danger, as with all charity work, is that the superficial trappings of giving, and the 'vanity of the giver', take precedence over concerns about the substance of achievement.

Development as a 'deliverable' by rich country governments: As DFID's budget has risen so the tendency has grown to justify aid in the same way as other areas of public expenditure, such as education, health and pensions (more than half of UK government spending), as 'public goods' that government delivers. Again, the more that government spends the more that it can claim to be meeting its responsibilities. Seeing aid as another state responsibility to be delivered invites it to be managed and perceived in the same way. Hence, DFID:

- Has introduced the 'business case' process, used throughout government spending departments, to examine programmes.
- Emphasizes 'direct deliverable' targets in its operational plans – children supported in schools, vaccinations delivered, malaria nets distributed, jobs created etc. – in the same way as other departments in the UK.
- Highlights 'value for money' (VFM) as a central mantra in all its work, and with it stresses the efficiency of delivery.
- Now makes a proportion of contractor payments conditional on direct deliverables.

The problem with these efforts to normalise and assimilate DFID spending and make it directly comparable to other areas of expenditure is that it misunderstands and distorts the fundamental essence of what development is.

Aid and development are not 'normal'. The UK government cannot deliver the development of other, sovereign countries in the same way that it can, for example, a better education system in the UK. Indeed, the more it tries to play a delivery role the more it may undermine the essential goal of development, to allow countries and people to develop themselves.

Reason 3: Higher budgets draw us away from the core, facilitating task of development

The essential role of development, ultimately, is to enable others to do, rather than do itself. This, of course, can be frustrating. For some, talk of facilitation and sustainability is self-indulgent sophistry, nuanced nonsense that excuses inaction. However, the core mission of development is nuanced. It is not about delivering insecticide-treated malaria nets directly; it is about developing sustainable systems of net provision. It is not about paying for children to attend school; it is about developing more inclusive, higher quality school systems. It is not about subsidizing loans; it is about developing better functioning financial markets. It is not about doling out seeds; it's about developing sustainable, high outreach agriculture input supply networks. But following a facilitation path faces considerable hurdles. Development as facilitation:

- Does not immediately lend itself to easy messaging. Much easier to talk of lives saved, to proffer images of kids in school etc., than attempt to communicate the progress of something as apparently amorphous as the development of self-reliant functional systems. Not impossible – but more difficult.
- Can be undermined by too much direct support, especially in the weakest economies. Individuals and organizations in both public and private sectors become accustomed to 'support' – financial, technical – and behaviour and incentives (logically) become skewed towards the expectation of more aid flows.
- Is more difficult. Much easier just giving things to people – and responding to the symptoms of under-development – than dealing with the more complicated causes of why people are poor. 'Just do it' is the implicit message of a large swathe of the development world – with Jeffrey Sachs as their unofficial head – that rails against anything more than direct, intensive giving (nets, fertilizer, money, seeds, machines ...) and the short-term illusory imagery of 'progress' this offers.

Reason 4: Higher budgets are distorting the development process

Amongst the development world's secrets, the growing dysfunctionality of DFID and the UK aid bandwagon that it finances is perhaps the biggest and dirtiest. The overarching pressure to spend makes DFID and the contractors who work for it seek ever more creative, tortuous ways of spending money. New funds to dosh out grants are invented. Governments are loaded up to the limits of their absorptive capacity. Private sector firms of any size and importance are offered support. Cash is given directly to households, shelled out like some extension of the UK welfare state. Some smaller countries – such as Malawi and Nepal – are simply saturated, full up, with development initiatives from DFID and other donors tripping over each other. The spending hot house creates a range of grotesque distortions: costs escalate, salaries inflate, the best people are attracted (at the expense of the real economy), government officials demand cash for any interaction with projects – a parallel, artificial aid world develops.

The contortions within DFID are most striking. Staff incentives are aligned not with 'good' development but with meeting spending targets – and with the ability to deliver politically appealing symbols of progress. Contractors, taking their cue from DFID, know that success in spending money is very likely to be rewarded with budget increases. At the same time, the level of stultifying bureaucracy around (larger) DFID projects grows, with two consequences: (a) demands for tight delivery-oriented accountability steer projects to pursue change that is most easily measured, rather than change that is most important; and (b) although with more resources, spending, paradoxically, becomes more difficult, with decision-making processes clogged in VFM fears. The grand transformational ambitions of development flounder and fold amidst DFID's organisational realities.

And shaping this organisational paralysis, the twin sister of higher budgets, is the heightened politicisation resulting from DFID's more visible profile. The ex-Development Secretary Andrew Mitchell boasted of the UK being a *'development superpower'*; David Cameron says *'aid makes me proud to be British'*; DFID issues detailed instructions over when and how to put the Union Jack on anything touched by UK aid; DFID officials obsess over the 'optics' of new initiatives (ie. what they look like). Inevitably, as it has become more political and prominent, DFID has become more concerned with the superficial and saleable, with what aid looks like to the government's key audiences: generous and large-scale ('heed that, compassionate conservatives') but also cost-cutting, pro-British and delivering ('we hear you, sceptical right-wingers').

For all of the above reasons, the size of DFID's budget has pushed the UK's development effort into a political space which has twisted its incentives and functioning. This new political economy of aid makes effective development increasingly difficult, and often impossible. Never has the contradiction between the high aspirations of development and its absurd, unworkable processes been more obvious. There is of course no guarantee that cutting the aid budget will remedy this situation, but certainly without a cut there is little possibility of consistency between the objectives and practices of UK development.

Reference

M.A. Clemens and T.J. Moss (2005) *Ghost of 0.7%: origins and relevance of the international aid target*, Working Paper No. 8, Washington, DC: Center for Global Development.

Market facilitation is the way ahead, but it needs to do more

Editor's note: This article originally appeared on CGAP's website on 27 March 2017 at <https://www.cgap.org/blog>

Kenya is a good place to start when considering market facilitation. It is the poster child of financial inclusion, with access to formal finance growing dramatically from 27 per cent in 2006 to 75 per cent in 2016. But, more than this, the last 10 years have also witnessed the influence of FSD Kenya (FSDK), an organization which, from the outset, has sought to follow a facilitation approach. Now, with the publication of an independent case study on FSDK, we have a chance to draw out lessons from this experience. What does this tell us about market facilitation? I'd suggest three takeaway points.

Market facilitation can (and does) work

By any reasonable reference point, FSDK has been a highly successful program. For example, it has contributed substantially to changed business models and the momentum of corporate growth and inclusion – notably the phenomena of Equity Bank and the M-Shwari product. It has been a key influence on the development of a policy and regulatory environment conducive to the era of digital finance. Its research has percolated throughout the sector and raised an understanding of financial inclusion. Its work on key 'public' functions, such as payments systems, is now beginning to bear fruit. Notwithstanding the presence of other favorable factors, without FSDK, change would have been reduced or would have been much slower or simply would not have happened.

So the essence of market facilitation – that addressing underlying systemic issues that constrain the development of functional, inclusive financial markets will achieve greater, more lasting change than conventional interventions – has, to a large extent, been fulfilled in Kenya. The case study is replete with evidence; the premise behind systems approaches is validated. And that's positive.

But, of course, there are caveats. In a number of spheres, such as service markets and cooperatives, FSDK has had limited impact. In some areas of intervention 'success', FSDK finds itself still playing an active role – for example as an adviser on regulation, as the main driver behind research, and as a technical adviser and 'de-risker' in innovation. All of this raises questions about the sustainability of change.

More fundamentally, there is a jarring disconnect between, on the one hand, advances in headline financial inclusion and the conspicuous growth of the financial sector in Kenya and, on the other, the stark fact of persistently high poverty levels. And that's less positive.

Market facilitation is a process we can understand (and therefore improve)

What explains the above picture? The main reason for success is that FSDK got the big things right as a facilitator. Its work has been analysis and knowledge-led; it has employed good-quality people who are close and credible to the market; it is seen to be independent, as a 'third party' able to engage with multiple players; it is flexible, able to adapt what it offers to fit different situations; and it is able to engage on tasks that require a longer time perspective. Its status as an independent trust rather than a conventional project arrangement (a position supported by its funders) has also helped.

Where FSDK has been less successful has often been because of failings in operationalizing the approach. For example, not using systems analysis correctly to identify key constraints means actions can have the wrong focus. Similarly, not giving sufficient weight to motivations in understanding market behavior can lead to (ill-fated) technical solutions to more deep-rooted political and institutional problems. And not having a sufficiently clear picture of how a future system should function can allow drift into the continuation of direct delivery roles. The lesson from these experiences is that there are operational disciplines and frameworks that should be used in putting market facilitation into practice. And these can be learned.

Successful facilitation is likely to take us into difficult issues on the role of finance

Most of FSDK's work has been technical in scope, concerned with capacities, information, coordination, etc. Yet it is clear that key systemic constraints to inclusive finance in Kenya are also political in nature – concerned, in particular, with incentives.

Most important here is the central 'So what?' question for all organizations engaged in financial inclusion. Kenya's finance market may well now be working slightly better for poor households and allowing them to manage their lives better. But it is clear that it is working even better for others – for middle-income consumers and, in particular, for the supply-side of the finance market which, with higher revenues and profits, has prospered throughout Kenya's 'inclusion years'. As pointed out in Mayada El-Zoghbi's blog, finance which is more transformational for poor people (i.e. inclusive) would need to connect better with the real economy (like agriculture) and real services (like health).

But why should banks change and innovate into riskier areas when there are easier ways of making money?

In this context, any valid change process has to be rooted in the incentives shaping market players' behavior. This includes not just the regulatory environment for banks but the broader, implicit social contract shaping the role finance plays in economies and societies. Working in this space may be new and uncomfortable for development agencies, but the experience in Kenya suggests that it is a necessary direction of travel if finance is to become genuinely inclusive. And while this is challenging, fortunately the frameworks and guidance used in market facilitation have equal relevance in considering how to engage in this new frontier.

This African aid initiative starts with a village ... but what happens next?

Editor's note: This article originally appeared on the *Guardian* website on 17 December 2009 at <https://www.theguardian.com/commentisfree/2009/dec/17>

A dewy-eyed view of charity work in Katine may just end in debilitating dependency Patrick Barkham's overview of the Katine experience covers the familiar mixed pattern seen throughout the *Guardian*'s two-year African initiative (One step forward ..., 6 November). The glimpses of village life offer genuine insight into an African reality. But the development response to this – an African Medical and Research Foundation (Amref) project that is typical of many NGO endeavours – risks giving a misleading impression of the nature of the challenge.

The 'integrated form of rural development' approach which the project preaches is not new – it was pursued widely 30 years ago and is regarded as having been a failure. While the relatively intense direct delivery of inputs – schools, seeds, water, health services, storage facilities – obviously has an immediate impact, this intensity of input can easily slide into a debilitating dependence.

On sustainability, the project emphasizes voluntarism to keep things going – built on prodigious amounts of training (the 'software' that is apparently a key strength). But it doesn't foster structures or mechanisms grounded in people's incentives and capacities – or appear to consider how and why things should work beyond the end of the project.

The causes of Katine's woes probably lie in the world outside – in national systems of financial services, input supply, information and services. As Barkham notes, 'the fact is that eight new boreholes in a sub-county of 66 villages is not many. But even this has inhibited government investment in the area', and that charities 'may find their good deeds a convenient excuse for the authorities to do nothing'. The project has to engage with underlying causes. In this context, the mantra 'it starts with a village' – at best a dewy eyed view of the world – in practice is likely to mean 'and ends with very little'.

Joshua Kyallo, Amref's Uganda director, says: 'The challenge for [Katine] is resources', as if to say more aid combined with noble intentions is inherently good and will succeed. There is simply no evidence to support the view that more is always better – either in Katine or in Africa as a whole.

The causes of poverty lie in the systems in which poor people – as producers, labourers, consumers and citizens – exist. Understanding and addressing these 'systemic constraints' (to use the jargon) is what development should be about.

Programmes that do so, some of which my centre advises, have generated large-scale and sustainable change. Millions more people's lives have been improved – with access to financial services, using better information to improve their farm output – and they are now earning higher incomes. All are different experiences, but with a common starting point – that the agencies' role is to bring about systemic change. With anything less we fool ourselves that the changes we see are significant and lasting. More seriously, we lead the people with whom we work down a similarly deluded path.

Binary choices, Obaman bubbles, Trumpian times ... oh, and the future of UK aid

'Divided' times? 'Fractured' might be a better term. *Trumpian* – or one of its many variants – even better.

Whatever terms we use for the opposing sides in this contested era – in vs out, mono vs multi, love vs hate, Obaman smooth vs *Trumpic* rough ... the main features of the emerging political landscape have been set. International aid in the UK is part of this Brexit-*Trumpist* world and is not immune to the forces that have shaped it. What does UK aid look like in this context and how should we respond to 2016's political eruptions?

Let's look at the context. The underlying drivers behind recent changes have been poured over endlessly. Amidst the benefits of globalisation, a substantial *Left-Behind* class has developed who have borne disproportionately the costs. Stagnant real wages and the decline of 'old' industries and regions have been accompanied by rising inequality. Much of this group's resentment is directed against those seen to be prospering, the *New-Included*: more urban, educated and wealthier. The former is characterized as white, incoherent, and annoyed – grimly battling it out against migrants in low-end labour markets; the latter as cosmopolitan, articulate, and optimistic – contented consumers of the low-cost services fuelled by diligent migrant labour. Generalized descriptions, not without caricature, but largely accurate.

These differences have found manifestation in political choice, buttressed by sources of information. For the *Left-Behind*, the political class represent liberal values and pursuit of a distant politically correct agenda in a politically correct vocabulary, none of which is theirs. Their media of choice – commercial and social – feeds their preconceptions and instincts. For the *New-Included*, embarrassed by 'the other's' ugly reactionary ways, different political choices are made fed by different information sources. Political polarization results, with little shared ground of fact to allow 'objective' exchange between groups. In his farewell address, Barack Obama characterized this polarization as society retreating into different 'bubbles', where individuals are *'surrounded by people who look like us and share the same political outlook and never challenge our assumptions'*, where we *'accept only information, whether true or not, that fits our opinions'*. This is the new 'post-truth' world; what matters is what feels right – this is the 'truth' that counts.

In this context, referenda and elections force a binary choice between two polar opposites. Not a place for nuanced debate but rather one which requires that misgivings are set aside and sides are chosen. And so, in the UK, we (liberal-minded development people) suppressed those awkward EU questions ('Just remind me again where accountability is here?') and doubtless in the US the same happened with inconvenient Clinton issues ('Tell me again how chummy $225,000 speeches to Wall St quite mark her out as a woman of the people?'), and feeling aghast at the *Trumpish* alternative, we make our 'progressive' choice.

And so where does UK aid fit into this? Look closely and we see that, in its own way, it is marked by familiar features of polarization and self-serving, self-referential bubbles of debate. Although in a different way from the current *Trumpeusian* shenanigans, the goings-on in UK aid are equally extraordinary. Fed by the (then) government's desire to rebrand itself (as 'kinder' and 'caring') UK expenditure on overseas development assistance (ODA) has grown from 0.5 per cent Of GNI in 2009 to 0.7 per cent (£12.4 bn), a 50 per cent growth in real terms. This spending growth is exceptional first because it has happened at a time of austerity with most domestic budgets static in real terms at best. And second, and without precedent, because since 2015 ODA spending at 0.7 per cent of GNI has been enshrined in law, further real ODA growth is guaranteed. Cementing spending at this level, as advocated by the UN, has been a step change in scale and in status for UK ODA. Moreover by establishing a tangible issue – the 0.7 per cent spend – around which binary views (for or against) can be formed, it has also placed UK international aid in the same *Trumpovian* world where allegiance prevails over reason.

It is worth reminding ourselves of the origins 0.7 per cent spending target. This does not lie not in any rigorous analysis or model which demonstrates that this, somehow, is the 'right' amount to trigger development. On the contrary, the original financing gap model that lay behind the target and articulated in the 1950s has long since been discredited (notably by Clemens and Moss,). Nor is there a compelling argument based on efficacy; on the contrary, the Independent Commission for Aid Impact's (ICAI) regular assessments of DFID's work show, at best, a mixed picture of success. Rather, it emerged in the UN (almost 50 years ago) as a result of opaque processes between different countries' officials, lobbyists and politicians. And somehow, through the passing of time and the absence of challenge, it has acquired a stature of permanence and authority. Indeed, ironically, there are parallels with the murky process that European colonialists went through 130 years ago when they carved out African 'countries' on a map, a process without transparency or developmental merit but whose outcome commanded widespread acceptance.

And so the principal argument for the 0.7 per cent spend is that it is, somehow, the *right thing* to do because, well, intrinsically, it *feels* right. Never mind that it is essentially a made-up target imbued with spurious intellectual weight, if we all say it often enough it will be right. *'We should feel proud'*, Britain is *'leading the way'* as an *'aid superpower'*. In other words, 0.7 per cent aid spending is the right thing to do because we so want it to be so. In classic post-truth, *Trumpegian* style, this is justification by *feel*, and not much more. (Oh, and the UN says so, so it must be right).

The net effect of this conspicuous spending growth and the palpable thinness of the rationale for it has been to give the impression of UK aid as the pet vanity project *par excellence* of the political class. A *cause celebre* of leftie and luvvies where agreement with the 0.7 per cent spend is *de rigueur*. And to invite scrutiny. With so much money swilling around the aid system – which, above all, has to be spent – it has not been difficult to find many examples of projects of questionable worth. More tangibly, the high financial rewards claimed by some have attracted outraged headlines and editorials – 'Scandal of our wasted foreign aid', 'Meet the begging bowl barons'. Among *Trumparistas*, the foundations of the 0.7 per cent spend are seen as brittle self-righteousness and greed rather than selfless generosity.

Quite quickly public views on UK aid, beyond the technical exchanges between researchers and practitioners, have descended into Obama-like bubbles. On the one hand, are the critics of aid who focus on spending profligacy, high fees and profits, the hypocrisy that lies beneath these, and apparently undeserving causes that receive aid. This is juxtaposed with the frugality of public spending on social and health services. The attacks are led by the instinctively hostile *Daily Mail* but others at the broadsheet end of the media – *The Times* and *The Daily Telegraph* – have entered the fray. Undoubtedly, a momentum is being built in *Trumpland*.

The other bubble, pumped up hugely by aid's new scale and prominence, are the defenders of aid and the 0.7 per cent spending boom (the two being seen as indivisible). This focuses on aid's apparent impact (lives saved, roads built, children educated etc.), with large numbers cited as evidence, and how (as above) the UK should be proud of the role it is playing. This is led by *The Guardian*, mouthpiece for internationalist sentiment, with supportive quotations from NGOs. There is generally little attempt to respond to the charges made by the aid critics, revulsion for all things *Trumpistian* is not hidden. and the validity of the 0.7 per cent spend is seen to be self-evident, a moral certainty not requiring explanation.

In true binary style, disconnected, parallel bubbles have developed. Each to his or her bubble. Of course, those of us engaged in international aid are assumed to be loyal adherents of the 0.7 per cent spend and all that goes with it. Yet our refusal to acknowledge publicly what is known privately on the effects of the 0.7 per cent target means we vacate the space for nuanced, reasoned analysis. For example:

- That for DFID, too much money is their biggest problem. Privately, informally, senior DFID staff recognise the (unnecessary) burden of the spending pressure.
- That while aid requires good people and organizations paid appropriately, high budgets have created a fairly lucrative 'poverty industry', distorting incentives far beyond the usual suspects of private consultants.
- That in a context where remittances and investment dwarf ODA, the efficacy of aid is as much about quality, insight and process as quantity.

- That, unlike domestic public expenditure (education, health etc.), where government is a 'deliverer', aid for other (sovereign) countries is about 'enabling' others, and this is not simply a function of financial resources …
- … but delivery in domestic 'public goods' *is* resource dependent. For example, notwithstanding debates on the *modes operandi* of UK health care, outcomes are unlikely to improve as long as health spending (8.5 per cent of GDP) lags the European average (10.2 per cent) so substantially.
- That while the world seems beset by crises, in relation to standard indicators of progress, global conditions have never been better. Many countries – most of Latin America and SE Asia – have grown beyond the gamut of traditional aid. Others will follow.

What then for UK aid? With the political environment which gave birth to the 0.7 per cent of GNI spending law now gone, it seems inconceivable that it will survive into a new parliament, or even get to the end of this one. Nor should it. You don't have to be a rabid *Trumper* to see that the arguments for the 0.7 per cent spending level lack validity. The failure of UK aid organisations to recognise this but instead keep within their 'more is better' bubble is a mistake in three respects.

First, the cause of international development is diminished, being seen as laced with the self-interest and hypocrisy of (elements of) the aid industry. For aid organizations to emerge cleanly from this entanglement will not be straightforward.

Second, an outmoded view of aid is prolonged that hinders us getting to more valid issues. International development *can* work and does have an important, if different, role to play in shaping a better future, and a better world. Removed of the 0.7 per cent burden might allow a more honest and effective discourse on what this role is and how it should be played.

Third, and last, an unwinnable argument is supported. To be a loser, to be *Trumped*, is not a position from which to influence the way ahead for UK aid.

Soapbox: Zip goes a million

In 1902, an American novelist named George Barr McCutcheon, penned the amusing work of fiction, 'Brewster's Millions'. At the turn of the year, in 1906-07, a Broadway stage adaptation followed, and some time later, a musical, re-named 'Zip Goes a Million'. Adapted ten times over, perhaps the best-known version of the storyline is Richard Pryor and John Candy's 1985 renewal of this far-fetched work of fiction, where Pryor plays the lead character, Montgomery (Monty) Brewster.

In this version, Monty's mad great-uncle sets him a challenge in his will: spend $30 m within 30 days such that you have nothing to show for it at the end of the month, and if successful, you'll inherit $300 m as your reward. Monty accepts, and is accompanied by para-legal, Angela Drake, from his great-uncle's specified law firm to keep an eye on his spending.

In this, my 2013 tongue-in-cheek, development industry themed re-write, the role of the mad great-uncle will be played by the UK Cabinet, Monty's shoes will be filled by a development contractor and the para-legal character will be assumed by a DFID staffer from one of their country offices. The new challenge: spend 0.7 per cent of national GNI on aid as soon as possible. The prize? Well, a concert at Wembley, some colourful rubber wrist-bands, and a signed Polaroid picture of politicians shaking hands, naturally!

Has setting this 0.7 per cent target and fostering its cult-like worship set us on an identical storyline to Brewster: having to burn through a lot of money, whilst having nothing to show for it when all is accounted for? After all, spending more money than ever before in fewer countries with fewer staff resources to direct this expenditure is sold to the general public as a good thing, isn't it? We'd be a generous citizenry, but better still, and appeasing the frothing *Daily Mail* lobby, we'd be doing it with less 'overheads' on the government's accounts!

But, how do you spend 0.7 per cent of GNI in such circumstances, year on year? Carelessly, would be my guess. In the absence of the people, insight, strategy, and persistence required to stimulate permanent transformations in the way that developing country systems perform, what else other than 'careless' could I have said? To protect myself from being branded an 'aid-hater' at this juncture I should declare that my problem is not with having an aid budget, it is with blowing a big one and being little further forward in the fight against poverty.

Having more money available now and more in the pipeline will not motivate contractors to search for solutions to age-old shortcomings – that development programme outcomes are rarely sustained, nor are they often 'developmental' (as opposed to distortionary). Shouldn't programmes whose aim is 'development' be judicious in their use of resources, spending funds intelligently on ventures that actively encourage and incentivise the individuals and institutions of developing countries to invest in and organise around upholding their own indigenous transformations? To do this, however, programmes and donors need to possess the human resources (skill) and time (patience) required to identify these ventures and instigate the necessary changes that bring them to fruition, and not conversely, to be systematically stripped of both 'luxuries'. Shouldn't we be asked to try and get more out of less, rather than being set up to in fact get less out of more?

Programmes with true developmental objectives – i.e. those that aim to transform developing country systems for the long-term – have particularly suffered under the heavy-handed pressure to spend existing budgets quickly whilst simultaneously being force-fed expanded budgets, linear spending patterns, and additional programme components. It is not only the programmes that have swollen beyond their natural limits. The absorptive capacities and incentives of developing country institutions and market players as counterparts and co-investors are equally tested. Meanwhile, DFID continues to engineer further means of spending money quickly and predictably (perhaps commissioning a new Challenge Fund), arguably with less interest in development validity and more in the resonance of the political narrative that can be sold to the general public.

It is, after all, the UK's prerogative to spend X per cent of GNI and developing countries must receive it. Our targets are setting the pace of 'giving' but also 'receiving'. Just to get money out the door, these same targets, however, risk jeopardizing existing efforts by some programmes in the DFID portfolio to spend in a way that is more conscious of capacities and incentives of the recipient. Meanwhile, programme leaders are increasingly absorbed in battles with afore-mentioned Angela Drake types over spending more and targets, perhaps more than they are absorbed in battles around higher quality and more durable outcomes. Sadly, it seems, politics is doing its level best to reduce quality for the sake of quantity. UKAID – 'Zip Goes a Million'.

Addressing the strategic black hole at the heart of DFID's PSD work

Let's use a metaphor that fits the moment. If DFID were a football team, the Independent Commission for Aid Impact (ICAI) would be rowdily leading a chant of 'You don't know what you're doing' from the terraces, aimed both at its struggling management and slightly bewildered group of players. Not especially pleasant. But not ignorable either, and unlikely to fix itself for the next game. *'DFID'*, pundits would conclude sagely, *'may be giving 100%, but the gaffer needs a rethink'*.

The ICAI (2014) report on DFID's private sector development (PSD) work published in May, and scoring it Amber-Red (*'the programme performs relatively poorly'*), is a severe criticism of DFID's PSD work. At its heart is the charge that DFID's work lacks essential coherence such that its achievements and impacts are much less than the sum of its many parts. For an agency which is rapidly increasing spend on PSD, it is a damning indictment. But the report, inadvertently perhaps, might also provide a starting point to address the black hole – lack of clarity in strategic rationale, positioning and role – which undermines DFID's PSD work. And, to continue the football theme, allow DFID, and all of us engaged in PSD, to *'take the positives'* from an otherwise difficult situation.

First, let's acknowledge the insight and honesty of the ICAI report in identifying aspects of DFID's situation that are widely known but seldom articulated. The culture of targets (and inevitable cheating), buying short-term results at the expense of longer-term efficacy, the saga of the business case process, lack of clarity in management structures, capacity limitations of the new PSD cadre ... the fact that ICAI has highlighted these suggests that it is doing its job. This doesn't always happen with 'independent' assessment agencies. Springfield's own experience in leading an 'independent' review for the Office of Development Effectiveness (ODE) at AusAID was that any criticism should neither be direct nor candid. When we refused to self-censor, another consultant was brought in to do so. We took our name off the report and AusAID ... now, what did happen to AusAID?

Second, the report also correctly identifies positive aspects of DFID's PSD world. DFID is seen as (relatively speaking) a leader among funders. It has a stronger private sector orientation. Many of the individual DFID-funded projects visited by the ICAI were 'making a difference'. And DFID has been associated with major innovations in PSD, most notably (both in terms of the report and from a Springfield perspective), in developing and applying approaches aimed at systemic change. In PSD, DFID is important.

But these points, while significant, form a backdrop to the main charge – that DFID's efforts are scattered, lack coherence and don't come close to the high ambitions set out for them. Why does this significant underachievement happen? The main reason, according to the report, is that *'ambition for PSD is not supported by practical guidance'*. Country offices and staff are unclear about *'DFID's particular role'* in PSD and often directionless in shaping country portfolios. There is no overarching view defining the role that DFID should play in its work. It might have been expected that this would be contained in DFID's Economic Development Strategic Framework (EDSF) published in January and the basis of the recently announced doubling in budget. However, this highlights overall priorities and objectives and doesn't guide DFID on 'how' it should engage or what its role should be. As the report notes, there is no *'theory of change that clarifies how DFID's activities cohere as a consistent endeavour'*; consequently the EDSF does not provide useful strategic guidance.

So what should that practical guidance be? Having identified the general issue, this is where the report is not as strong.

- The report wrongly pigeonholes the market systems (M4P) approach into a meso- or mid-level change box. M4P is about the regulations, norms, services, infrastructure and information that together shape the systemic (macro and meso) context for 'micro' level performance. In practice, macro and meso are often arbitrary distinctions. What matters is that M4P is about getting to underlying causes and therefore about systemic change. The report's classification is all the more bizarre when three of the five 'macro-level' projects it visited (PEPE and LIFT in Ethiopia and FDST in Tanzania) and therefore supposedly not in the M4P sphere of influence are openly M4P in origin and orientation.
- The report sees the world of PSD through the flat descriptive lens of a macro-meso-micro map. Its view of strategic balance, somehow, is that there should be a range of interventions across these in important sectors of national economies. The net effect is to suggest a kind of 'doing-a-bit-of-this-and-a-bit-of-that' at each level – a picture with a splash of macro colour, a bold flurry of micro endeavour and perhaps a delicate pastel of meso intent. Somehow this adds up to balance and coherence? This is symptomatic of an underlying conceptual and practical problem – the report doesn't distinguish analytically between (1) strategic role and focus – the role that an agency sees for itself in pursuing development goals and (2) the operational/intervention tactics it employs in playing that role – who it works with, how, doing what. Strategy leads tactics; if the first is wrong, the second can't be right.
- The report doesn't follow through its own arguments on micro-level support. While acknowledging the immediate (and often easy) tangible gains from micro support, it questions how sustainable/scalable these are. Logically, it might then be asked, why support (and indeed plan to ramp up funding!) interventions that are inherently micro in

orientation (such as challenge funds) – unless they're undertaken along with other supporting activities addressing other issues in the wider market system? Or does DFID see development validity lying in fluffy transient impacts (tokenistic could be another term)? Presumably it doesn't.

In practice, DFID has no meaningful strategic position which says 'this is our role'. What does DFID *stand for* in PSD? Implicitly, the report says that DFID doesn't know. It has no overarching theory of change that brings cohesion to its work. It has aspirations and diverse activities – with no obvious coherent link between them both. (The report's 29 references to 'coherence' indicate where it sees the problem lying).

So that's where the report gets to. And where it rather jarringly stops. To the obvious question, what should DFID's strategic guidance be, disappointingly the report offers little.

So let's help out.

The only credible, strategic, developmental position for DFID to take in relation to PSD (and indeed other fields) is that it is concerned with addressing underlying causes – rather than superficial symptoms – which in turn means it should focus on the systemic factors inhibiting the development of market systems (in the broadest sense). This would build on the more progressive aspects of DFID's PSD track record and escape the 'bit-of-this-bit-of-that' characteristic that undermines its performance now and is common in organizations shaped by political expediency rather than valid mission clarity.

This would still mean a range of different interventions (at different levels) but within a strategic framework that allowed impacts to be bigger and be more enduring. It would mean replacing a flat descriptive framework (macro-meso-micro) with an analytical lens that diagnoses underlying causes and directs DFID to seek to address these. This would be built as a requirement into all DFID's country strategies and projects and – as a common, overarching theory of change – would be a major step towards coherence and away from the basic contradictions seen across current portfolios and even within individual projects.

Interestingly, DFID is not the first agency to be confronted with this critique of its role. 'Good practice guidance' for funders of the financial services field globally over the last two decades has come from the 'Pink Book' published by CGAP (the Consultative Group to Assist the Poor). The essence of this is that any interventions anywhere in the macro-meso-micro spectrum are okay. However, CGAP now understands that this has reduced scale and sustainability and has distorted markets. In contrast, CGAP's (2013) new five-year strategy, acknowledging past (and current) sins, emphazises systemic change as the guiding rationale for intervention – '*a catalytic role in market development*'. DFID can learn from this example.

What cannot be disputed from the ICAI report is that DFID needs a more coherent, explicit, articulated view of the role it seeks to play in PSD. It needs to raise its game. This *Soapbox* makes the case for DFID to focus on systemic

change – the underlying causes preventing the development of market systems –as the overarching central theory of change that should shape all of its
work. This would be good for DFID and, given its size and influence, good for
the wider development cause. And if it's not that – if systemic change does
not become DFID's organizing principle – what is it going to be for DFID?
Certainly, as the report makes clear, the current situation is not working and
is not tenable. It certainly doesn't offer a platform from which to build (as
DFID plans to double its spend in this area); rather a bottomless pit in which
to fall (taking much of this spend and, worse still, the opportunity for greater
development impact along with it!).

References

ICAI (2014) *DFID's Private Sector Development Work* <https://icai.independent.
    gov.uk/report/dfids-private-sector-development-work/>.
CGAP (2013) *Strategic Directions FY2014–FY2018* <www.cgap.org/sites/default/
    files/cgap_strategy_20141018.pdf>.

Ten years of the Scottish government's international development programme: Distinctive role or 'me too' gesture?

Summary

In the last ten years the Scottish government (SG) has spent a total of £60–70 m on its international development programme. Although cited as a success and as being unique in its approach, closer analysis reveals a different picture, and raises fundamental questions over the rationale for the programme and over its future direction. This includes whether, in the context of unprecedented growth in aid spending from the UK government – now equal to £450 per household from £270 ten years ago – and widespread cutbacks in other public expenditure, why spend £4 more per household on aid?

International development is a reserved power – therefore there is no statutory requirement for an SG. In this context, the origins of the SG programme lie in a spectrum of factors – developmental (contributing to reducing poverty globally), 'formal'-political (a greater international presence for the SG) and 'informal'-political (for politicians, the easy distraction and vanity of development projects).

The programme itself is characterized by a diversity of activity. It consists primarily of a series of small projects (57 in 2016) and core funding to three Scottish-based coordination and networking development NGOs. Malawi is the main focus of activity, reflecting the historic close ties between the two nations, and consumes around half the programme's £9 m current annual budget.

The SG reports on the programme in positive terms. However, in practice there has been little assessment of its efficacy – especially in terms of the SG's own key criteria of 'impact' (has this changed poor people's lives?) and 'sustainability' (will change last?). The only part of the programme which allows this level of insight is its flagship and largest initiative – the Malawi Renewable Energy Acceleration Programme (MREAP). MREAP can be seen as a window into the performance of the whole programme and is frequently cited as a success, especially its headline achievement of increasing 80,000 people's access to affordable renewable energy.

But more detailed scrutiny, from MREAP's own analysis, shows that most of these gains will not be sustained. Rather than make a significant, lasting difference and meaningful change in the lives of poor people, MREAP's performance, especially its lack of sustainability, bears all the hallmarks of the wider development experience in Malawi – a country awash with, and dependent on, aid resources, most of which have been ineffective.

After ten years, what can be concluded about the performance of the SG's international development programme?

- Politically, it has been a 'success'. There exists an implicit consensus between the political parties that this is, somehow, a 'good thing' to do. The common manifesto positions of the main parties at the 2016 Scottish parliamentary election confirm international development's political acceptance. Pronouncements on the programme referring to its success and its innovative character, and to this being evidence of Scotland's compassionate and influential role, are largely accepted.
- With regard to its support for the Scottish Malawi Partnership, there seems no doubt that the programme has helped catalyse wider interest in and funding for Malawian causes – and this, in itself, is a positive outcome.
- But overall there is little evidence of achievement of substance – meaningful change in the lives of poor people in Malawi or developing countries. From a development perspective, it has not been a success and the SG's repeated assertions of the programme's virtues have an empty quality that serve a political rather than any developmental purpose.
- The development rationale for an SG international development programme remains unclear. Especially now, in the light of the unprecedented growth in aid spending from the UK government – now equal to £450 per household from £270 ten years ago – and widespread cutbacks in other public expenditure, why spend £4 more per household on aid?

For the future, answering the core question – what is it that Scottish aid can do that UK aid cannot? – is critical. If there is no credible response to it, the Scottish international development effort runs the risk of being seen as a 'me-too' gesture, tokenism dressed up as idealism, cosy political self-interest as development concern.

Introduction

In 2005, prompted by the devastation from the Asian Tsunami, the Scottish government (SG) established its international development programme. Since then, over the last ten years, £60–70 m has been invested under the programme in seven main countries in Africa and South Asia, and in particular in Malawi.[1]

International development is referred to commonly in SG communications in a positive light, as being successful and as an example of Scottish international leadership. And it is accorded importance by the SG, even to the extent of awarding it ministerial status. Yet it is anomalous in a number of respects. It is not a statutory responsibility of the SG, nor is it, relatively speaking, a significant budgetary item. Nor, despite the claims made of its success, has it been the subject of serious independent scrutiny.

Now, with the SG in the throes of a consultation exercise on future priorities, is a timely moment for an independent view of the programme, of its rationale and its effectiveness. And to consider some of the bigger issues which receive comparatively little attention from the SG, the media or from the aid community in Scotland. Why have an aid programme? Does it do any good? How is it serving the cause of international development? This brief paper seeks to throw light on some of these questions.

Its specific objectives are to consider:

1. The origins of and rationale for the SG's international development programme.
2. The overall changes brought about by the programme, including changes to the institutional context for aid in Scotland.
3. The efficacy of the Malawi programme, which has consumed most programme resources, and in particular the 'flagship' Malawi Renewable Energy Acceleration Programme (MREAP).
4. In light of the above, the extent to which the programme is meeting its original rationale and objectives, and on this basis, some preliminary conclusions and potential implications for the future.

The paper does not examine the operational details of how the existing programme works. Its focus is the bigger strategic questions facing the programme. It draws on information in the public domain, and on the author's extensive experience in international development work.

1. The international development programme – origins and rationale

Under the terms of Scotland's devolution settlement – defined in the Scotland Act (1998) – international development is a reserved power for the UK government. In other words, the SG is not required to have an international development programme – it chooses to.[2] The initial prompt for the SG to create such a programme may have been the desire to have a better coordinated response to the Asian Tsunami – and more generally a desire to offer help at a time of great need – but the underlying question of why spend resources, from a limited pool, on international aid still stands. Why do this? More than a generic wish to contribute to global development, three sets of reasons appear relevant.

First, the (Labour) SG of the time (2005), felt that Scotland's *'devolution journey'* would not be complete without the establishment of a permanent international development fund. In other words, the defined set of devolved responsibilities were not *enough*, and that for the SG to be *valid* – and to do the kind of thing that *proper* governments do – it had to have more than this (Keating, 2014). This wish for a bigger international role and voice is not uncommon in sub-state units (Hepburn, 2015) in Europe and North America but is more likely to take other forms – such as culture and foreign investment promotion (which Scotland also does) – rather than an international aid programme.

Second, and related to the above, the decision to develop an international development programme was sourced in a desire to take a more prominent role internationally and establish a stronger identity, or brand, in doing so. The International Development Policy Paper of 2008 (Scottish Government, 2008) spoke of *'advancing Scotland's place in the world as a responsible nation by building mutually beneficial links with other countries ...'*. And the current consultation paper (Scottish Government, 2016) articulates an ambition for Scotland to be seen as a *'compassionate'* nation contributing *'as a good global citizen to reducing poverty and inequality globally'*, as a *'voice for humanity, voice for progressiveness, voice for tolerance'*.

This desire for a more visible role in the international development arena has been matched by a view that the country *'has a distinctive contribution to make in its work with developing countries'*, so that better, more effective development is supported. This distinctive offer is referred to variously as expertise in particular fields such as renewable energy and higher education and as the knowledge stemming from cultural and institutional bonds, especially in Malawi. Within this view of uniquely Scottish expertise and knowledge which could be tapped into by a Scottish aid programme is an implication that these resources could not be utilized effectively by the broader UK aid programme, and that something extra is required to draw on them. This should be seen in the context of a UK aid programme which has changed vastly in the last ten years.

In 2005, the UK aid programme totalled £6.7 bn, equivalent to £270 per household. By 2015 this had increased to £12 bn, £450 per household (Figure 13.1). The UK is now the second biggest bilateral donor (after the US) and, aside from some smaller, European countries, spends more on aid as a proportion of GDP than other comparable economies. This unprecedented growth – 50 per cent in real terms since 2010 – in spending comes at a time of significant austerity and large-scale cutbacks in many domestic budgets,

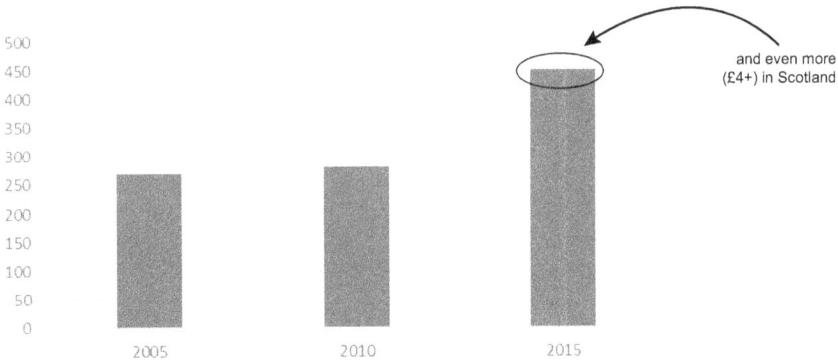

Figure 13.1 UK aid spending per household (£), 2005–2016

affecting all parts of the UK including Scotland. Scottish taxpayers of course bear this burden as much as their counterparts elsewhere in the UK but have the extra load of the Scottish government's aid budget – at £9 m equivalent to roughly £4 per household. Notwithstanding the reasons for this spending explosion at a UK level, still less its efficacy, the rationale for a Scottish aid programme – at least in part because UK aid wasn't 'enough' – might have been challenged by the new reality of a vastly expanded UK aid programme. However, there has been little open debate on this.

The third reason for a Scottish international development programme lies in the realms of the informal and of realpolitik. For politicians, international aid provides a soft distraction from other, more pressing concerns. Aid recipients are not constituents. Comparatively speaking, aid is not exposed to the same level of scrutiny, by the media or parliamentarians, as other areas of public expenditure. Aid taps into a very human desire to 'help' and offers many easy (and visible) opportunities to demonstrate that 'help' is being offered. For some critics, international development is therefore an ideal place for politicians' (and celebrities') vanity projects (Birrell, 2015). Harder questions on the longer-term impact of aid – such as its real contribution to low-income economies and to sustainable development – are seldom asked. This is less so in the UK as a whole where the vast amounts devoted to aid means that it cannot escape some examination, but here too, much critical comment is superficial and about (apparent) waste rather than efficacy. Certainly, in Scotland, if aid is not a criticism-*free* zone it is criticism-*lite*. Protected by an aura of virtue and selfless idealism, aid's intentions are frequently seen to outweigh more humdrum considerations (such as achievements). In such a context, analysis which is remotely critical is deemed unfair, as disloyal to the greater charitable cause of *'doing our bit'* to *'make a difference'*.

This 'doing our bit' rationale was much to the fore when the SG – with the backing of the UK government – instituted the international development fund in 2005. As the First Minister at the time, Jack McConnell, explained, Hillary Benn, then Department for International Development (DFID) Minister *'responded strongly backing our commitment to use the opportunities of devolution to make a difference elsewhere. He said "There is more than enough work to go round and everyone can contribute to tackling global poverty"'* (McConnell, 2013).

McConnell, under whose stewardship the international development programme was launched, and fiercely criticized in other spheres of government work, received little criticism for this policy, which was adopted and expanded by his (SNP) successors. Indeed, even although it was a minute part of his government's work and not part of its statutory responsibilities, international development came to be seen as a McConnell area of expertise. McConnell, now Lord McConnell of Glenscorrodale, was widely expected to be appointed as the British High Commissioner to Malawi had Labour won the 2010 election and he has since set up the McConnell International Foundation to promote development work.

The origins and rationale for the SG's aid programme therefore lie in a combination of factors: government desire for more legitimacy; an ambition to take a more independent place in the world and a belief that in doing so better aid will result; an implied critique of the limitations of the existing (and much expanded) UK aid system; and a political preference to be involved in the comparatively safe and expedient waters of international aid.

2. Changes (overall) from the Scottish government aid programme

The SG international aid programme comprises a series of components (Table 13.1). The largest of these is for projects in Malawi (approx. half the budget) with other significant amounts aimed at South Asia (India, Pakistan and Bangladesh) and sub-Saharan Africa (Kenya, Rwanda and Tanzania). Smaller amounts are available for an open small projects window and scholarships. In addition approx. £0.5 m is provided as core funding to support three networking/advocacy organizations in Scotland: the Scottish Malawi Partnership (SMP) and its sister organization in Malawi, the Malawi-Scotland Partnership (MaSP), the Network of International Development Organisations

Table 13.1 Key spending components of the international development programme

Description	2014–15 funding
Main Development Programmes	Malawi Programme (£4.2 m) Sub-Saharan Africa Programme (£1.22 m) South Asia Programme (£1.46 m)
Renewable Energy Programme	Malawi Renewable Energy Programme 2012–15 (MREAP) (£349,878)
Small Grants Programme	3-year pilot Small Grants Programme, launched 2013 (£431 k)
Sport Relief Partnership	Partnership with Sport Relief and UNICEF in Malawi & Bangladesh (£165 k)
Scholarships	The Pakistan Women Scholarships (£150 k) The Pakistan Children Scholarships (£110 k) The David Livingstone Scholarships programme in Malawi (£100 k)
Core funding for international development networking/fair trade organisations	The Network of International Development Organisations in Scotland (NIDOS) (£135 k) The Scotland Malawi Partnership (SMP) in Scotland and its sister organisation the Malawi Scotland Partnership (MaSP) in Malawi (£231,542 in total) Support for fair trade via the Scottish Fair-Trade Forum (SFTF) (£155,600)
Humanitarian funding	In 2014/15, donations to: Gaza; Ebola in West Africa; and Malawi floods appeals

Source: Scottish Government (2016)

in Scotland (NIDOS), and the Scottish Fair Trade Forum. The current annual budget is £9 m, an amount that has been unchanged since 2010 – having started at £3 m before growing to £6 m in 2008.

In reality, the programme mainly comprises a number – 57 in 2016 – of small projects in different theme areas such as health, education, renewable energy and water, with the specific themes varying from one region to another. After ten years of support, worth £60–70 m, what do we know about the effectiveness of this aid? What can be said about the efficacy of this aspect of government policy?

The first thing to be noted is that the SG's national performance framework[3] for assessing 'progress' in Scotland doesn't apply to aid. Of the 55 listed indicators only one, Scotland's international reputation, might be said to be linked – and then tenuously – to international development. So international development is, in this sense, an 'off-the-books' anomaly, in terms of accountability and performance.

Second it is difficult to assess performance. To do so properly means gaining insight into two related broad aspects of change: 'impact' – meaning change in poor people's lives and 'sustainability' – meaning the capability of the systems around people to continue to deliver benefits.

For example, in education this would mean not simply training teachers but looking at the effectiveness of teachers in terms of child learning and the ability of teacher training systems to provide and develop further appropriate training. Or in renewable energy, this would mean not simply looking at the use of solar-powered electricity and the benefits people derive from this but the functionality of the system of demand and supply (in a market) for solar panels and its ability to adapt and grow in the future. The SG itself has identified sustainability as a critical indicator of success – *'Long-term viability/ sustainability is absolutely crucial'* – allowing development to continue without further infusions of aid.

In this light – given the accepted importance of impact and in particular sustainability – it is notable that, after ten years, so little is known about the efficacy of the government's international development effort. The only overarching independent review of the programme was conducted in 2008 (LTS International, 2008). However, this was early in the programme's life and the review's focus was primarily on process – whether projects were being delivered according to their plans (it found they were) – and had little substantive to say on impact and sustainability. In the absence of rigorous attempts to assess impact and sustainability, at times the programme conflates 'impact' with 'activities delivered' to give a misleading impression of achievements. For example, in 2015, the SG's report to a parliamentary committee on its 'achievements' in international development highlighted its commitment to supporting *'critical global concerns'* and to projects that *'would be funded'* – not changes that it has caused (European and External Relations Committee, 2015). More specifically, in 2013, on the occasion of a visit from the International Development Minister Humza Yousaf to India, the SG issued a press release entitled *'Impact of aid on India'* (Scottish Government, 2013). This provided a list of activities that had been undertaken through supported projects:

- *'Trained more than 350 physicians and surgeons in diabetic foot disease management.*
- *Helped more than 3,200 farmers to develop better farming techniques.*
- *Supported almost 200 young entrepreneurs.*
- *Supported around 30,000 women to expand their businesses.*
- *Provided rights awareness training to 600 women.'*

In all cases this then was about things which had been done (trained, helped etc.). But whether any of this had any meaningful impact on people's lives let alone whether it was sustainable – more than a simple puff of subsidized activity, virtuous in intent but hoping for the best in terms of meaningful change – was not assessed. To assert this to be 'impact' is factually incorrect. This is more than nit-picking pedantry; the 'so-what' challenge – does it make a difference? will change last? – is fundamental to 'good development'. Projects' focus, and what they report on following the guidelines laid down by the SG to grant recipients, is on activities delivered; they don't (and can't) ask the more difficult 'so what' question. Of course, all projects are able to cite – and to show visiting dignitaries – examples of people who have benefitted from aid. But the majority of projects supported by the SG have little more than a perfunctory view of their longer-term impact or sustainability. The one project that has looked at these issues in more depth is MREAP in Malawi which we explore in more depth below.

If substantive enduring changes to people's lives are not evident from the international development programme, one area of change is more visible and more clearly attributable to the programme. Core government funding is provided for three organizations – SMP, SFTF, and NIDOS. Though different, in each case their role is concerned with networking among other development and civil society organizations, with providing information and educating the Scottish public, and with influencing decision-makers. In each case the prominence of the organisation has risen and they have become more established fixtures in the development institutional landscape over the last ten years. But in doing so, each organization has become financially dependent on the government. NIDOS for example, formed in 2000, has grown from an organization with an annual income of £35,000 in 2003 to a one, ten years later in 2013, with an income of more than four times this amount (£161,000), but has done so almost entirely on the basis of grant funding from the Scottish government. In recent years this has accounted for three-quarters of their funding.

The effect of SG support, it might be argued, has been to raise the capacity of NIDOS to do its work more effectively. But a more insidious effect is possible as well. Part of NIDOS' role is to be an advocate on aid issues but its ability to play this role with the SG – for example to hold it to account – is undermined by its crushing financial dependence. The potential dangers of NGO dependence on state funding is an ongoing debate in development circles (Banks and Hulme, 2012), in particular the risks to NGO legitimacy and independence. In the case of NIDOS it has, *de facto*, become a quasi-state organisation. Government support therefore may have increased the prominence and role of Scottish-based development organizations – and developed an aid constituency for the SG – but in doing so it has undermined the plurality of voices within the sector.

Overall, the international development programme has unquestionably increased the volume of development-related activity from a plethora of small projects and the raised profile of key coordinating NGOs. However, the latter may have been at the expense of organizations' independence while there is no evidence to show that the growth of project activity has resulted in meaningful or sustainable outcomes amongst poor people. In general, there is an absence of detailed data on the effectiveness of projects. The exception to this situation is in Malawi where the greatest concentration of activity and budget has been made. If the Scottish government's international development programme was successful anywhere one would expect it to be here – and it is the Malawi programme that it is the focus of our analysis in the next section.

3. Unpicking the Malawi experience

Scotland's international aid is aimed at seven priority countries in South Asia and sub-Saharan Africa, with Malawi being by far the most significant of these. The SG signed an overarching Cooperation Agreement with Malawi in 2005 and at that time, all of the international development budget (then £3 m) was for projects in Malawi. Currently a minimum of £3 m per annum is spent there, and this is closer to £5 m in reality. With other climate change projects in addition to this, Malawi is the main focus of funding. This prioritisation reflects the considerable historical connection between the countries, stemming from David Livingstone in the nineteenth century, manifested in continuing strong personal and institutional networks and linkages between the countries.

The SG regards its approach in Malawi, building on these links, to be *'unique in world terms'*. Its so-called *'relational approach'*, it believes, using the extensive links between the two nations, brings greater efficiencies and impact. Its emphasis on *'people'* and *'partnerships'* and on being *'needs-based and culturally sensitive'* contains within it a rebuke to other development practices and their *'top-down'* and *'impersonal'* ways. The SG's approach therefore is seen to be 'better' and logically to be more likely to generate better results.

The decision to focus efforts on Malawi primarily stemmed from the strength of the relationship but is also justified on the basis of developmental need. A raft of indicators show the impoverished and parlous state of the country. In relation to the Human Development Index, which assesses countries with respect to income, education and health achievements, Malawi ranked 170th out of 176 countries in 2013; life expectancy is barely 54 years; more than 40 per cent exist in severe multi-dimensional poverty; more than

80 per cent survive on less than $2 per day; ill-health is prevalent and child mortality rates are high. It is also subject to periodic drought and in 2016 faced its worst food shortage in a decade.

Malawi's economic development weakness is compounded by weak institutions and poor governance. Although it is more than 20 years since the demise of Hastings Banda, who ruled for 33 years, the era of multi-party democracy in Malawi has not delivered either competent government or rulers of integrity. In 2013 these flaws came to a head when the so-called 'cashgate' scandal was exposed (BBC, 2014). After a series of incidents including the shooting of the Finance Ministry's Budget Director and the discovery of bales of cash in the car boots and homes of junior civil servants, a broader and long-established case of corruption around a computer-based financial information storage system emerged. Some donors, including DFID,[4] temporarily suspended aid in the light of the scandal. Since then the Malawian government claims to have rooted out the problem. However, there remains little confidence in the political class, the culture of corruption is widespread and, given the disparities between the aid world and the 'real economy' world, the incentives for corruption are strong and often irresistible (The Conversation, 2015).

3.1 The diverse Malawi portfolio

In the 2013–2016 period, 24 different projects were supported in Malawi under the international development programme with an allocated budget of £8.1 m. These covered projects under three sectors – health (ten), education (five) and sustainable economic development (nine) – and were implemented by NGOs, academic organizations and commercial contracting firms. They covered a range of activity, for example:

- *Transforming the Education and Training of Clinical Professionals Delivering Maternal and Child Healthcare*; the University of Edinburgh: in partnership with the University of Malawi, supporting the development, delivery and management of masters degrees in maternal and child health.
- *Developing a Sustainable Programme of Cervical Cancer Screening*; NHS Lothian: developing a sustainable cervical cancer prevention programme through: increased provision of screening clinics; a 'train the trainers' skills model; and, improved staff skills in data collection and monitoring.
- *Mary's Meals School Feeding Programme Expansion*; Mary's Meals: establishing school feeding operations in 18 primary schools, in turn increasing access to education and improving nutrition for children.
- *Social and Economic Empowerment of 19,200 Smallholder Producers*; Oxfam: addressing the inter-related problems of economic and social insecurities faced by 19,200 poor households, by improving skills and access to technologies and financial services, and capacities for advocacy.
- *Mangochi Livelihoods and Economic Recovery Project*; Scottish Catholic International Aid Fund: working with vulnerable groups to support

3,000 households in to increase their income and food security through effective crop and livestock productivity and small-scale business.

- *Chancellor College Masters in Primary Education*; Strathclyde University: developing a diploma in primary education aimed at encouraging more trained teachers to teach in primary schools.

The supported projects are diverse. They include those aimed at specific aspects of public sector strengthening – typically in health and education – and, with Malawian public sector partners, others that work more directly with the poor – often organized in groups – and are concerned with economic and social development, and others (notably Mary's Meals) which are more welfare-oriented (feeding children). Generalizing over the portfolio of projects of course runs the risk of drawing inappropriate conclusions, but certainly it is the case that with none of these has there been the depth of analysis to throw light on their impact or sustainability. MREAP (see below), not included in the above list and costing an additional £2.3 m – the largest single programme in the portfolio – has been more shaped by analysis and allows more detailed learning and conclusions to be reached.

The resources expended in Malawi – £10.4 m over three years – represent the greatest concentration of Scottish aid resources. But it is important that this is put into the wider Malawian aid context. In the same three-year period DFID has spent approximately £270 m[5] in the country – 'official' SG aid, even here at its point of most intense focus is therefore less than 4 per cent of the DFID total. In Malawi, as elsewhere, DFID spending has generally increased but, privately, aid officials are known to be concerned about the absorptive capacity of Malawian institutions. To say that Malawi is 'full up' in relation to aid is a simplification but the dangers of aid – in the absence of appropriate partners (in the private and public sectors) – becoming a means of direct delivery only, and of inducing not development but dependence, are openly acknowledged.

Concern over Malawi's dependence of foreign aid is hardly a new topic – indeed, one authoritative analysis of this was published in 1975! (Morton, 1975). But there is no indication that it is diminishing. The statistics are revealing; per capita aid spending in Malawi at $70 per head in 2013 is on a par with other comparable countries in Africa. But because the economy is so weak, its aggregate dependence on aid is much greater. Aid to Malawi is equivalent to 30.3 per cent of gross national income,[6] much higher than in neighbouring countries – in Zambia the figure is 4.5 per cent, Tanzania 7.8 per cent, and Kenya 5.9 per cent. Aid accounts for around 40 per cent of government expenditure in Malawi.

3.2 The Scotland Malawi Partnership – the core of the relationship

At the heart of the Scottish government's international development programme in Malawi is the Scotland Malawi Partnership (SMP). Set up in 2005, the SMP exists to *'help coordinate, support and represent Scotland's many civic links with Malawi'.*[7] These links are numerous. The SMP has 800 member organisations. 94,000 Scots are said to have personal links with Malawi; 46 per cent of the Scottish population are estimated to personally know someone with a connection to Malawi.

The SMP's activities take different forms – cultural, economic, social – but as an umbrella, coordinating body are as much about promoting their members' endeavours as their own. A number of broad points can be made in relation to the SMP:

- It has helped to instigate a growth in activity and linkages. The number of members has increased from 450 in 2010 to 800 now – including NGOs, businesses, education organizations, churches, local authorities, and individuals. There is a higher profile to the Scotland–Malawi relationship than ever before; there is more and more diverse activity than ever before. There is evidence that the SMP has helped to catalyse this growth.
- Given its diversity it is difficult to measure the strength or value of this relationship precisely. However, a study by the University of Edinburgh (Anders, 2014), using a 'social return on investment' framework, estimated that the value of inputs, including in-kind donations, finance and volunteering was £40 m per annum. This has clearly not all been caused by the SMP or by SG support to the SMP. But the SMP itself has stated that it believes support has been very important, *'unleashing a powerful and enviable multiplier effect', 'a virtuous circle between Government and people where popular support inspires Government efforts while Government support stimulates popular engagement'.*
- Leaving aside reservations over the 'additionality' of this £40 m amount, there seems little doubt that the SMP has been successful in stimulating more activity and 'buzz' around Malawi and a rare level of civic engagement for a developing country.
- However, it is also notable that the University of Edinburgh report did not estimate the 'return' from the 'investment' made by the SMP's members. It was concerned with putting a value on inputs only. Accounts of the impact of the SMP's members' activities are anecdotal and subjective and, as with so much else in the SG aid story, say little or nothing on longer-term sustainability.
- The SMP has also sought to develop an ethical framework to shape the many activities undertaken, based around a belief in *'dignified partnership'*. Underpinning this is a series of partnership principles including appropriateness, mutual respect, sustainability, trust and transparency. Although not a methodology for intervention, these principles are seen to be important in guiding activities, and as an embodiment of the *'relational approach'* advocated by the Scottish government.
- The SMP is more than 90 per cent funded by the Scottish government, as it has been from its inception. A partner organisation has also been

established in Malawi, the Malawi Scotland Partnership (MaSP). This exists *'to support Malawi's many civil society links with Scotland'*. It sees itself as a *'Malawi-owned and Malawi-led network'*[8] – which may be true, but it is also entirely SG-funded. The SMP and MaSP are, to a considerable degree, creations of the SG and dependent on it.

Overall, the picture that emerges on the SMP and the Malawian dimension to the Scottish government's international development efforts is certainly that there has been a significant growth in aid activity. Some of this has been supported by the SG directly but much of it has been separate from 'official' aid, tapping into personal and institutional networks, and a deep well of goodwill. But on the efficacy of this – real and lasting achievement to enhance the lives of poor people in Malawi – there is little analysis. For that we need to turn to MREAP.

3.3 MREAP – the troubled flagship

If Malawi is the central country focus of the Scottish government's international aid effort, the lead initiative within this is the Malawi Renewable Energy Acceleration Programme (MREAP). MREAP is the showpiece, the programme which has attracted most attention and which has been the recipient of more public funds than another initiative. As an action research programme, it has also – and unlike most other aid activities supported by the SG – been the subject of a relatively high level of scrutiny and analysis, much of which is available publicly. MREAP therefore provides a unique window into the overall SG aid experience.

MREAP was a three-year programme that, in its initial phase, ran from 2012 to 2015 and received £2.3 m. Its overall objective was to improve the prospects for renewable energy (RE) in Malawi. More specifically, it sought to improve the 'enabling environment' for RE – the institutions and services supporting the development of RE – and increase the access of poor Malawians to affordable and appropriate energy. The key thrust of the programme was enhancing 'community energy' (CE) which (although there is no universal definition) refers to projects based on collective action to manage and generate energy and emphasize engagement and control by local communities who benefit collectively from outcomes.[9] Scotland was seen to have relevant competence in this sphere that could be of benefit for the Malawian context. The programme was implemented by a consortium of eight organizations in Scotland and Malawi, led by the University of Strathclyde. From the Scottish 'side' this also included Community Energy Scotland (CES), a membership and support organization for the community energy sector and IOD PARC, a consulting firm. The Malawian side included NGOs, academic organizations, and the Malawian government.

MREAP was delivered through four related components:

- The Community Energy Development Programme (CEDP) – instigating new community RE projects – especially solar electricity, biomass and

cookstoves – and developing a new community energy network and support organization.
- Renewable Energy Capacity Building Programme (RECBP) – developing Malawian capacities, especially in higher education institutions (for example a new course on RE), related to training and research on RE.
- Wind Energy Preparation Programme (WEPP) – concerned primarily with feasibility and other technical analyses to support wind energy projects.
- Institutional Support Programme (ISP) – monitoring and evaluation of MREAP's work to ensure that activities were grounded in detailed analysis and to provide an evidence base for learning and policy advice.

Implementing these components involved a range of activities but at their core, and the uniting feature of all the various workstreams, and the headline indicator for the SG, was the objective of improving access to more affordable renewable energy.

From the perspective of 2016, with the programme (at least the first phase) completed, what can be said about the performance of MREAP? Certainly, a plethora of activities have delivered a range of outputs – for example, 46 different CE projects in 11 different districts, a new CE support and network organisation (Community Energy Malawi – CEM), toolkits and handbooks on RE, a new MPhil on RE, a grant-giving RE entrepreneurship fund, research and feasibility studies ... the list is long. By the project end, 80,000 people, according to MREAP's own analysis, have benefitted through improved access to RE, from these activities. It shows also that, six months after RE technologies were provided through MREAP, 93 per cent of these were functional and being used, for example, in improving lighting for schools and health centres and providing cookstoves for households.

The achievements of MREAP, at first sight at least, appear significant. Certainly, the view from the SG on MREAP is positive. The Minster has commented on MREAP's 'success' (British High Commission Malawi, 2015), MREAP features prominently in government discussion, and a successor to MREAP focused on RE in a new phase of funding for 2015–18 is being developed. Press coverage has also been largely positive (Didcock, 2015).

Closer study of the MREAP experience, however, suggests a more nuanced view is appropriate. MREAP was always conceived as an action-research type programme from which lessons – 'the good and the bad' – could be learned.

The SG's own criteria for 'good development' centres on the degree to which sustainable outcomes are being achieved, allowing external aid, as a temporary input, to exit. This emphasis on sustainability echoes wider views in international development on sustainability (and scale) as being the essence of what development is about. It is of course particularly apposite in Malawi where, as noted above, limited impact and increased dependence (i.e. lack of sustainability) have characterized the development experience.

In this light, closer analysis reveals a picture markedly different from the positive image presented. Of critical importance here, the community enterprises which have been supported/instigated – and which are central to the initiative – are very unlikely to be sustainable. According to MREAP's own analysis (Currie, Davies, and Young, 2015) two-thirds of projects are likely to fail within three years without further support. Community enterprises lack the capability (financial, technical, and organizational) to maintain and further develop their projects. The envisaged means of support to remedy this was the establishment of CEM as a provider of technical and other services to projects. However, CEM itself is completely dependent financially on MREAP – and therefore the SG. There is no realistic chance of it being financed from local sources; if it has any future it can only be as a foreign-funded entity. MREAP's own analysis provides a brief review of potential funding sources for CEM but these are highly speculative, and it describes CEM's position as *'over-whelmingly vulnerable'*. In other words, the aid dependence that has marked Malawi's experience is inherent within MREAP's approach to promoting RE.

MREAP's support for cookstoves raises particular sustainability concerns. Cookstoves accounts for more than half of the stated MREAP beneficiary outreach of 80,000 people. Benefits from use of energy-efficient wood fuel stoves are environmental (less fuel required) and social and economic (less time required to collect wood) in nature – and these benefits are being realized. However, stoves are finite; sustainability requires that sustainable systems for making and selling stoves are developed. MREAP's own evaluation found that *'producer groups' sustainability will depend on increasing adoption rates and rolling out appropriate marketing'*. It also found that the development of local markets was proving to be very problematic. That this should be the case is not surprising. Although MREAP sought to have an action-research emphasis, its approach on cookstoves mirrors common failings – going back many years (indeed decades) – that have characterized the experience of international development organizations. The traditional approach of setting up and working with women's producer groups as community enterprises, tried in many countries, has generally resulted in limited impact and sustainability. This experience – much of it of failure – prompted the largest agencies and organizations to develop a different, market development perspective based less on groups as producers but more on individual entrepreneurs and on the stimulation of demand. German development organizations, for example the Global Alliance for Clean Cookstoves,[10] have been at the forefront of this evolution. MREAP's approach appears to have bypassed this learning.

Similar concerns are raised in relation to solar lanterns (for lighting). As with stoves, real sustainability requires that systems of supply and demand (a market) for these are established. MREAP's approach has been to develop group community enterprises as the key player in developing this market. But its analysis highlights a range of fundamental problems with this approach. Community groups/enterprises are *'associated with charity work'* and people fail to pay off the outstanding balances on loans given for lantern purchase, with many regarding them as donations from distant aid benefactors. MREAP's own evaluation concludes that sustainability would have been better pursued if solar lanterns were seen as a 'normal' business rather than one that was the preserve of community groups.

The sustainability challenge in Malawi was one that MREAP was aware of. As part of the programme, although strangely towards its end (June 2015 – and therefore too late to influence its activities), MREAP studied the sustainability of other previous solar photovoltaic initiatives throughout Malawi. It found that *'the majority of installed projects can be considered "unsustainable" and at risk of failure. Many projects are now unsupported, are partially or completely non-functional and are without reliable and effective means to resuscitate performance'* (Frame and Daunhauer, 2015). In practice, this description could be seen as equally applicable to MREAP's own experience.

Notwithstanding the immediate value of many of the outputs generated and the relevance of the technical expertise brought to bear, and even taking a positive view of the longer-term benefits of other aspects of MREAP's intervention – for example its work with academic organisations – its approach has been seriously flawed. Like much of the historic development experience in Malawi, the rush from immediate impacts is likely to recede quickly as benefits – and the systems that can deliver these – are shown to be unsustainable in the longer-term without further direct infusions of aid. Obviously, given the profile of and optimism around MREAP this is a disappointing finding. Why has this happened? Two underlying causes can be highlighted.

First, MREAP's approach has been based on the false premise that the Scottish experience in promoting community renewable energy has particular relevance for Malawi. Scotland's overall record in relation to renewable energy is well-known. In 2014 production from renewable sources was equivalent to almost half of the country's gross electricity consumption, having been only 20 per cent in 2007. Renewables output has doubled in a seven-year period. Testing targets to reduce greenhouse gas emissions, the significant renewable energy resource in the country and further investments in preparation mean that the share of electricity from renewable energy will continue to grow. RE is seen as a policy priority by the SG and is central to its energy and environmental strategies.

Scotland is also a formal partner in the UN's Sustainable Energy for All (SE4ALL) campaign having been requested by the UN's Secretary General to sign up because of its *'international leadership on renewable energy and climate change'*. In this context, it might be understandable therefore that RE should feature in Scotland's 'offer' in relation to international development (and climate change).

But if renewable energy is important – and is a success – in Scotland, and potentially offers some relevant experience and expertise from which other countries can benefit, it does not follow that *community* RE is either important or relevant. In 2015, the total 'community and locally owned' renewable energy capacity in Scotland was 508MW (Young and Georgieva, 2015) out of a total for RE overall of 7444MW, equivalent to 7 per cent of the total.

However, the majority of this capacity was actually owned by private business and estates. If this is taken out, the actual total owned by community groups, charities, housing associations and local authorities was 146MW, less than 2 per cent of the total. At best therefore, community ownership is a peripheral part of the overall Scottish renewables story. More than this, the prevailing mode of renewable energy community enterprise that has developed has been dependent on major public subsidy and investment, with over £40 m of essentially grant funding being provided from public sources. Community enterprises are also assisted by a membership organization that provides ongoing technical and other services, CES. According to its annual accounts, CES is 40 per cent funded by grants, from both public and private sources. Indeed, its single biggest grant in recent years has been through MREAP to promote the community energy model in Malawi!

These facts on the role of community enterprise in renewable energy in Scotland – overall, its marginal significance – and the 'model' of community energy that is supported, especially the expectation of continual external support, raise major questions on why this should be seen as relevant to Malawi, a country whose energy sector is fundamentally underdeveloped and where aid has often caused increased donor dependence rather than self-reliant development? The SG clearly sees community energy as being a success story – *'Scotland leading the way across UK in how we support local and community ownership of renewable energy'*. Irrespective of the validity of this view, which is not the focus of this paper, the promotion of community enterprise RE in Malawi appears to owe more to a domestic agenda – the apparent virtues and success of community RE – rather than any analysis of the appropriateness of this to address the needs of Malawi. This has been development as ill-considered supply-side push – the aid-giver's agenda – rather than analysis-based response to Malawi's situation.

The second reason for MREAP's weak performance in relation to sustainability is that its approach has taken little or no cognisance of wider learning in international development. Given its fractured and increasingly politicised nature, there is seldom harmonious consensus on 'good practice' in development among donor agencies and implementing organizations such as NGOs. One clear trend however, voiced with growing force over the last twenty years, has been recognition of the failure of development interventions that focus on group/community enterprises. From the 1980s-onward, especially among NGOs, loosely categorized as the sustainable livelihoods approach, this was a common approach to development. At its heart this seeks to focus financial and technical resources on groups of beneficiaries with the objective of developing them into socially oriented entities that drive development – managing 'public' resources (such as water), providing services and inputs (such as finance, seeds, storage etc.), and advocating to governments on behalf of their communities. However, in practice the difficulties of group management, limitations in capacities, and most important, the mixed incentives inherent with a group setting undermined their functioning and meant the experience was, chiefly, one of failure, addressing symptoms rather than underlying causes (DCED, 2001; Dorward et al., 2002; Clark and Carney, 2008).

Learning from this failure has contributed to major reassessment of the fundamentals of development and in the last 10–15 years, to the emergence of new 'systemic' approaches. Variously termed market systems or market development approaches (Springfield Centre, 2014), the essence of these is that development agencies should (a) focus their attentions on the functioning of the overall systems or sectors within which poor people exist and concentrate on addressing the underlying constraints that prevent these from working effectively and (b) exit once this has been achieved – with an overt priority given to sustainability. The emergence of these approaches also illustrates development agencies' recognition of the reality in Africa of far-reaching changes in people's lives from market development – such as mobile phones – which have had little or no involvement from development agencies.

Operationalizing a systemic approach often means working with a range of partners, including government and established businesses, as well as communities. It has been – and is being – applied in a range of contexts, for example with considerable success in the Kenya financial sector where eight million more people have access to services than was the case ten years ago (Gibson, 2016). Although not applied extensively in the energy sphere, Kenya also offers a flavour of the potential here as well. M-KOPA is a business which provides pay-as-you-go solar installations for off-grid households, developed with some initial support from development agencies. 300,000 households in East Africa currently use M-KOPA solar systems for electricity. M-KOPA was launched commercially around the same time as the commencement of MREAP in October 2012, but its achievements (2000 households per week are now reported to be buying M-KOPA) – stand in marked comparison to those of its Malawian counterpart (small-scale projects sliding into 'failure' and dependence without continued external support).

M-KOPA is now expanding into clean burning cookstoves.[11] M-KOPA does not operate in Malawi but there are organizations there – such as SolarAid[12] – that recognize that innovative new business models offer hope in addressing the country's energy plight (McGrath, 2016).

Overall, thanks to its relatively detailed level of analysis and documentation, MREAP offers a useful and transparent basis for lesson-learning. This would have been strengthened had the SG followed MREAP's own recommendations and commissioned an independent evaluation at the programme's conclusion. However, they chose not to do this, on the basis that it was too soon for such an exercise.[13] While of course the perspective of several years hence will be valuable, not to have an evaluation of this, the SG's flagship programme, before then is a surprising decision in two respects. First, it assumes that the likely impact and sustainability are results that somehow, mysteriously, happen, and that it isn't possible to develop a real insight into projects' effectiveness prospectively, a position which does not stand up to considered analysis.[14] Second, it means that learning – perhaps hard but necessary – is, *de facto*, postponed for several years. In the meantime, policy decisions are taken without the benefit of this learning, a consequence that seems at odds with the SG's *'ambition to improve the International development programme'*.

The decision not to have an independent evaluation has also allowed MREAP's headline 'impact' – 80,000 people benefitting from improved energy access (mainly cooking stoves) – to be highlighted without challenge and without the essential caveats which MREAP's own analysis reveal: most of these gains are not likely to last without continued 'propping-up' support from the SG. In other words, the same limited-impact – dependency-creating development that has characterized Malawi for decades – has been largely replicated here.

What then can be learned from MREAP? Overall, it has done much of what it said it would do – and communities throughout Malawi are currently benefitting from the multiplicity of projects supported. But in the longer-term the impacts from these projects are unlikely to be sustainable. Given that *'long-term viability/sustainability'* was seen by the SG to be *'absolutely crucial'* for MREAP, this is an obvious and fundamental weakness. In this sense, MREAP – flagship programme in the international development programme – has not succeeded, and if appropriate learning is not extracted from the experience it will have failed as an action-research programme too. This analysis shows that this 'failure' has happened for two underlying reasons.

1. The programme was based on the incorrect premise that the Scottish experience in community energy provides a useful model for Malawi (it doesn't).
2. The design of and approach of MREAP, especially its ill-conceived focus on community/group enterprise, ignored basic learning that has taken place in the international development arena over the last 10–15 years.

Both of these problems were set into the conception and design of MREAP and meant that, no matter the diligence and commitment of the assorted partners, to a large degree, the programme was bound to fail.

4. The international development programme: Conclusions and the way ahead

4.1 Overall conclusions

As noted in Section 1, a spectrum of objectives ranging from the political to the developmental, lie behind the SG's international development programme. After 10 years, what has been achieved with respect to these and what can be learned from the experience?

1. As a political project, the international development programme has been 'successful' ...
Politically, international development is not an actively debated policy area but there exists an implicit consensus between the political parties that this is, somehow, a 'good thing' to do.[15] In the 2016 Scottish parliamentary elections, all the main parties represented in parliament offered their tacit or overt support for the international development policy. Indeed, both the ruling SNP and opposition Conservatives stated that they would increase its budget to £10 m – an 11 per cent increase (Scottish Conservative and Unionist Party, 2016; Scottish National Party, 2016). The SNP government's decision to create a ministerial position for international development is further confirmation of its political acceptance. This has happened despite its non-statutory status and its small budget size – £9 *million* out of a total budget of £37 *billion*. Beyond Parliament, the core funding of coordinating/networking groups – and a range of organizations for small projects – has created a constituency that is generally (and naturally) very supportive of the SG's efforts in international aid. In this sense, the original rationale for an international development fund of completing the *'devolution journey'*, to allow the SG to be more nation-like in its appearance, has further advanced. The political class, it would appear, are in unison.

2. ... and created a positive appearance, supported by much self-acclaim
The consensus on the validity of the international development activity extends to the media, where aid is seldom exposed to deeper or more critical analysis, and policy researchers. In May 2015 an internal government report was critical of the international development programme's arrangements and management capacity – currently 11 civil servants – and this received some media exposure (Hutcheon, 2015).

At the same time, a more detailed article on Mary's Meals in Malawi – a key recipient of SG support who provide food for one quarter of Malawi's school children – questioned the extent to which this was contributing to a long-term solution (Smith, 2015). But these are exceptions – the norm is for media coverage, if there is any, to accept broadly the message that emanates from the SG.

And that message is unremittingly positive! As the budget has increased to £9 m and as the policy area has assumed a ministerial level of importance, so the language used typically to describe the international development programme has ascended to new heights of (self) acclaim and congratulation. So, SG documents refer to the programme variously as *'successful'*, *'leading'* and *'ground-breaking'*, a programme that has *'been praised globally'*, as a *'pioneer'*, as evidence that – much as was originally intended – the programme shows that *'Scotland recognises its place in the world as an innovative, influential and caring nation'*.

3. But there is little achievement of substance to match this appearance ...
Beneath this barrage of apparently ceaseless achievement, there are few if any specifics cited to merit such glowing prose. If there is one 'achievement'

that is mentioned repeatedly it is the 80,000 people in Malawi that now have improved access to energy because of the flagship MREAP programme. This features in the current consultation paper, in First Minister speeches and in press releases. Yet, mentioned without caveat or context, this is an extremely misleading figure. MREAP's own analysis shows that in practice, far from being unalloyed success, without continued external support, most of the projects that contribute to the 80,000 are likely to fail. Far from being a paragon of self-reliant, sustainable development, the evidence suggests the opposite; the impact is likely to be similar to the bigger aid experience in Malawi – a short-term burst of impact which, without continued infusions of external support, will dissipate quickly, inducing cloying dependence rather than instigating development. While MREAP's own analysis is commendably transparent, an independent end-of-programme evaluation, especially important for this flagship programme and recommended by MREAP itself, would have been expected to bring out this learning more clearly. Although the decision by the SG not to go ahead with this – or indeed an independent assessment of the wider programme – may be politically expedient, from a development perspective, it is an opportunity missed.

The international development programme has therefore placed greater emphasis on appearance than substance. Whether or not it has contributed to enhancing perceptions of Scotland's role in the world is a moot point beyond this paper's scope to address; what is less debatable is that there is little evidence to show that it has resulted in meaningful change in the lives of poor people in developing countries.

4. ... And the oft-mentioned 'different' approach does not translate into good development practice
Where does this leave the claims of the SG having a distinctive approach and offering to international development? Well, there is clearly a different relationship between Scotland and Malawi, and the programme, through the catalysing efforts of the SMP, has tapped into and stimulated a wellspring of good intentions and energy – seen in the growth in funding for a multiplicity of Malawian causes. In itself, this is a positive development and potentially a strong resource to promote change. Unfortunately, there is little evidence to show that this is having a significant impact. Still less is there any evidence to support the efficacy of the much-vaunted distinctive approach that the SG follows. Characterized by repeated reference to key principles – partnership, dignity, respect, personal, etc. – none of these translate into a coherent approach to development practice. On the contrary, the MREAP experience illustrates that interventions which are wrongly conceived and take little cognisance of wider practical learning in the international development sphere, are more likely to fail. Self-declared principles can easily descend into the realms of self-righteous platitude. In this light, the SG's repeated assertions of its programme's virtues – without substance or evidence – have a hot air

self-righteous quality, a 'what's like us?' bluster that serves a political rather than developmental purpose.

5. Leaving the essential development question – what is distinctive/better about the Scottish government's international development programme? – largely unanswered

Despite the assurance that it collaborates closely with the UK government, decisions and discussions on the SG international aid effort appear to have proceeded without adequate recognition that the aid context in the UK (including Scotland) has changed. The unprecedented, astonishing growth in aid spending – which is set to continue because of the UK government's commitment to maintain spending at 0.7 per cent of GDP[16] – has changed the context for SG aid. With UK households now contributing £450 each to international aid – from £270 ten years ago – the rationale for spending more (the £4 Scottish international development levy) needs to be clear. Even in Malawi, Scottish aid amounts to less than 4 per cent of UK spending. In many countries, DFID struggles to spend its hugely enlarged budget. Developmentally, what is it that Scottish aid can do that UK aid cannot? This basic question is largely unanswered and as long as this is the case, the Scottish international development effort runs the risk of being seen as a 'me-too' gesture, tokenism dressed up as idealism, political self-interest as development concern.

Regrettably, this changed context has not sparked any notable reassessment of what Scottish aid is there to do. Indeed, if anything it appears to have only triggered a political race to pledge to spend more. In 2014 Minister Yousaf stated that Scotland (were it independent), and not content with the UK level of effort, would seek to go further than the UK government in terms of aid spending – *'not only will we ensure that we meet the 0.7% target, but we'll look to go to 1%'* (Allan, 2013). It was, he said, a matter of *'showing our political intent'*. Self-evidently, it is the political objectives of Scotland's international development experience that have been prioritised – but development goals are a secondary concern.

4.2 Suggestions for the future

Given the above conclusions on the SG's international development experience, what are the implications for the future? Three broad suggestions are made.

1. Make a decision – but for the right reasons: Does Scotland have a distinctive offer?

The SG should decide if it wishes to have an international development programme or not. That decision should not be based on an abstract notion of 'wanting to help' – a have-a-go instinct that confuses amorphous intentions with specific achievements, and whose essence is that more is always better. Rather it should be based on an analysis of what additional value such a programme can offer relative to other development spending, especially in the context of the UK's expanded aid effort.

- Saying no here would not imply a closed insular view or one that is morally inferior; it would merely be a recognition that the SG's capacity to *do* international development well doesn't exist now and that, anyway, at £450 per household, Scottish citizens already contribute significantly to development goals.
- Saying yes would require that there is a considered analysis of what the oft-referred to 'distinctive' Scottish offer to international development really is in practice. What is it that Scotland can potentially do/do better that bigger programmes cannot? Malawi might well feature in this search for a Scottish aid unique selling point but other features may emerge, for example, related to being small, flexible, specialized, and focused? One implication of this would be that a programme would be narrower and tighter and less broad-based, and that fewer of the broad constituency of organizations that currently feed off the programme would find a role or funding. In such a scenario, developmental concerns would take precedence over political factors.[17]

2. Assuming it is yes, put analysis and measurement at the heart of any future programme
From the outset, any such programme should be based on rigorous analysis, measurement and learning. The current programme's claims to be based on a unique relational approach are unfounded. Its claims on effectiveness are optimistic veering to disingenuous. Yet, in the absence of a commitment to be more analytical, development interventions can slide into an ambiguous grey zone of doubt, claim and counter-claim. Certainly, any programme which is seeking to be different and more specialized – and more effective because of this – has to be strongly analytical and focused.

3. Locally based perhaps – but shaped by international experience
Any future programme should be informed by wider development experience and learning on successful practice emerging from this. A careful balance has to be struck between, on the one hand, a programme that draws on 'national' strengths – that are common/specific to Scotland – and on the other ensuring that relevant experience and expertise from elsewhere is not excluded. Without this there is a danger of a limiting, 'backwater-ism' setting in – undermining the prospects for achieving significant change.

Notes

1. If the Climate Justice Fund is included, the total figure is closer to £100 m.
2. The Scotland Act, while listing international development as a reserved power, also gave the Scottish government *'powers of assisting Ministers of*

the Crown with international relations … including in relation to international development assistance', thus providing a space for action.

3. The national performance framework <https://www.webarchive.org.uk/wayback/archive/3000/https://www.gov.scot/Resource/0049/00497339.pdf>.
4. Scottish government aid does not go directly to the government of Malawi – and Scottish aid was not stopped in this instance.
5. This figure covers only country office spending and excludes centrally managed programming resources, such as the Africa Enterprise Challenge Fund. Inclusion would take the figure closer to £300 m.
6. Net overseas development assistance as a proportion of gross national income <http://data.worldbank.org/indicator/DT.ODA.ODAT.GN.ZS>.
7. <http://www.scotland-malawipartnership.org/>.
8. <http://www.malawiscotlandpartnership.org/>.
9. <https://www.gov.uk/guidance/community-energy>.
10. <http://www.cleancookstoves.org/market-development/>.
11. <https://m-kopa.com/impact/>.
12. <http://www.solar-aid.org/>.
13. Private correspondence with author.
14. It is standard practice in most development agencies to have an external, independent end-of-project review.
15. This mirrors the consensus that has characterised the UK political parties on aid, all of which, officially at least, support the UK government's increased aid spending.
16. Although now fixed in law by UK parliament, it is not certain that this commitment to further substantial increases in aid spending in a context of continued public expenditure frugality can be maintained.
17. According to informal reports referring to the Chancellor George Osborne, one of the reasons for the UK government's aid spending growth, has been to 'keep the charities off our backs'; Ian Birrell, 'We can't pay 0.7% on foreign aid'; *Mail on Sunday*, 3 April 2016.

References

Allan, V (2013) 'SNP aims to make Scotland a world leader in aid', *The Herald*, 13 January 2013

Anders, G (2014) *The value of Scotland's links with Malawi: building on the past, shaping the future*, School of Social and Political Science, University of Edinburgh

Banks, N and Hulme, D (2012) *The role of NGOs and civil society in development and poverty reduction*, The University of Manchester Brooks World Poverty Institute, BNPI Working Paper No. 171

BBC (2014) *Cashgate – Malawi's murky tale of shooting and corruption*, 27 January 2014 <http://www.bbc.co.uk/news/world-africa-25912652>

Birrell, I (2015) 'Britain should stop wasting money on foreign aid', *The Telegraph*, 22 July 2015

British High Commission Malawi (2015) *We've brought new energy access to almost 80,000 people in rural Malawi*, 18 October 2015, British High Commission Malawi Press Release

Clark, J and Carney D (2008) *Sustainable livelihoods approaches – what have we learnt? A review of DFID's experience with sustainable livelihoods* <http://www. eldis.org/go/home&id=41798&type=Document#.VyCCzPkrKM8>

Currie, C, Davies, G and Young, EW (2015) *Process Evaluation of Community Energy Development Programme Projects*, MREAP, University of Strathclyde

Didcock, B (2015) *Scots university team give Malawi clean energy boost*, The Herald, 27 July 2015

Donor Committee for Enterprise Development (2001) *Business development services for small enterprises: guiding principles for donor intervention*, DCED

Dorward et al. (2002) *Critical linkages: livelihoods, markets and institutions*, Paper presented at the seminar on *Supporting institutions, evolving livelihoods*, Bradford Centre for International Development, UK

European and External Relations Committee (2015) *Connecting Scotland: how the Scottish Government and its agencies engage internationally, 4th Report*, The Scottish Parliament, Edinburgh

Frame, D and Daunhauer, P (2015) *Sustainability of solar PV institutions in Malawi*, MREAP, University of Strathclyde

Gibson, A (2016) *FSD Kenya: Ten Years of a Market Systems Approach in the Kenyan Finance Market*, FSD Africa, Nairobi

Hutcheon, P (2015) *SNP foreign aid policy under fire in internal report*, 24 May 2015

LTS International (2008) *Independent review of Scottish Government international development fund projects focused on Malawi*, Scottish Government Social Research, Edinburgh

McConnell, J (2013) Mutual respect and the Scotland-Malawi Partnership; Progress Labour's Progressives, 17 October 2013 <http://archive.progressonline.org. uk/2013/10/17/mutual-respect-and-the-scotland-malawi-partnership/>

McGrath, M (2016) *Can 'pay as you glow' solve Malawi's power crisis?* 8 April 2016 <http://www.bbc.com/news/science-environment-35935754>

Morton, K (1975) *Aid and dependence, British aid to Malawi*, Routledge, London

Scottish Conservative and Unionist Party (2016) *A stronger opposition – a stronger Scotland; Scottish Conservative and Unionist Party Manifesto,* Edinburgh

Scottish Government (2013) *Impact of aid to India: Funding is making a real and lasting difference to poor communities*, Scottish Government, 12 October 2013

Scottish Government (2016) *Meeting global challenges and making a difference: aligning our international development policy with global goals*, Edinburgh

Scottish National Party (2016) *Re-elect – SNP Manifesto 2016*, Edinburgh

Smith, M (2015) 'The appetite for change', *The Herald*, 23 May 2015

Springfield Centre (2014) *The operational guide to the making markets work for the poor (M4P) approach*, DFID and SDC

The Conversation (2015) *What drives corruption in Malawi and why it won't disappear* <http://theconversation.com/what-drives-corruption-in-malawi-and-why-it-wont-disappear-soon-48183>

Young, F and Georgieva, K (2015) *Community and locally-owned renewable energy in Scotland at September 2015*, a report by the Energy Saving Trust for the Scottish Government, Energy Saving Trust

PART V

Tributes to Alan

A tribute to Alan Gibson 1961–2018

Jim Tomecko

Last week a light went out in our world. A light for which there is no replacement. Alan Gibson spent his life shining this light into so many areas and illuminated so many mysteries for us, in a profession that has so few certainties. To many Alan was known for his lucid and eloquent writing, facilitative teaching style, and hard-hitting frankness in his consultancies. But, for me it will be his quick wit, public repartee, and incisive humour that will forever stand out, as quintessentially Alan.

In the 18 years that I knew him Alan was always somehow a critical influence on my thinking every time I started a new project and needed an impartial confidant to sort out what should and should not be done; an oasis of reason in a desert of confused and disparate interests. Alan and his colleagues at Springfield have continued to uphold a long tradition of preeminent teaching institutions serving the needs of those us, in international development, that focus on what, these days, is called the bottom of the pyramid. In the 70s SIET in Hyderabad, with contributors like David McClelland, was the Mecca for innovations in small business and entrepreneurship promotion, this mantle was passed on to the UPISSI in Philippines and the Cranfield School of Management with Malcolm Harper in the 80s. Then in the 90s Alan Gibb and the Durham Business School took over this role, until in 2000 when the Springfield Centre offered its first course. Because of its outstanding quality and its commitment to practical applications, this course has become a 'must' for any professional in our métier. Though there are others that try to copy training in market development, no one even comes close to Springfield. Alan was an essential driving force in making this all of this happen, and over so many years.

But there is one quality for which I will always respect, honour and remember Alan; that is, his conviction to 'doing the right thing'. In this regard he was fearless! Some may have called him obstinate, but Alan was never rash in reaching in conclusions. Once he had thoughtfully researched his position he was always eager to draw up a course of action, enlist whatever support he could get and confront the demons or windmills that stood in his way. In an age when this kind of challenge can frequently result in reputational risks and even personal financial loss Alan was a faithful warrior and champion for doing the right thing. He was a standard bearer! The world, or at least our

http://dx.doi.org/10.3362/9781788531443.014

corner of it, would be a better place with more people like Alan. The light went out on Alan far too early and we are all the poorer for it having done so.

Jim Tomecko
12 February 2018

Tributes for Alan Gibson

The world has lost someone so very special, so iconic that no words can ever capture the beauty of this man.

Marshall Bear

The field lost a great leader, an original thinker, and a mentor to so many people across the globe. I am privileged to have known Alan and learned so much from him. I regret others will not have that very precious opportunity to emulate his crunchy-ness.

Heather Clark

It is difficult to find the right words. Alan was brilliant, funny, knowledgeable and always so very interesting. Being a mentor is a challenging path but Alan had the gift. I think about him often and remember what I learned during the program. Alan, you will be missed. My deepest sympathies go out to Alan's family and friends.

Aida Musagic

He was such a force of nature. Passionate, funny, combative, and thoughtful in equal measure.

Adrian Stone

Alan Gibson was my facilitator for training in Bangkok. Alan's face was the first I saw, and I was immediately introduced to his wit and sense of humour as he cracked a Trump joke after he learned I was American (a theme that was repeated throughout my two weeks with him). He had a unique ability hold our class's attention while discussing some admittedly dry topics. I admired Alan's willingness to embrace every question and response from participants while challenging responses that were inadequate or incorrect without stepping on anyone's toes. I spent time individually with Alan, and he readily answered my every question and made connections with others that could help me on some of the thornier problems we faced. I have thought of Alan every day since I learned of his passing.

Sheldon Yoder

I will remember Alan as a hugely valued colleague but also for his sense of humour. I was once going through Nairobi airport without the required dollar notes to purchase a visa and the man in the queue in front of me lent me the $20 to get me through to the cash point. The gentleman who graciously lent me the money was in fact from the IMF and so Alan and I had a great discussion that we had witnessed a World First: a loan from the IMF with no conditions attached.

David Smith

Very few losses in our lives leaves behind such an immense void that is hard to fill.

Raji Rajan

Alan was visionary with a passion for the market systems methods and principles but a flexibility to imagine, to create and to envision a future where low income people were better off, had better access, had more information, had better lives. Alan was intuitive. I sat across from him in November in Bangkok and I poured my work out in front of him with pointed questions. He listened patiently and then he gave me such honest, distilled advice. Like he could see between all that I was getting caught up in and open a path forward. We are currently taking that advice but I wish he was here to share that process. I immediately missed his wit and humour, the way he kept everyone on the same page despite at least 10 countries represented in the room. After the course, I followed up with him by email to continue to learn from him. He offered a lot of himself in doing that. He is sorely missed but he left glimmers of his vision and optimism in each person he taught and met.

Jennifer Oomen

I hugely admired him for his extraordinary frankness and fearlessness – he put me well in the shade. And also for not taking a swing at me in Kampala in the late 90s, I think, when we had the most ferocious of arguments about the value of what I was encouraging DFID to do with the Ugandan extension service. That blazing row was the beginning of my enlightenment. And in later years I reveled in wheeling Alan in to deliver the necessary hard message medicine that our world of development so often need, but fail, to hear ...

Alwyn Chilver

Absolutely devastating. Alan's contribution to development over his career is immeasurable and inspiring.

Alyna Wyatt

Everyone needed, and benefited from, a bit of Alan Gibson.

Sarah Barlow

It goes without saying that work means even more this morning.
    Deep breath.

Dan Nippard

My heart sank when I saw the news about Alan's untimely death. He was a keen spark, igniting and illuminating the field of market system development: always challenging, acutely articulate, and full of passion. I was constantly inspired by his incisive writing – his ability to communicate the critical messages with wit and precision. Alan will be very sorely missed.

Mike Albu

I first met Alan in 1992 when I was unemployed, and he and his colleagues granted me a free place on a one-day course. Then I joined David Wright at DFID, Alan set up Springfield with Mark Havers, and Alan, Rob, and all at Springfield generated a disruptive buzz in our then rather complacent 'small business in development' world. Springfield has always since had an 'edge' that bureaucrats and governments need to step up to, rather than drift back to ignorance and inertia. Alan's drive was invariably in top gear, and I have been very privileged to see him in action across the globe and reaching out to hundreds of colleagues. And I'm personally grateful for knowing him and his generosity of spirit, e.g. when, with no notice, he and Rob once dropped everything and rescued my southern daughter from Durham station platform when a piece of northern grit had disabled her! A very special man.

Richard Boulter

It is just so sad to lose such a brilliant person who has done so much.

Mayada El-Zoghbi

I found Alan such a remarkable man, so intelligent, so witty, a wonderfully fair and respectful trainer who found something in all of his students. All of our core skills class were so happy to have landed in his class and felt we had won the jackpot (no offense to the other great trainers!).

Regarding my own personal situation, Alan was so very generous with his knowledge and ideas of how I could progress in the world of market systems development. In addition, I sensed he was quietly watchful of my health during the course, noticing when I was getting uncomfortable or needed to raise my legs. I am quite sure he got a kick from the fact that my baby's first kicks occurred during his session – and we both joked about the fact that the baby was as disgusted by the video we were all watching at the time.

I will try to honour Alan's commitment to long-term systems development through my work in the future, while also remembering to keep a twinkle in my eye.

With my deepest sympathies,

Susan Hennessy

He made an enormous contribution to the field. I personally learned a great deal from him. But, more importantly, I was – and will continue to be – inspired by his unwavering passion for helping poor people.

Aly Miehlbradt

A truly unique person to enjoy learning from. A true thinker – constantly thinking while doing. When working with us at the Small Business Centre at DUBS he would regularly challenge with his colleague Mark Havers the attempts at 'wisdom' that in academe seem only too often to come from papers and not from the equal ability to learn from experience. We had a motto at the time drawn from TS Elliot's Four Quartets that 'it is possible to have the experience but to miss the meaning'. This meant that it was our comforting task to try to provide, through reflection, greater meaning to the experience of entrepreneurs.

Yet Alan, I always thought, saw it the other way round, that we ourselves would only gain true 'wisdom' not through 'knowledge alone' but through its application in practice.

He was a great person to debate with as long as you did not have the expectation of winning except by means of later reflection. An equally robust (but not unskilled) centre half on the football field! I was always glad I was never a Centre Forward!

That he should die challenging nature is truly tragic but perhaps unsurprising.

Allan Gibb

Alan's clarity of thought, fluency of expression and keen sense of humour were inspirational. The qualities that impressed me most, though, were his courage and leadership: when enthusiasm for market systems cooled in the mid-noughties, he continued to bet the firm on it. When uncomfortable things needed to be said in evaluations, he said them. The inevitable pushback took its toll, but Alan's life was an example to us all. He used his talents well.

Jim Tanburn

Alan's thinking, along with his wit, was razor sharp. The work he did during his life was transformational, particularly in relation to supporting the most disadvantaged. Such a huge loss.

Dinah Bennett

I remember him as a brilliant and ground-breaking thinker.

Frank Matsaert

A bright light is snuffed.

Jon Burns

I met Alan at a time in my career when I was searching for that something that would last beyond serving the common good of the people, for a while. I sought a legacy for the many poor people of low income, in communities far from the centre of key resources. It had to be managed by them and making a difference in their lives and earning power. Meeting Alan and the Springfield team of M4P Purists changed the story for the communities in Kano, Kaduna, Jigawa states of northern Nigeria impacted by the ENABLE MEDIA work. It's only natural to continue to do it the purist way, right? Exactly. It has always been about empowering local people and tangible, long-term benefits. That was Alan's heart. He believed and lived to guide people like me to work with the grassroot people to light that one lamp. Alan, you brought the light, you helped light the lamp, we carry on because, in that light, your greatest moments shine through beyond today.

Helen Bassey-Osijo

Alan's intellect, challenge and wonderful cynicism made the world of private sector development and our commitment to poverty reduction a better one. The world has lost a great thought leader. Long may his great passion for growth and ideas for continued improvement in our business live through the work of all of us committed to this great cause.

Mavis Owusu-Gyamfi

He was a legend and an inspiration to many, many people and I will always consider myself lucky enough to have interacted with him.

Richard Waddington

A wonderful teacher. It was a great privilege to be taught by Alan during the Springfield M4P training. His virtuosity was remarkable and will always be remembered.

Sarah Ayu

Alan was a mentor to me. In my very first job in Katalyst back in 2004, I was given a pile of reports to read. There was one Alan Gibson who was cited every now and then. I asked my manager, who is this person? I was told, he is the man behind what we are working on. We met several times since then. In 2008, the OP guide was being written and Alan was in Bangladesh to hear from us. We spoke wholeheartedly about our experience, our failures. Alan with his bright wide smile continued probing and I learnt that day the power of listening and the power of being inquisitive. Cheers to Alan for leaving behind a legacy!

Md. Rubaiyath Sarwar

He pioneered what we regard today as our daily business and influenced the livelihood of millions.

Goetz Ebbecke

Mourning the loss of Alan Gibson … Reflecting on how much we learned from him and his 10-year review of FSD Kenya. Can only imagine what a review of his life and work would be!

Tamara Cook

Alan exemplified moral courage in our field; he stood by his principles even when it made his job harder. He brought intellectual clarity and originality into every assignment, always daring to ask big questions.

Combining his talents with humour and modesty, Alan was also excellent company. I'll always respect how he valued people for their character and not their rank.

In so many ways Alan was, and is, inspiring.

Kevin Seely

Alan is one of those people you meet in life that the more you know them/ spend time with them the more thankful you are. Hearing the news was really a jolt and made me pause and reflect on what is really important such as families and friends.

Mike Field

It is with great sadness that I have read the news about Alan and his brother's sudden and tragic death today. Our thoughts and prayers are with his family and all those to whom he has been a dear colleague and friend.

Matthias Herr

Alan was and remains a towering giant in the world of development policy. Whether or not he coined the M4P term, he and close colleagues certainly were responsible for much of the thinking and insight that gave rise to this paradigm. As a result, governments, development practitioners, policy makers, and funders are able to work more cost-effectively and with greater impact in applying public resources to overcome poverty.

Paul Zille

Words cannot express the disbelief and shock on hearing about the tragic passing away of dear Alan. We are deeply saddened to lose such a unique person. He was indeed a gem, and his teachings and sense of humor during the training will be greatly missed. Spending two weeks with him at Springfield was life-changing – his wisdom shed light on so many wonderful things we could do with M4P in all our contexts.

Our sincere condolences to the entire Springfield team from Msingi EA. We pray for his departed soul to rest in peace.

Mandeep Shah

He was such a great man. May his soul RIP.

Addis Alem

Dear all, lets light a candle during the week as we celebrate the great life of our very own … Alan Gibson. You were a great man and surely Springfield will miss you Alan.

Prossy Adong

Alan was a mentor, a teacher, and a friend to many in our field. At the SEEP Network, we consider ourselves direct beneficiaries of his influence. Our learning agendas have strived to incorporate much of the practice and theory that Alan worked so hard to promote. Similarly, many our members have been influenced by his passion and insight. Together with our staff, board of directors, and organizational members, we express our deepest appreciation. We are certain his legacy will continue to inspire.

Sharon D'Onofrio

His virtuosity was remarkable and will always be remembered. Deepest condolences for his family, friends, and loved ones.

Sarah Ayu

My deepest condolences for a Goodman Alan. RIP lecturer and mentor.

Deogratias Chubwa

He was a pioneer in development and had so much more to contribute. He was a very good motivating and inspiring lecturer. My deepest condolences. RIP Alan.

Pada Senin

I am so saddened by the news of Alan's death. My thoughts are with you during this difficult time. Alan, as you know, had such a profound impact on so many people and on good practice in our sector – including in my organization. This morning we (at WUSC) are thinking very fondly of our interactions with him and the learning that this engendered in us.

Chris Eaton

Alan was a friend and a highly respected professional that led many of us down a market systems adventure that defined much of our work over the last 20 years or so – quite a legacy to leave behind.

Hugh Scott

Sending my condolences to you all. Whilst I wasn't in Alan's class, I got a sense of the type of person he was from his very humorous introductions to the team at the closing session. No doubt he will be sorely missed and will be remembered with fond memories.

Chim Chalemera

Indeed a true loss for the development world and for all of us who had the opportunity to meet and enjoy time with Alan. My condolences and thoughts are with his family and friends at The Springfield Centre, RIP.

Ivan Idrovo

I've known Alan as a friend since the end of the last century when he was a consultant on our GTZ project in Zimbabwe. I like so many have sat in a lecture room in Glasgow and watched him weave a web of the intricacies of business development in a market driven way that helps the poor through days of PowerPoint slides that all came together in the final presentation. Leaving us all to marvel at the clarity of the reasoning and the presentations – truly brilliant. We are all gonna miss him. He and the rest at Springfield Centre have changed development in a very important way given us the right to use words like sustainable and systemic with meaning. Thanks for that Alan.

Kevin Billing

Alan was the person who unlocked the world of M4P for me and set my development journey on a different trajectory. For all of Mercy Corps, he was instrumental in pushing us to adopt M4P widely, by training many of our staff over the years and providing his trademark thoughtful, blunt, and honest advice. All of the market systems development work we do is a tribute to Alan's impact and the best honour we can pay him is to never stop thinking critically and honestly about the impact we are having in the world. Thank you, Alan, for your passion, integrity, and sense of humour.

Sasha Muench

What a contribution, what a legacy. A wonderful guy. Our work in Lagos was a special piece for me. Alan's clarity of thought and writing, his convictions about good and bad development have endured far beyond the short time we worked together. Above all it was his irrepressible wit and wicked humour that just shone through, often with caustic honesty. How can I forget 'wholesome and meaningless' describing some new policy pronouncement? Alan – so long, and thanks for all the fish!

Roger Cunningham

Alan was my group lead in the Glasgow training and joking with him through-out the week, I felt I had developed a bond. I respected him sincerely for his brilliant mind and humble heart. Even though I hadn't stayed in touch, the news really shook me to the core. It's such a loss for us all.

I hope God gives his family and friends the strength to cope with his absence and enough of us out here can carry forward his sincerity and passion for development.

Zannatul Ferdous

I feel incredibly fortunate having had the opportunity to meet and work with Alan earlier this year, and to benefit from his clarity of thought, ability to help us navigate complex issues (with humour and grace), and his deep, irreplace-able expertise that has had such a profound impact on our sector over the years.

Camilla Nestor

It's a very sad day for so many people around the globe who were touched by Alan's work. Alan wasn't just an excellent trainer, he was a great supporter and mentor when asked for guidance. I was privileged to be trained by Alan in

May 2017. Alan's style, extensive knowledge, and sense of humour were key to making the training transformational.

I will plant a palm tree for Alan. Palm trees are beautiful, strong, tall, and steadfast trees and that's how we try to be in the face of challenges. Be strong. RIP Alan.

Safa Abdel Rahman-Madi

Epitaph on a Friend – Robert Burns

> An honest man here lies at rest,
> The friend of man, the friend of truth,
> The friend of age, and guide of youth:
> Few hearts like his, with virtue warm'd,
> Few heads with knowledge so inform'd;
> If there's another world, he lives in bliss;
> If there is none, he made the best of this.

David Elliott

I first came across Alan Gibson through the cases he wrote for the Katalyst programme. From then on I followed his cases for their articulate examples and his soap box articles for their frank, hard hitting and conceptual clarity. When I met him at a Springfield training, overwhelmed by the 'wow factor', I barely managed a hello. Sadly, that was the last I would see of him. I will miss having something to read that is able to express our frustrations as practitioners so clearly. It is a great loss to lose a voice like his in this field.

Sadia Ahmed

It's not just a loss to the Springfield Centre, it is a loss to the global development community.

Eric Momanyi

Alan Gibson family history and roots

Dave Gibson

Alan Thomas Stuart Gibson was born on 3 July 1961 in Irvine Central hospital in Ayrshire, south-west Scotland. He was the fourth son of Janet and Cameron Gibson and younger brother to Neil, Ian, and David. Alan's father, Cameron, had been a veterinarian but in mid-career felt a call to become a minister of the church. His mother, Janet, was a maths teacher and homemaker. Alan's parents both grew up in Minishant, a small village just south of Ayr.

Alan's first seven years were spent in the historic village of Fenwick 11 miles south of Glasgow where his father was minister. In 1968 the family moved to the town of Nairn in the north of Scotland where Alan would spend the rest of his childhood and teenage years.

At school Alan excelled academically and athletically, particularly at football. In 1978 Alan left school aged 17, to attend Napier College in Edinburgh for the next four years. He graduated from there in 1982 with a first-class honours degree in Technology with Industrial Studies.

On the morning of Thursday 6 February 2018 Alan and his eldest brother Neil left Nairn in the Highlands of Scotland to go hillwalking in the Achnashellach area. When they did not return by evening their mother raised the alarm. An extensive search was immediately launched with mountain rescue teams helicoptered into the remote area.

Alan's body was found on Saturday 8 February on the northern slopes of Beinn Liath Mhor. The body of his dog Archie was found close by. The search for Neil was abandoned due to extreme weather. Neil's body was found six weeks later in the remote valley to the north of Beinn Liath Mhor.

The Springfield Centre was established in 1995 as an independent consulting, training and research firm. Springfield has always sought to marry a strong business perspective with practical knowledge of the development context and a commitment to sustainable development objectives. Springfield believes that development intervention should be transformative, and has been at the forefront of new thinking and practices aimed at making markets work for poor and disadvantaged men and women. Springfield works with a range of public and private partners to sustainably change the economic systems that provide disadvantaged people with the goods, services, jobs, and incomes that they need to improve their livelihoods – without recourse to perpetual development assistance. In 2019 Springfield became part of Swisscontact.

Swisscontact is a leading partner organization for the implementation of international development projects.

We promote inclusive economic, social, and ecological development to make an effective contribution towards sustainable and widespread prosperity in developing and emerging economies. With this objective in mind, we offer the chance to economically and socially disadvantaged people to improve their lives on their own initiative.

The independent, non-profit, private foundation was established in 1959 in Switzerland.

We strengthen the competencies of people, improving their employability; increase the competitiveness of enterprises, growing their business; and foster social and economic systems, promoting inclusive development.

www.ingramcontent.com/pod-product-compliance
Lightning Source LLC
Chambersburg PA
CBHW060347050426
42336CB00051B/2417